6.

TWO HUNDRED POPULAR FLIES

Two Hundred Popular Flies

AND HOW TO TIE THEM

Tom Stewart

ERNEST BENN LIMITED
London and Tonbridge

Published by Ernest Benn Limited
25 New Street Square, London EC4A 3JA
and Sovereign Way, Tonbridge, Kent, TN9 1RW

The text of this book was originally
published in the late author's four books,
Fifty Popular Flies, volumes 1 to 4

First published in this format, 1979

© Tom Stewart—Book One 1962
      Book Two 1964
      Book Three 1969
      Book Four 1973

ISBN 0 510–22527–6

Printed in Great Britain

British Library Cataloguing in Publication Data
Stewart, Tom
 Two hundred popular flies, and how to tie them.
 1. Fly tying
 I. Title   II. Fifty popular flies
 688.7'9   SH451

ISBN 0–510–22527–6

Contents

5

Publisher's Note

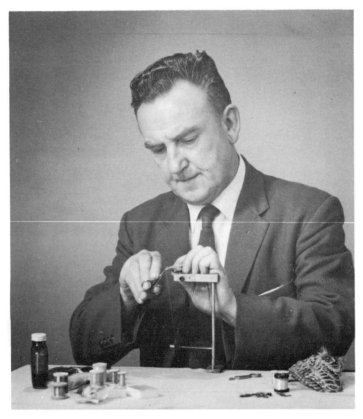

THE AUTHOR

The articles and sketches in this book aroused a great deal of interest when they were first published in *Trout & Salmon* magazine. They were later republished, in book form, in four paperback volumes entitled *Fifty Popular Flies*, between 1962 and 1973.

Sad to say, Tom Stewart died in 1975, but as a result of the continuing, steady demand for his books it was decided to issue this omnibus edition of his four volumes of fifty patterns, under the title *Two Hundred Popular Flies and how to tie them*. We know that Tom Stewart was thrilled when his first book appeared, and we would like to think that he would have been equally pleased with the appearance of this compendium of information, advice and hints on the dressing of all types of game fishing flies. We hope it promotes his desire, which was to encourage others to take up this fascinating hobby with profit and pleasure.

BOOK ONE

No. 1

The Butcher

CREDIT for the introduction of the Butcher is most often jointly accorded to Messrs. Jewhurst and Moon of Tunbridge Wells.

When the fly was originally dressed it was apparently known as Moon's Fly, but, about 1838, if the story be true, its name was changed to the Butcher. And since Mr. Moon was a butcher by profession it is assumed that the pattern derived its new name from his calling rather than from its fish-killing propensities!

There is still another claimant for the honour of inventing the Butcher. The *Glasgow Herald* of 6th December, 1929, in a reference to St. Mungo Angling Club, founded in 1881, asserts that one of the club's original members "achieved immortality by inventing the Butcher".

His name was Andrew Hamilton and he had a butcher's business in Pollokshields.

In view of the 43 years' difference between 1838 and 1881 it is reasonable to assume that the fly originated in Tunbridge Wells. Quite possibly Mr. Hamilton created one of its variations—the Bloody, Gold, or Kingfisher Butcher. Hardy's Gold Butcher was a product of the well-known Alnwick tackle dealer of that name.

It is impossible to say what the original Butcher was meant to imitate. Most certainly it wasn't a fly. Probably it was a small fish or even a beetle, but whatever it was there is no denying that it is one of the deadliest artificial flies that can be presented to trout or sea trout.

Generally fished as a bob fly or top dropper it will often do well on the tail or point of a wet fly cast.

As my sketch shows, the fly is easily tied. The requirements are a small piece of white feather dyed pillar box red, a small strip of flat silver tinsel, a black hen or cock hackle, and paired pieces cut from the corresponding quill feathers of a crow, rook, magpie, or mallard ("blue").

Fig. A shows the red feather tail, the tinsel, and the hackle tied in, Fig. B the Butcher Spider before the wings are added and Fig. C the completed fly—closed-winged version.

But if you wish to make the split-winged pattern (Fig. D) the drill is slightly different. Here you roll two pieces of the requisite feather between the fingers and tie them in before the hackle is applied.

Split them in criss-cross fashion with the tying silk and then put on the hackle—in front of the wings. If you wish you can also put

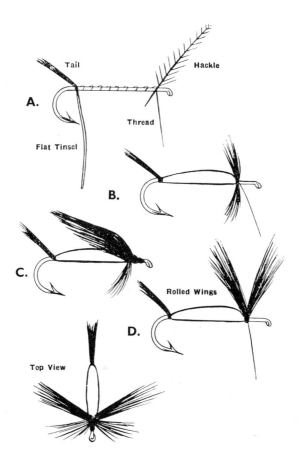

the hackle behind the wings and cause them to slant, advanced-wing fashion, towards the eye. Since split-winged flies are meant to be bobbed on the surface it pays to use tiny cock hackles, which help to keep the fly on or near the top of the water.

No. 2

Greenwell's Glory

WHILE the Greenwell's Glory perpetuates the Durham Canon of that name, the real credit for the introduction of this fly probably goes to James Wright, of Sprouston, Roxburghshire.

For it was Wright, not Canon Greenwell, who first tied the fly that few dry and wet fly trout fishers nowadays would care to be without.

Perhaps it would be fairer to say, however, that this fly owes its birth to a joint effort. The Canon picked a natural fly off the water and took it to James Wright, who copied it, and a Sprouston schoolmaster named Brown christened the new pattern Greenwell's Glory.

The fly has been in existence for over 100 years, for it was first tied and used at the River Tweed in May, 1854.

Fundamentally, the dressing has never changed. Wright tied the fly with a blackbird wing (inside or outside), a Coch-y-Bondhu (red-black) hackle, and a well-waxed yellow silk body ribbed with gold wire or left unribbed.

Later variations have given the fly a red or yellow, silk or feather tail, but the pattern used by most anglers today, whether they fish lakes or rivers, has neither of these refinements, and it appears to do just as well without them.

It is not widely known that in the premises of the Trout Anglers' Club in Rutland Street, Edinburgh, there are original copies of letters which Canon Greenwell wrote in connection with the fly.

In one of these letters he wrote (commenting on an offer of the Fly Fishers' Club that he should sit for a portrait): "I scarcely think that my merit as the originator of Greenwell's Glory entitles my portrait to be hung in your club, but if enough brothers of the rod wish it, I have no objection . . . I have no heirs more grateful to me than the disciples of Isaak Walton".

12

Tie in a small piece of fine gold wire to the hook shank with well-waxed yellow silk (not floss) and wind the silk towards the eye of the hook. Now rib the body with the wire and tie in hackle as shown in the diagram. This is the Greenwell **Spider,** a very useful nymph-suggesting pattern.

Now take two corresponding pieces of feather from a hen blackbird's wings (you can use the blae feather from a teal duck, the unspeckled, dark blae feather from grouse wings, or the dark or pale feathers from a starling's wings) and tie them in as shown.

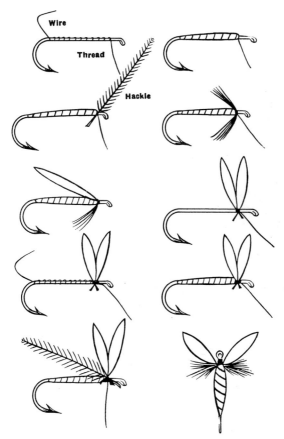

If you wish to tie the split-wing Greenwell's Glory you tie in the wings first and split them with a few criss-crossings of the tying thread. Now tie in the wire, rib the body, and apply the hackle close up to the wings so that they slant, advanced fashion, over the eye of the hook. The split-wing pattern is particularly good as a bob fly.

13

No. 3

Peter Ross

RED and black are acknowledged by many wet fly fishers as the colours likeliest to attract trout. And since the Peter Ross has a partly red body and a black hackle with sufficient silver tinsel added to give it brilliance it is scarcely to be wondered at that it is such a popular pattern.

It is commonly supposed to be taken by the trout for a fresh-water shrimp—a view to which I cannot subscribe, for having handled many thousands of shrimps in the course of introducing them to various waters I have never been able to see the relationship.

Moreover, I do not suppose that Peter Ross, the Killin, Perthshire, man who gave his name to the fly, was greatly concerned about what the trout took it for so long as they showed a taste for it!

I am inclined to suppose that the fly is taken for a small fish and that it is no more than a very deadly variation of the old and well-tried Teal and Red.

It is a tail fly which fishes best when well sunk and worked through the water in long, slow drags and erratic jerks.

The original Peter Ross had a red and silver body, a black hackle, and a barred teal wing, but Ray Bergman, the American author of *Trout,* mysteriously defines it as a fly with a gold-ribbed yellow silk body, a ginger hackle and no wing!

The late James Orr, of Greenock, a noted West of Scotland fly-dresser, once told me that a Peter Ross dressed with a bright orange hackle instead of the usual black one makes a pattern that is not only beautiful in the angler's eyes but attractive to trout as well.

Components of the standard dressing of the fly are: flat and oval silver tinsel (or wire), a few orange, black-tipped tippets from the neck feathers of the Golden Pheasant, a pinch of red wool or seal's fur, a black hen hackle, and a piece of barred teal duck plumage.

Tie in the wire (oval tinsel), flat tinsel, and tippets. Wind the flat tinsel about a third of the way up the hook shank. Tease out the wool and roll it on to the tying thread between the fingers.

Now wind on the wool and thread towards the eye of the hook and tie in with a couple of half-hitches at the hook's neck, leaving room, of course, for the hackle and teal wing.

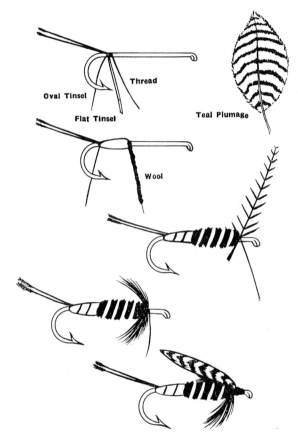

When the wool has been tied down, wind the oval tinsel (or wire) in ribbing fashion towards the fly's head, ribbing the flat tinsel and then the wool with good tight turns.

Tie in the black hen hackle and wind round the throat of the hook.

There are two ways of putting on the wing. With small flies, cut corresponding pieces from either side of the teal plumage; for larger patterns use the whole feather folding it over so that the two sides match.

No. 4

Wickham's Fancy

IT might be said that this extremely popular fly, which is used for wet and dry fly fishing with equally good results, owes its birth to a simple accident. And this is how it came about.

Dr. T. C. Wickham, of Winchester, a noted River Test angler, wanted a copy of a fly known as the Cockerton. He went to his fly tying friend Jack Hammond, also of Winchester, who busked the wanted pattern to the doctor's instructions.

But either the fly tier erred, or the doctor did. For when the fly was completed it did not quite correspond to the Cockerton the doctor had known in his younger days.

It seems it had more gold and less hackle than the Cockerton, but the doctor tried it just the same. And it was a killer. Fished wet or dry it quickly established a reputation for itself and ever since then it has been regarded as one of the deadliest patterns in the angler's fly box.

Credit for the invention of the fly was also claimed for George Currell, also of Winchester, who was said to have tied the fly for a certain Captain John Wickham in 1884.

The Pink Wickham, which has corncrake instead of starling wings, was first tied by Francis Francis in 1885.

I find Wickham's Fancy particularly attractive to trout when there is a glint of sunshine on the water to catch its gold, but it is also a first rate fly for dusk fishing when its style of dressing might very well cause it to be taken for a sedge fly. In loch fishing it is a grand fly in a big wave.

The dressing I like best is:—Wings, medium blae (starling for small sizes and mallard, inside out, for larger patterns); body, flat gold, ribbed with finest gold wire; hackle, bright red to gingery cock carried from shoulder to tail; setae or whisks, same as hackle.

Tie in several hackle fibres for setae at point opposite to hook barb, and put on flat gold tinsel and gold wire at the same time.

16

Now wind the flat gold tinsel up the hook shank towards the eye and tie in firmly. Tie in the hackle, using one of good taper, and wind it towards the barbed end of the hook in neat, tight turns, so that each turn ribs the gilt body of the fly. Tie down the end of the hackle with the wire and snip off waste fibres.

Then work the wire in ribbing fashion over the top of the hackle towards the eye. When the wire has been securely tied in put on the wing, as prescribed, and finish off with a whip knot.

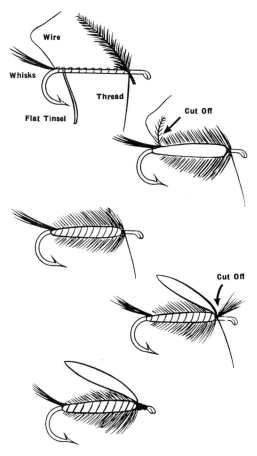

The Wickham will take on every place on the wet fly cast so that if it should be killing as an intermediate fly another one can be put on the tail for, perhaps, even better results.

The dry fly is dressed in much the same fashion, either with split wings or wingless with an additional hackle at the throat to give the fly greater buoyancy.

No. 5

Black
Zulu

ANY fly that was once banned from competitive angling—as the Black Zulu was—merits its place on the angler's fly list.

There are at least three types of Zulu, the gold, blue, and black, the last-mentioned being the most popular.

They are essentially lake flies though the Blue Zulu as well as the black one can be put to good use in rivers where there are sea trout. In fact, the Blue Zulu, which is referred to in some quarters as the Blue Devil, is one of the deadliest patterns an angler can put before a sea trout or whitling.

I have not been able to trace the inventors of any of these Zulus so that I cannot tell when they were first tied. But in the case of the Black Zulu it is reasonable to suppose that it is a variation, whether so intended or not, of a Dove pattern created and used by Charles Cotton some 300 years ago.

Cotton's fly, which would also appear to be a forerunner of the Black Pennell and the Black Palmer, had a black ostrich herl body ribbed with silver twist and a black cock hackle over all. The only noticeable difference between these and the Black Zulu is that the Zulu has a short red tail, which may consist of red wool, mohair, floss silk, or dyed feather.

Used as a top dropper, or bob fly, the Black Zulu has proved itself to be best suited to dull, windy days though it will also take well at sunset, especially when trout are smutting. It should be made to trip along the surface, just tipping the waves, and appears to be taken for a fly in difficulties or about to take off from the water.

I do not place much faith in spider-type dressings of Zulus. The true Zulu is dressed palmer-style—that is, with the hackle running in a taper from shoulder to tail.

The hackle should be put on sparingly so as not to obscure the attractiveness of the tinsel over the black wool, herl, or seal's fur.

Like Cotton, I prefer black ostrich herl for the body which I rib with fine flat silver tinsel, the tinsel being used to bind in the tapering, black cock hackle. The hackle fibres are later teased out from below the tinsel with a pin. The process in tying the Zulu is outlined in the accompanying diagrams.

The only difference between the Black and the Blue Zulu is that the latter has an additional hackle, which can either be bright blue or pale turquoise, tied in at the throat.

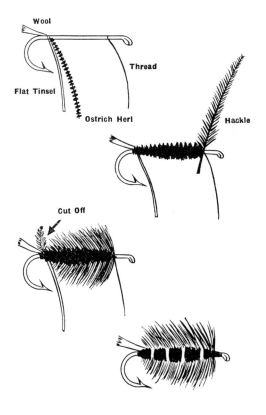

The Gold Zulu, which is also called the the Red Zulu, is a completely different fly. It has a bronze peacock herl body ribbed with fine flat gold tinsel and has a Coch-y-bondhu (red-black) cock hackle, once again rather scantily put on, from shoulder to tail. The tippet is the same as for the other Zulus.

All of these Zulus can be tied as tandem flies and fished in Worm-fly fashion on the tail of the wet fly cast in a good depth of water.

19

No. 6

Coch-y-bonddu

AS an all-round trout killer, which can be fished wet or dry with equally good results, there are few patterns in the angler's fly box to match the Coch-y-bonddu.

It is supposed to imitate a beetle and its Welsh name (interpreted as "red with black trunk") suggests that it had its origin in that country. But even in these enlightened days there is still an aura of mystery around the Coch-y-bonddu; no one appears to be quite sure what it represents.

The popular idea is that it is taken by the fish for the Garden Chafer or June bug (*Phyllopertha horticola*) which has a metallic, bluish-green thorax, black legs and body, and reddish-brown wing cases. It invariably appears on the water in late May or early June when large swarms of these land bred insects are blown or fall on to the surface.

Prototypes of the natural beetle, *Phyllopertha horticola*, are variously referred to in fly fishing nomenclature as Marlow Buzz, Coch-y-bonddu; and Bracken Clock, the last two being presumably variations of the first, the earliest record of which appears in Alfred Ronalds's Fly Fisher's Entomology, 1836, though it is possible that the fly was in use before Ronalds's time. Incidentally, Bracken Clock is a name given to the Coch-y-bonddu in Scotland, where "clock" is an old word for beetle.

Used as a wet fly the Coch-y-bonddu fishes best as a top dropper or bob fly and is particularly effective on a dull, warm day or at dusk.

Tie in two fronds of bronze peacock herl, taken from near the top of the "eye" feather, with a short piece of orange silk floss and a short length of brown thread, which is used for ribbing the body to prevent the herl from being torn off by the trout's teeth. Very fine copper wire can also be used for this purpose.

Twisting the two strands of herl together wind them on to the hook shank, working in the direction of the hook eye. Tie in the herl and rib the body with the thread or wire.

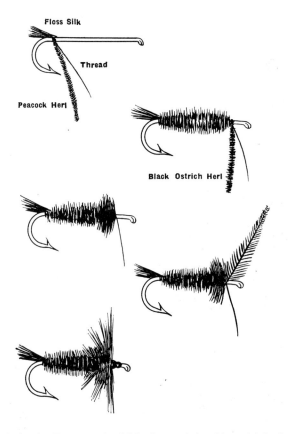

Now tie in the Furnace (red-black) cock hackle, which should be long enough to permit of at least four turns in order to make the pattern thoroughly buoyant.

Furnace hackles are rare and expensive nowadays, and a reasonably good substitute can be achieved by making a few turns of black ostrich herl or wool at the throat of the hook and overmounting this black patch with a ginger cock hackle fairly long in the fibre.

No. 7

Yellow Dog

THIS noted salmon fly is known by at least four names—the Garry, Minister's Dog, Golden Dog, and Yellow Dog. It was created by the late John Wright, of Sprouston, Roxburghshire, whose father dressed the Greenwell's Glory to the specification of Canon Greenwell.

The Yellow Dog is, of course, a hair-winged pattern. As its name suggests, the wing was first obtained from a tuft of hair from a dog. This dog, which belonged to a minister, was called Garry; hence two of the names for the fly.

My first acquaintance with the Yellow Dog was during a visit to the River Stinchar in Ayrshire, where I heard that an angler had taken four salmon with the pattern from a small pool in one afternoon. This is an ideal fly for a slightly coloured water.

The Yellow Dog ranks high as a salmon fly on the Ayrshire rivers, but its real claim to fame lies in the Tweed where it is used with deadly effect from the beginning to the end of each salmon season.

It is a fairly easy fly to dress though care has to be taken that not too much hair is used for the wing or a top-heavy fly will result.

Wind on a small tag (three turns) of flat silver tinsel and tie in a small Golden Pheasant topping (from the crest of the bird). Then wind on several turns of yellow or gold floss silk and tie in a red ibis tail.

Now tie in the flat silver tinsel and the black floss silk. Wind the floss up the hook shank to the neck of the hook and rib the black body evenly with the silver tinsel. Try to achieve a nicely tapered body.

Tie in a well-speckled guinea fowl hackle dyed blue and apply the winging fibres.

The winging hairs must be tied in tightly. The best way to do this is to smear the end that is to be tied down with a little celluloid varnish or shellac. This keeps the fibres together and facilitates the tying down of the hairs.

22

The necessary bucktail or deer hair (or yellow bear fur) used for the fly's wing can be obtained from any reputable supplier of fly dressing materials.

For the Yellow Dog you need hair of two colours—bright yellow and blood red. Build the yellow hair on top of a few fibres of the red hair and holding the composite wing along the back of the fly's body tie the hair in firmly, touching the hair roots once more with clear varnish to give them a secure foundation.

Now taper the head of the fly with the necessary turns of black tying silk and touch up the head with black celluloid varnish.

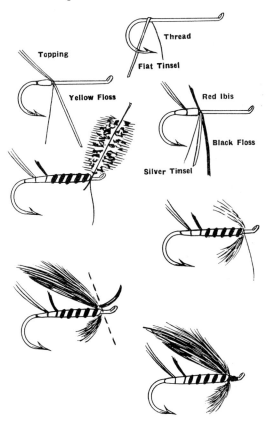

No. 8

Mallard and Claret

UNDOUBTEDLY this pattern is a variation of our old friend the Grouse and Claret—one of the best artificial flies that the lake fisher can put before a trout. It is also a very good sea trout pattern.

The origin of the Mallard and Claret has been ascribed to William Murdoch, an Aberdeen angler, who is also credited with the creation of the Heckham Peckham series of flies.

It is possible that Murdoch created the Grouse and Claret, too, but this is by no means certain, for many of our oldest flies had their origin in Ireland.

It is much more reasonable to assume that Murdoch stumbled on the Mallard and Claret in the course of dressing a large pattern of the Grouse and Claret. As is well-known, grouse feathers are rather short in the web and while they are perfectly suitable for small flies they are not quite large enough for the winging of the biggest flies.

The Mallard feathers supply the answer as they are long in the web and closely resemble grouse feathers, especially when they are wet.

Quite the best of the dressings of the Mallard and Claret is one with a very dark claret wool body, ribbed with oval gold tinsel. It has golden pheasant tippets, and a black hackle.

The fly, however, can be dressed with a brown hackle or a claret one—slightly paler than the body. And there are patterns which have a silver-ribbed body instead of the gold one. Some dressers go farther in the use of silver, and tie Mallard and Clarets that have silver butts in the style of the Peter Ross.

Then, again, I have a very deadly pattern of the fly from an Irish tackle firm, in which the tail is a small piece of swan feather dyed bright yellow.

The accompanying illustration shows how to dress the Mallard and Claret. And if the fly dresser has any difficulty in pairing the pieces of mallard feather he should very lightly smear the tips with thin celluloid varnish which helps to hold the points of the wing together. Only enough to cover the tip of a needle is necessary and it can be scraped off once the wing has been set in place.

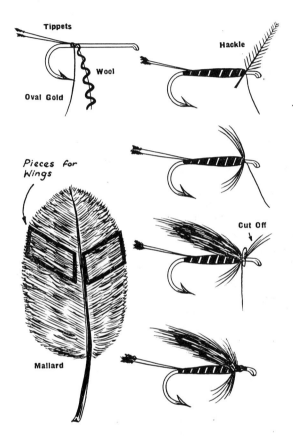

No. 9

Sam
Slick

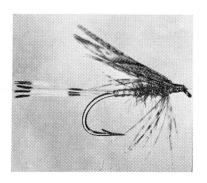

THIS can be a very deadly lake pattern. It is not a particularly imposing fly—so few really taking patterns are—but it has a good reputation for taking trout in difficult conditions and when they appear to be looking at nothing else.

In my experience it does its best work when the weather is dull and scoury and there isn't much fly life about the water. On such days trout invariably take the artificial fly deep down.

For this reason it is advisable to fish the Sam Slick fairly well sunk, the size of fly being determined by the state of the water and conditions of light.

On a day of very rough waves it is worth trying a size 10 pattern on the tail of the cast but in normal conditions a size 12 (these are old numbers) is large enough.

The Sam Slick will also kill sea trout. It is especially useful when the water is dark from being stained with peat.

Presumably it is its yellow tag clearly focussed against the inky water that makes the fly so attractive at such a time.

The first thing to do in tying a Sam Slick is to tie in a few Golden Pheasant tippet fibres (or a small topping from the same bird). Then tie in a piece of oval gold tinsel for ribbing the body.

One third of the body (nearest the tail) is formed of yellow floss silk and the remainder with brown seal's fur (or fairly dark fur obtained from a hare's ear). The entire body is then ribbed with the oval gold tinsel.

Don't make the body too thick.

The hackle is speckled brown partridge from the back of that bird and the winging feather is also speckled, being obtained from the tail of the partridge.

26

A very good nymphal representation of this fly, which bears some relation to the March Brown, can be made by simply omitting the wing.

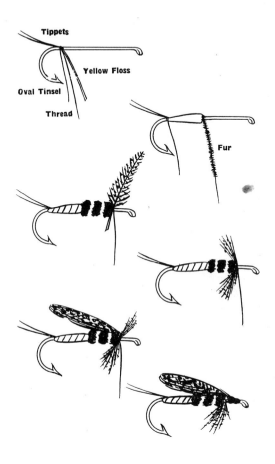

No. 10

Silver
Wilkinson

IT is generally agreed that the Silver Wilkinson is very much the
same fly as the Silver Doctor. The exception is that the hackle
of the former is magenta while that of the latter is blue. Both are
followed by a throat hackle of widgeon or lightly barred teal.

The scarlet head used in the Silver Doctor is often omitted from
the Silver Wilkinson. Sometimes, too, a piece of Indian Crow is
added to the topping and Blue Chatterer used in the tail. Indian
Crow is frequently incorporated with the Blue Chatterer "cheeks".

Except in competitive fly dressing these and certain other refinements, especially in the wings, can very well be done without. For
instance, if Blue Chatterer feathers have to be represented at all it
is just as useful to employ the tips of blue cock hackles.

The wings and bodies of the Silver Doctor and the Wilkinson are
identical and if one is killing salmon it is a pretty safe assumption
that the other will do the same. Some fly dressers add jungle cock
cheeks to the Wilkinson's sides.

After tying in the tag of flat or round tinsel and golden yellow
floss, add a small golden pheasant topping with a small blue hackle
tip on top as the tail.

The butt should be made of scarlet wool. Dyed ostrich herl can
also be used but it is so soft that it is liable to be torn off by the
first fish that takes hold of the fly.

Flat silver tinsel is used for the body, this being ribbed with fine
oval tinsel. To make sure that the flat silver tinsel goes on evenly
it pays to put on an underbody of fine wool or floss silk.

The wing consists of golden pheasant tippet fibres in strands with
strips of the mottled tail feather from the same bird placed over
them. Then add married strands of scarlet, blue and yellow swan,
bustard (oak turkey), and barred teal on each side.

Such feathers as florican bustard, light mottled turkey, and barred
Summer Duck have been omitted from this dressing as they are not
considered essential to the fly's success.

To finish the fly the tips of blue cock hackles are fitted in with jungle cock 'cheeks' on top and a topping is fitted over the full length of the wings. Then the fly's head is painted with black celluloid varnish.

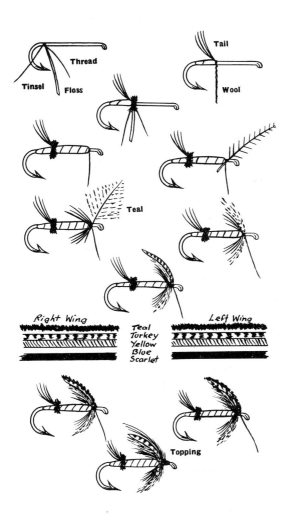

29

No. 11

Grey Duster

BY all accounts this pattern had its origin in Wales, but it now owes its over-all popularity as a dry fly to the publicity it was given by the late A. Courtney Williams in his *Dictionary of Trout Flies.*

It is not surprising—when you consider its trout killing qualities —that it almost tempted Mr. Williams to become a "one-pattern" angler.

While it enjoys a great measure of popularity just before or when the Mayfly is on the water I have to confess that I use it throughout the season from May onwards and count it among the best dry flies that were ever invented for trout.

It has proved especially useful to me as a floating pattern for lake and river fishing. In the early evening, when the sun is just leaving the water and rising trout are dimpling the surface I have found the Grey Duster to have few equals.

When I first used this fly I hackled it in the normal way, round the throat, but after a while I tried it with a horizontal hackle—the "Parachute" style, perfected by Alexander Martin, the Glasgow tackle-dealer—and found it even better in its performance.

As a stem on which to wind the hackle horizontally I used the thick end of a hackle stem, but one may use a small piece of stiff wire or gut instead.

It is a very easy fly to dress, and for the guidance of those who wish to try it I would suggest they make it up on several hook sizes —from 12 to 15 (old numbers).

The smallest size (15), although slightly more difficult to dress in "parachute" style, is particularly attractive to trout when they are midging in near-calm water and for all its smallness it is remarkable the number of big trout that come up for it—even in the absence of a rise.

Use brown tying silk for the tie, dubbing it with light rabbit's fur, with or without a touch of the blue under-fur.

Then put on a distinctive black and white badger hackle, fairly stiff in the fibre to give the fly buoyancy.

Before snipping off the protruding hackle stem (shown as "A" in the sketch), put a drop of celluloid varnish or shellac at the base of the stem, taking care, of course, that the varnish does not get on to the hackle.

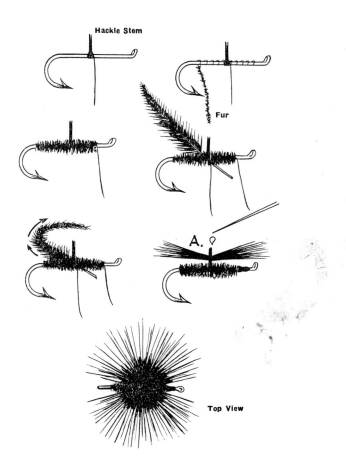

Hackle Stem

Fur

A.

Top View

No. 12

Houston Gem

HERE is a fly which enjoys a considerable reputation as a trout killer in the West of Scotland.

It was a red letter day in the life of the village postman when he delivered the Houston Gem. The postman was the late James Houston, who lived in the little Renfrewshire village of Kilmacolm.

Houston was an expert trout fisher. He literally haunted the nearby narrow waters of the River Gryfe and there are anglers in Renfrewshire who still talk of the tremendous catches he made with his home-tied spider flies.

Fortunately, Houston did not confine his fishing attentions to the Gryfe. He liked loch fishing and it was for this purpose that he invented the Gem.

As he first tied it the Houston Gem had Golden Pheasant tippets, a black silk body ribbed with flat silver tinsel, and a black hen hackle.

The wing was taken from what fly dresser's term the "church window" feather from the cock pheasant's neck. These are reddish-brown, tipped with dark brown, almost black, and pale fawn markings.

But later versions of the fly had a small piece of red feather (as used for the Silver Butcher) substituted for the Golden Pheasant tippets, which appears to improve the pattern's attractiveness.

The Houston Gem can be used with good results for sea trout as well as trout.

However, in dressing it for sea trout, it is necessary—the pheasant winging feather being so short in the web—to use two full feathers placed together.

Small pieces from either side of the feather are all that are needed for the wing of the trout fly—but be sure that they are well marked.

I fish the Houston Gem on the tail of the cast, where it appears to do its best work. It is a fly that does well at any time.

The method of dressing, as detailed in the sketch, is as follows:—
Tie in the red feather tippet (red silk would serve at a pinch), the
flat silver tinsel, and the black body silk.

Wind the silk up the hook shank and rib it with the flat tinsel.
Tie in the black hen hackle, and surmount this with the pieces of
pheasant back feather for the wing.

Mr. William Leckie, of Edinburgh, tells me that he received a
copy of a fly identical to the Houston Gem from a Penicuik man
pre-1914 and that it proved a most useful fly in the summer months
at Gladhouse Reservoir. It was known then as Pheasant Back and
Black.

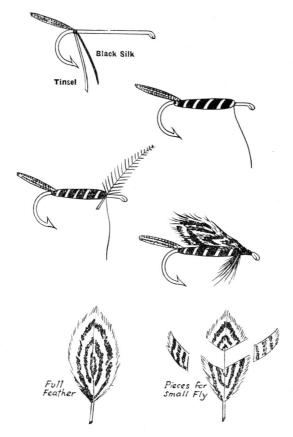

This, as Mr. Leckie states, would suggest that a fly dressed from
observation of natural insects may have more than one place of
origin.

33

No. 13

Thunder and Lightning

THREE things contribute to the lasting popularity of this fly. One is that it is easily dressed. Another is that it is a fly that can be relied upon to give a good account of itself on almost any salmon river where it is fished. Thirdly, it has an intriguing name.

It is particularly successful on a rising water, on rivers that are naturally dark, or when a spate is running off and the water has a dull porter colour. Yet its efficacy as a low water fly should never be overlooked when a river has fined down.

The dressing I give for the fly omits such feathers as Indian Crow (often used in conjunction with Golden Pheasant topping for the tail) and blue and yellow macaw (horns) not only because these are hard to secure, but because I feel they are not strictly necessary. Some fly dressers also omit the jungle cock cheeks—without apparently impairing the fly's efficiency—but I consider these add to the fly's attractiveness.

The first step in building this fly is to tie in the tag of flat (or round) silver tinsel, then a strip of yellow (gold) floss silk and a piece of black ostrich herl (for the butt).

Now tie in the flat (or oval) gold ribbing tinsel and black floss for the body. Once the body silk has been put on tie in a bright orange cock or hen hackle and wind it down the body towards the tail. Tie in the tip of the hackle with the ribbing tinsel and wind the tinsel in tight even turns towards the head.

Tie in the tinsel at the head, pick out the hackle fibres with a needle, and put on the throat hackle which can be either Blue Jay or a Guinea Fowl speckled hackle dyed bright blue.

The wing feathers are bronze mallard. These are difficult to manipulate by the novice so I suggest he place the corresponding feathers together and slightly smear the tips with celluloid varnish, which keeps them from splitting up. The varnish can later be removed with celluloid thinners.

Having tied in the wings and cut off the surplus, put in the jungle cock cheeks, one on each side of the wings.

All that remains now is to put on the Golden Pheasant topping, taper the head, finish off with a whip knot, and paint the head with black varnish.

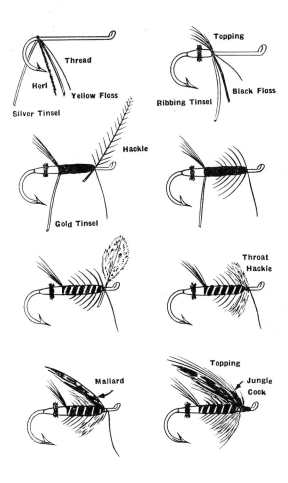

No. 14

Alder Fly

ONE of my favourite dry flies is what an angling acquaintance once described as a "forty-second cousin" to the Alder fly. I agree with the description, for this pattern of mine is without wings and is far removed from the original dressing of the artificial Alder fly supplied by Charles Kingsley.

The variation I use is more akin to the peacock and black spider introduced by T. C. Ivens in his very worthwhile book *Still Water Fly Fishing*, the exception being that my pattern is dressed with a cock hackle instead of the long-fibred hen hackle recommended by him. A further difference is that Mr. Ivens fishes his pattern deep sunk whereas the one I use is a floater.

The Kingsley dressing of the Alder fly gave the fly a dark freckled game-hen feather for the wing, a black hen hackle in front of the wings, and a body of peacock herl dyed magenta. And it was on this pattern that G. E. M. Skues killed as many as 60 trout, most of them over 1 lb. in weight in two days' fishing!

However, the Alder fly most commonly used today has an un-dyed bronze peacock herl body, a black cock or hen hackle, before or after the wings, and either grouse or brown speckled hen feathers for the wing. It seems to do just as well as the original.

I cannot agree with those who say that the Alder fly has never proved much of a success as a dry fly. I have, in fact, taken more fish with it as a floater than as a wet pattern, but that may be because I have used it more as a surface fly than a sunk one. I would certainly not be without it on my cast when the natural fly is on the water.

My sketch will serve to show how to dress the ordinary pattern of the fly, but in the case of the variation on which I pin my faith the details are as follows:—

Tie in a hackle butt on the centre of the hook stem. Build the tying silk round the butt to give it strength. Then put on the peacock herl body and tie in the black cock hackle. Wind the hackle in an anti-clockwise direction round the hackle butt. Tie down the end of the hackle and cut off the surplus. Finish off with a whip knot, raising the horizontal hackle fibres to do so.

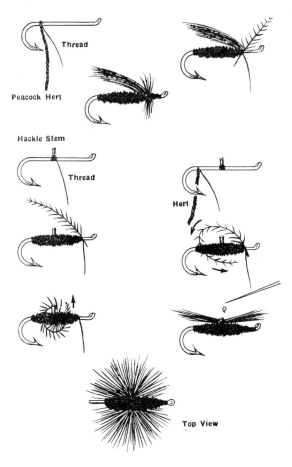

Put a drop of celluloid varnish or shellac on to the hackle butt and when this is dry snip off part of the hackle stump and press the hackle fibres flat with the fingers—and you will have a very deadly horizontally hackled fly.

No. 15

Alexandra

IT always seems a bit odd to me when anglers tell me that they
have never been able to take a fish on an Alexandra. For of all
the fancy flies that can be mounted to the tail of a wet fly fisher's
cast this is one of the deadliest.

I class it with the Peter Ross as a pattern that must be operated
in a certain way to make it more attractive. Obviously it does not
imitate a fly, but it could be taken for a minnow or beetle and for
this reason it should be worked in what might be described as dance
time—slow, slow, quick-quick, slow !

Vary the pace of line recovery so that the fly darts and hesitates
as a minnow or beetle might behave in the water. Keep it changing
course so that its flashiness may be seen to the best advantage by
the fish.

I prefer to fish the Alexandra deep-sunk and I find it does best
on wild, windy days when fish are taking the fly well below the
surface.

The Alexandra is essentially a lake fly. I don't say that it will not
fish well on a river, but its old name—Lady of the Lake—infers that
it was originally dressed for stillwater fishing. And I must say that
it enjoys a much better reputation on lochs or lakes than it does
on running water.

The Alexandra, or Lady of the Lake, as it was then called, was
introduced some time around 1860. It was re-named in honour of
Princess Alexandra.

There seems to be a bit of doubt about who created it. Some
think it was W. G. Turle, of Newton Stacey; others that it was Dr.
John Brunton, inventor of Brunton's Fancy.

The original dressing was:—Body—flat silver tinsel ribbed with
fine silver wire or oval tinsel; wing, several strands of green sword
peacock herl with strips of red-dyed feather tied in as cheeks to
the wing. The hackle was black hen and the tail a red feather tippet
with or without a short piece of the winging herl.

38

There are variations of this dressing. Some tie the fly with a pale turquoise hackle in place of the black one. Others surmount the green wing with a topping from the Golden Pheasant. The late Pat Castle, author of *Trout and How to Catch Them,* once told me that he preferred the fly to have small jungle cock cheeks in place of the red ones and I am informed that this makes a very attractive sea trout fly.

It was the Alexandra, I think, which gave rise to Paddy's Fancy (also called Erin's Pride), which only differs from the former in having a gold body and a yellow or hot orange hackle.

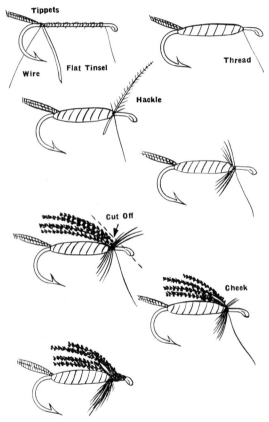

Here (with the help of a sketch) is the method of dressing the Alexandra:—Tie in red tippet, flat tinsel and wire. Take thread to neck of hook and wind flat tinsel up hook shank to form body; rib the body with wire to keep it from unravelling. Tie in black hen hackle and the strands of peacock herl (the number and length of the strands depends on the size of the fly) and tie down. Finish off with a whip knot, and varnish the fly's head.

39

No. 16

Coachman

FOR dark, calm nights, when trout are rising to sedges there are few flies to equal the Coachman. It's an odd thing, too, that although this white-winged fly would appear to be unrelated to any natural insect found on the water during daylight it has been known to kill fish in brilliant sunshine.

I have found it a particularly good pattern when trout were smutting at dusk or when caddis flies were capering on the water. Fished in a small size (14 or 15) it will also account for grayling.

Credit for the creation of the fly has been ascribed to either Tom Bosworth or John Hughes, both of whom were coachmen. The pattern, according to various writers, was originated in 1835.

However, there has recently come into my possession a faded cutting from a 1918 newspaper which states that *Salter's Angling Guide* (published in 1825) contains a reference to a fly much used at Watford in Hertfordshire. It describes this pattern as Harding's or The Coachman's Fly.

The first edition of Salter's book appeared in 1808 and if his reference to the Coachman was in this it would appear that the fly is much older than is generally supposed.

In its earliest dressings the Coachman is stated to have had a corncrake wing, and it is interesting to note that a fly so dressed is now known as the Dark Coachman.

Incidentally, writing 70 years ago, H. R. Francis stated that the Dark Coachman had a starling wing and was a deadly fly in brook fishing.

The Royal Coachman did not arrive on the scene till 1878. It was introduced by John Haily, an American, and was first used as a wet fly.

Modern dressings of the Coachman have a white hen or swan wing, but I find the white satin-like feathers obtainable from the inside of a mallard duck's wings to be much better because of their softness and durability. The body is made from bronze peacock herl, and the hackle is red-brown, cock or hen.

The dressing for the Royal Coachman, which is favoured a great deal more in America and Australia than it is in this country, is as follows: Body—bronze peacock herl tufts at throat and tail with dark red silk floss in between; wing—white swan; hackle—red/brown cock; whisks—the same as hackle. Incidentally, some fly tyers use Golden Pheasant tippets for the setae.

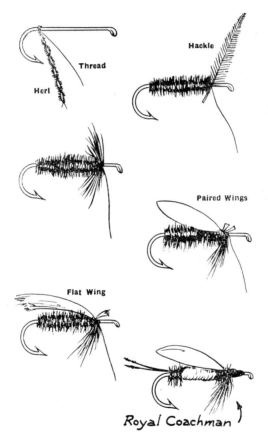

Royal Coachman

To dress the ordinary Coachman tie in two twisted strands of bronze peacock herl with any dark tie-silk. Wind the herl towards the neck of the hook and tie down.

Put on the hackle as shown in the sketch and tie in the wings The latter can be put on as paired feathers or in a small bunch, which can be pressed and tied down to lie flat across the fly's back

No. 17

Pope's
Nondescript

ONCE, when fishing the River Tweed at Norham, I put on a floating version of this fly and killed eight trout with it when the
fish were taking nothing else. Another time, using the pattern wet
on a nameless lough in the wilds of Donegal, I took a dozen trout
with it during a hatch of Lake Olives.

These experiences satisfy me that fished wet or dry Pope's Nondescript is a very useful pattern to have in the fly box.

It was first dressed by W. H. Pope, the noted Dorchester angler,
who fished it with marked success on the streams of Hampshire.
Presumably he produced the pattern as a variation of the much
older Blae and Green, which is a reasonable imitation of the Green
Midge (*C. Viridis*), frequently found on the surfaces of lakes and
reservoirs throughout Britain.

Pope's fly is a favourite chalk stream pattern, but its deadliness
has been proved on faster water as well. It should be dressed on a
small (15 or 16) hook.

Pope dressed his Nondescript with starling wings, a body of light
green floss silk, ribbed with flat gold tinsel, and with a bright red
cock hackle and setae.

The method of tying it is simple. Tie in several hackle fibres and
a short length of flat gold tinsel. Then tie in the green floss silk
and wind it tightly from tail to head in close turns, thickening the
body near the head to achieve a nicely tapered shape.

Take the matching pieces of starling wing—a snippet from two
corresponding primary feather quills—and fix them on to the hook
in an upright position. Then put on the cock hackle, which should
not be too long in the fibre, and criss-cross it before and behind
the wings taking care that you do not damage the wing feathers in
the process.

For wet fly fishing use a henny-cock hackle, shiny, but reasonably soft, and don't put on so many turns as you might do when hackling the dry pattern.

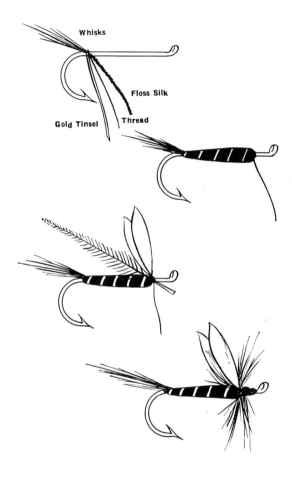

No. 18

Durham Ranger

THIS is one of those salmon flies which involve the use of whole feathers for the wings—the feathers, in this case, being the tippets from the neck of the Golden Pheasant. As a rule such patterns are easy to dress, and the Durham Ranger is no exception.

However, because its wings are made from whole feathers, there is a tendency to overdress this fly, so it is advisable to be sparing with the wings. Strip enough fibres off the sides of these to make them reasonably slim.

The first step in dressing a Durham Ranger is to tie in a piece of flat silver tinsel for a tag, following this with a couple of turns of yellow or gold floss silk.

Then tie in a small Golden Pheasant topping feather as a tail. The original dressing also insisted on a piece of Indian Crow in addition to the topping, but this is a refinement which can quite well be done without.

Now add a butt which can be made of black wool or ostrich herl. Then make two more turns of yellow or gold floss before tying in a longish badger cock hackle dyed orange.

Tie in this hackle by the tip. Then tie in a piece of oval silver tinsel which will be used to rib the body after the body hackle has been put on.

The body of the Durham Ranger consists of dubbed orange, fiery brown, and black seal's fur put on in even sections in that order from the tail end of the fly.

When the body dressing has been completed rib it with tight and even turns of the orange hackle and then with the oval tinsel. Don't make the fur body too thick; try, instead, to give it a nice taper. Then, when the ribbing hackle and tinsel have been applied, pick out the fur fibres with the point of a needle.

Now put on the throat hackle—a white cock hackle dyed bright blue.

Your next step is to put on the wings. These consist of two or three pairs of Golden Pheasant tippet feathers tied back to back, with Jungle Cock "enamelled" feathers intervening.

Begin by tying in two longish Jungle Cock feathers and surmount these with the tippet feathers, leaving the shiny pieces of the Jungle Cock feathers protruding slightly beyond the ends of the tippet feathers, as in the sketch.

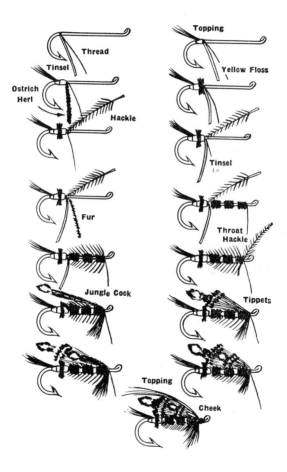

Now add the second pair of Jungle Cock feathers and put on a second pair of tippet feathers, leaving the Jungle Cock "cheek" feathers showing beyond the tips of the tippet feathers as before.

I invariably tie this pattern on 1 inch and 1¾-inch irons—sizes suitable for most salmon rivers in this country.

45

No. 19

Williams Favourite

THIS silver-ribbed variation of the Black Spider is a delightful fly to look at—and a deadly one, too, where trout and sea trout are concerned.

It was first tied by Alfred Williams who fished it consistently for the 60 years of his angling life and put more reliance on it as a trout killer than any other pattern.

His son, the late A. Courtney Williams, whose dictionary of trout flies is accepted as the standard work on fly histories and dressings, made no secret of the fact that the fly was his own standby from April to September and that he got more fish on it than any other pattern.

The fly bears more than a passing resemblance to that other splendid pattern, the Black Pennell. It fishes best on the bob and is particularly attractive when dibbled across the wavetops. However, it is the sort of fly that might be used with success almost anywhere on the wet fly cast.

Williams Favourite is, in fact, probably best known as a wet fly to be used when a river is clearing after a spate or when flooded burns have stained a lake or reservoir. But its creator's son, who got more pleasure out of dry fly fishing, has stated that it served him best as a floater—when the Black Gnat, and even the larger, but similar, Hawthorn fly, was on the surface.

I have used the fly on a 12 hook for sea trout on many Scottish rivers and can vouch for its killing powers even when the fish are not rising freely.

I like the wet fly sparsely dressed with no more than two or three turns of black hen hackle and the body distinctly tapered from head to tail. As a loch fly for trout I regard it as a fail-me-never.

Being a spider-type pattern Williams Favourite is easy to dress, the requirements being a few fibres of black hen or cock hackle for the setae, a piece of oval silver tinsel, a short length of black floss silk (wool, seal's fur or ostrich herl will do at a pinch).

46

Tie in the tail fibres, the silver tinsel, and the floss with black tie silk.

Now wind the floss up the hook shank in tight turns, thickening the body towards the head of the fly.

Tie down the body silk with a couple of half hitches and rib the black body evenly with the tinsel. Only three or at the most four turns of tinsel are necessary.

The black hen hackle is then put on in the way described for other spider-type flies. If required as a dry fly use a shiny, stiff, black cock hackle and whisks.

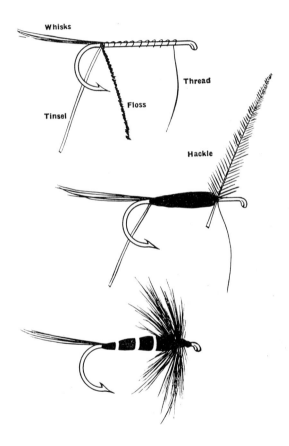

Tie the Williams Favourite on old number 14 and 15 hooks for trout and 12s and 10s for sea trout. Make a good stock of them for this is a fly which, once you have used it, you will never want to be without.

No. 20

Teal and Silver

WHETHER it is tied in tandem or single form the Teal and Silver is a deadly fly for sea trout. Few anglers who go after these migratory fish would care to be without it on their casts.

The view is held that it kills well because of its resemblance to herring fry or sprats on which sea trout and salmon are accustomed to feed in salt water.

At the same time, the Teal and Silver, tied in suitable sizes—14s to 10s (old numbers)—can be a very useful fly for brown trout. It is a special favourite for night fishing in high summer.

Some salmon fishers dress and use it as low water pattern with an abbreviated body and wing.

In some respects the Teal and Silver, or Teal and Blue, as it is sometimes known, is a simplified form of the Silver Doctor, a very popular salmon and sea trout pattern.

And, in fact, some amateur fly dressers try to imitate the latter by sheathing the teal wings with thin strips of yellow, blue, and red swan. The result is hardly a Silver Doctor, but a very good variation of the Teal and Silver.

To dress the ordinary pattern you require flat and oval or round silver tinsel, golden pheasant tippets or a small topping feather from the same bird (for the fly's tail), a white hackle dyed Cambridge blue, and a piece of barred teal plumage (for the wing).

Tie in the tippet fibres, then the oval and flat silver tinsel. Wind the flat tinsel up the hook stem towards the eye, and rib it with the oval tinsel. Now tie in a blue or turquoise hackle and wind it on.

Take corresponding pieces of the barred teal feather and place these together to form the wing, and tie down. Alternatively, you can take a whole piece of the teal plumage and fold it in two to form the wing.

Finish off with a whip-knot and paint the fly's head with black celluloid varnish.

Hook sizes for sea trout flies vary from 10s to 6s (old numbers).

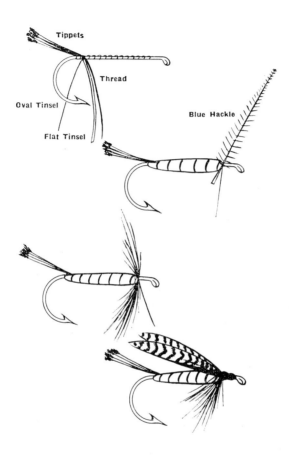

No. 21

The Poacher

THERE is a remote resemblance between the Poacher and the Coch-y-bonddu, previously referred to in this book. But whereas the latter is believed to imitate a beetle, the Poacher has no known natural counterpart.

It was invented in 1925 by Angus Robertson of the well known Glasgow firm of tackle dealers and was originally intended for sea trout fishing.

The Poacher had its baptism in Loch Lomond and it got its name simply from the fact that at the time it was introduced poaching was particularly rife in that area.

Its introduction to trout fishing came in rather amusing circumstances. A friend of Angus Robertson had gone to fish a well known loch in Sutherland and having a Poacher with him decided to put the pattern to the test.

The fly accounted for so many trout that its user was besieged by every angler staying at the lochside hotel to obtain copies of the killing pattern for them.

A telegram was despatched to Robertson. It was brief and to the point—"Send two dozen Poachers."

But a Post Office official who handled the message took it at its face value and promptly queried the ambiguous request. No one could blame him for wondering what anyone could want with two dozen poachers!

The tackle dealer promptly put the official's mind at rest and the Poachers were soon on their way.

Since that time the Poacher has been better known as a trout pattern than a sea trout one. It is particularly good as a bob fly where it seldom fails to interest the surface-feeding fish.

The dressing is—tail, a few fibres from the scarlet breast feather of the golden pheasant; tag, gold-coloured floss, mohair, or seal's fur; body, two strands of green peacock sword feather wound on as herl; and the tag and herl body ribbed with fine oval or round, gold tinsel; hackle, Furnace (red/black) cock or hen.

The whisks, oval tinsel, and floss are tied in at a point opposite the hook barb. Now wind the floss on to the hook shank for about a third of its length. Tie in the floss with a couple of half hitches of the tie silk and fasten down the green peacock herl. Wind the herl towards the eye of the hook and tie in, leaving sufficient room for the hackle, which I prefer to be slightly bushy.

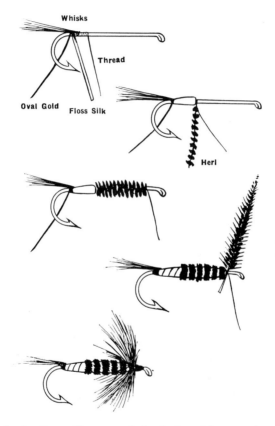

Now rib the floss silk tag and the body with several good tight turns of oval tinsel and put on the hackle. Strive to give the body a nicely tapered appearance.

The Poacher is a beautiful pattern and it can be used with equal confidence on lakes and rivers. It should be tied in sizes ranging from old number 14s to 12s for brown trout and 10s to 6s for sea trout. Dressed on a size 4 light wire salmon hook and thickly hackled it might do quite well as a dapping fly.

51

No. 22

Cowdung Fly

O N bright, sunny days, when there is a good wave on the water, there are few flies to match an artificial Cowdung fly for enticing trout.

A land-bred insect, the natural fly is familiar to every angler. In flight it appears to have an orange body, but actually, it has a brownish yellow body and two clear, distinctly veined wings each with a spot on them. The male fly is brighter in colour than the female.

One of the oldest dressings of the artificial fly is that supplied by Alfred Ronalds. He tied it with a yellow wool or mohair body with a pinch of brown fur added, landrail wings, and a ginger coloured-hackle.

This dressing is still used, but there is a tendency today to forget about the brown fur, make the most of a piece of dull yellow wool, and replace the landrail wing with pale starling. The hackle alone remains the same—ginger hen.

Nevertheless, I have seen dressings of the fly which had a light brown wool or seal's fur body and landrail wing. My own tie—a variation that I have used since I was a very young angler—has a mixed body.

The half nearest the tail of the fly is orange silk teased and wound on with the tie-thread; the other half is emerald green wool. The wing is made from the palest (almost fawn) feathers of a corncrake and the hackle is dark ginger and shiny (from a cock bird). No more than a couple of turns of this hackle are required.

I fish the fly as top dropper or bob and find that it gives of its best when it is brought tripping across the waves.

West of Scotland angler Ivan Calder has a distinctly different dressing. He ties the fly with a bright orange wool body, a dark ginger cock hackle (again shiny) and a very small bunch of speckled grouse hackle fibres, teased out, for the wings.

As will be observed in my sketches I use a closed-wing fly for wet fly fishing and a flat, folded wing for the floating pattern.

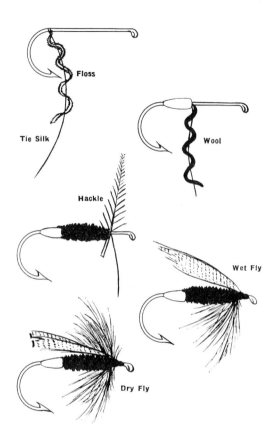

No. 23

Blue Charm

I KNOW successful salmon fishers who use the Blue Charm to the exclusion of every other pattern. They are content to fish it in various sizes—ranging from $\frac{3}{4}$-inch to $1\frac{1}{2}$-inch irons. And they maintain that by changing the size of fly to suit the water and light they have taken fish after a succession of other patterns have gone unheeded.

Fishing a river where the big runs of sea trout occur about the beginning of August it frequently pays to put a Blue Charm on the tail of the sea trout cast. It will not only prove attractive to sea trout but may interest any salmon that happen to be in the river. However, if you mix your salmon and sea trout fishing in this way be sure that you use gut or nylon of the necessary strength to cope with the bigger fish.

Here is a tip about preparing the wing of the fly. This was given to me by the late Tom Finlayson, of Houston, a professional tyer, who dressed many thousands of salmon flies in his lifetime.

Take a $\frac{1}{2}$-inch broad (or slightly less, depending on the size of fly) strip of mottled brown turkey tail feather. Draw a needle through the centre of the feather to make two halves. Then take a $\frac{1}{8}$-inch broad piece of barred teal feather of the necessary length and insert this between the two halves of turkey feather.

Smooth the fibres (turkey and teal) together between the fingers till they "marry." Then bend the entire feather so that there is a piece of teal on the upper edge of each wing. Leave the wings aside until you are ready to tie them in.

First step in building the body of the fly is to tie in a piece of round or flat silver tinsel as a tag. Then tie in a piece of yellow or gold floss silk, and when this has been wound on tie in a small Golden Pheasant topping for the tail.

54

Tie in a couple of fibres of black ostrich herl for butt and flat silver tinsel to be used for ribbing. Use black floss silk for the body, giving it a slight taper from the head downwards.

Once the black body has been completed, rib it evenly and firmly with the flat silver tinsel. Then apply the hackle for which I prefer a white cock hackle dyed bright blue.

Now put on the folded wings and surmount them with a length of Golden Pheasant topping. The result should be a very attractive fly—and a very deadly one.

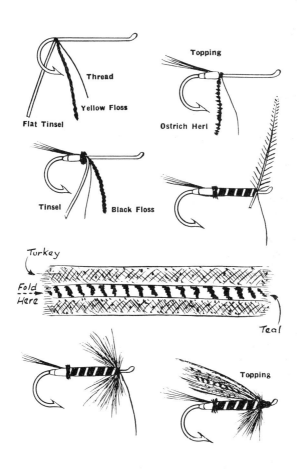

55

No. 24

McLeod's Olive

Dressings of the natural olives that skip and skate on the surface of almost every lake and river in this and certain other countries are legion, but I have yet to find one that kills so well as this one does at Loch Leven.

The natural Olive of which this fly is an imitation hatches out in greater numbers than any other insect on this loch, barring, perhaps, the extremely prolific White Moth.

It is so plentiful that on many summer evenings it is possible to find a mound of these Olives one foot deep under the light on the pier at Kinross!

According to George Scott, the noted Dunfermline fly dresser, whose knowledge of natural and artificial flies peculiar to Loch Leven is probably unmatched by any other angler, McLeod's Olive is a very old pattern. He produced a dressing of it about 30 years ago—the one I am about to describe—yet he can remember its being used much earlier than that. Many anglers, like Mr. Scott, regard it as a "must" on the wet fly cast from June onwards.

McLeod's Olive, which would appear to have been introduced by a person of that name, is not altogether unlike the Burleigh or Blae and Green, elsewhere mentioned in this book, and it is said that when one is taking fish it is a pretty safe bet that the other will do the same. But results prove that the McLeod's Olive kills much better.

This Olive is a pretty easy fly to dress. Materials required are: Medium olive green wool for the body; medium olive green hen feather for the hackle and setae; and snips of starling secondary feathers for the wings. No more than two turns of flat gold tinsel are added as a tip to the body.

Tie in the olive green tippet fibres or setae with pale olive or yellow tying silk, then add the gold tinsel for the tip or tag.

Now tease out a pinch of olive green wool or mohair and dub it on to the hook stem with the tying silk as shown in the sketch. Tie in the medium olive green hackle feather and wind on. Snip off the surplus hackle fibres and tie in the pieces of starling winging feathers. Finish off with a whip-knot and varnish the fly's head.

Dress the fly on a size 14 or 15 hook (old numbers) and fish it as a dropper. It is particularly deadly on the bob.

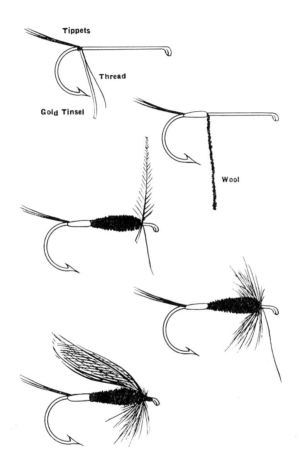

No. 25

Scott's Fancy

THIS pattern is an imitation of the so-called Fisherman's Curse— that little creamy-coloured fly that comes out in droves on summer evenings and drives anglers almost to distraction as trout dash and snatch at it with almost complete disregard for their assorted flies.

Loch Leven anglers refer to the natural fly as the White Moth, though it is in no way connected with the moth family.

It is not to be confused, moreover, with those little white "midges" (Caenis, known as the Little White Curse) that periodically appear in smoke-like clouds over the water.

The artificial fly I am describing was first dressed by George Scott, of Dunfermline, about 1940. He copied it from the natural insect.

In recent years we have not seen so many hatches of the Fisherman's Curse on Loch Leven, but I have known times when the natural flies were dipping and dancing in their hundreds above the water and the fish were coming eagerly to Mr. Scott's pattern, to the absolute exclusion of everything else.

One such experience was enough to make any angler at Loch Leven never to be without a Scott's Fancy on his cast.

Indeed, when there were big hatches on the loch there were any number of knowing anglers who could afford to discard all other patterns and fish four Scott's Fancy flies on their casts!

This artificial fly has a body of peacock herl dyed dark green. It has a yellowish green floss silk tip in imitation of the egg sac— tied in as a tag. No more than two or three turns of the silk are necessary.

The body should never be bulky. In fact the flue should be scraped from the herl before it is dyed.

58

The hackle is pale fawn and the wings are from the palest, almost creamy undercoverts of the corncrake's wings.

I have had success with this fly on many waters. Indeed, when and wherever, the Fisherman's Curse appeared in numbers I have enjoyed good sport with a pattern based on the one created by Mr. Scott. It should be dressed on hooks ranging from 15 to 12 (old numbers).

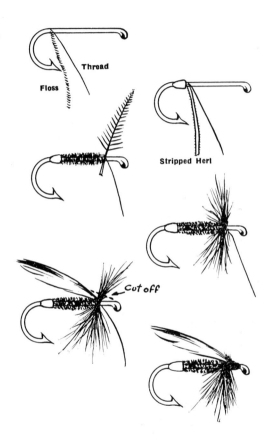

No. 26

Water Cricket

FOR lake fishing this is one of my favourite patterns. However, I have to confess that my dressing of the Water Cricket differs from that recommended by Alfred Ronalds in 1836. It would be fairer to describe my tying of the fly as a variation. It is the one most used in my part of the country.

Ronalds wound one or two of the longest of peewit topping feathers or a black cock hackle down the fly's body, after which some of the hackle fibres were snipped off, leaving only the leg hackle at the throat. But equally good results can be achieved with a small, wispy throat hackle of black hen. Also, while I use the orange floss silk body recommended by Ronalds, I rib it with thick black cotton thread.

The Water Cricket is a very good pattern for wet fly fishing during the hot days of summer when it and other small water beetles are much in evidence

I would not suggest, however, that the pattern I use is taken for the natural water cricket (*Velia currens*). I think that it is representative of quite a number of forms of life on which the fish feed.

The Water Cricket is essentially a wet fly. I use it on the tail of a three-fly cast and have found it to be particularly attractive when well sunk.

Here is my dressing of the pattern which is simply tied. Tie in a piece of black cotton thread (for ribbing the body), and a short length of orange or gold coloured floss silk. Wind the floss up the body as shown in the sketch and rib it evenly with the black thread.

Tie in a sooty black hen hackle and make no more than three turns.

I have also seen the fly dressed with the black crest feather of a plover or with a tiny blue-black feather taken from the outside of a rook's wing.

The fly is usually dressed on a size 14 hook.

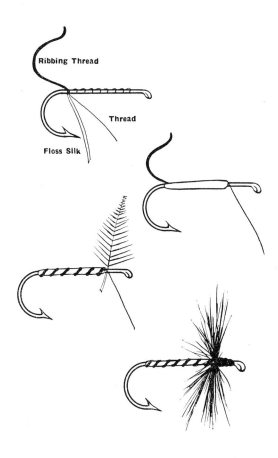

No. 27

Hairy
Mary

THERE are so many variations of the Hairy Mary—a very popular salmon fly for most of the rivers in this country—that the name is now applied to almost any hair-winged pattern.

One of the latest ties—and a very killing one on such Scots rivers as the Echaig, in Argyllshire, the Stinchar and the Doon in Ayrshire, and the Nith and Tweed—is the one I am giving now.

It was first dressed by the late Tom Finlayson, the noted Scottish fly dresser, whose much-lamented death, after a lifetime devoted to salmon-fly dressing, left a void in angling circles.

Mr. Finlayson fished two flies to the cast—the blue-bodied one under discussion and another with a crimson body.

The body material in each case consisted of Lurex tinsel, which has the advantage that it does not change colour or tarnish.

Both patterns are dressed on sizes 6 to 8 low water hooks, either singles or doubles.

The tag is made of silver and crimson floss silk. The tail is a topping with Indian Crow (or a small piece of dyed orange feather) on top, and the butt is black ostrich herl or wool.

Thinly pad the body with blue floss silk before putting on the blue Lurex tinsel. This ensures that the tinsel goes on smoothly and evenly. Then rib the Lurex tinsel with ordinary oval silver tinsel.

The hackle is black hen, very thinly put on.

The wing consists of dyed black bucktail topped with a few fibres of orange bucktail or deer hair.

In the case of the crimson-bodied pattern the hackle is a white hen hackle dyed pillar-box red with a throat one of lightly barred teal or widgeon added.

The wing is made up of black and white badger hair with a few fibres of orange bucktail on top. The tag in this case is silver (flat or oval) and golden yellow floss.

62

The two patterns are especially useful for greased line fishing. They can be dressed in smaller sizes for sea trout fishing.

There is also the original Hairy Mary, the dressing of which is as follows: Tail—Golden pheasant topping; Body—Black floss, ribbed oval silver or gold tinsel; Hackle—Blue; Wing—Brown bucktail or brown squirrel tail.

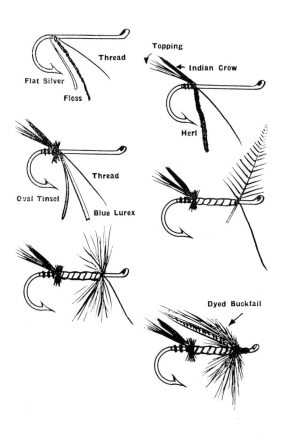

No. 28

Logie

THIS is one of the more popular low water salmon flies for use in greased line fishing in reduced water.

It is a particularly good pattern for small river fishing, its principal characteristics being the sparcity of the dressing and the colourful appearance of the materials with which it is built.

The lightness of the dressing serves two purposes. One is to give the fly a translucent effect, which becomes the more apparent when the bronze mallard feather used in its wing splits up and assumes a hair-like texture. It is for this reason that some anglers tease the mallard sheath winging feathers out with a pin before using the fly.

The other reason is to give the fly the requisite buoyancy to enable it to swim just below the surface, in which position it is most effective.

Low water flies of the Logie type have become established favourites on many rivers where the levels fall rapidly after a flood and the water takes little or no time at all in settling.

To dress the Logie, tie in a piece of fine round or flat silver tinsel as a tag. It should be positioned about half-way between the point of the hook and the eye, it being remembered that the body is greatly abbreviated in low water types of salmon fly.

Now tie in a piece of fine oval silver tinsel to be used for ribbing the fly's body, which consists of pale primrose floss silk (for about a third of the body) and bright red floss silk for the remaining two thirds. Make sure that the silk is not too thickly put on. A slim body is essential though some effort should be made to give it a slight taper from the head downwards.

Add a small Cambridge blue shiny cock hackle, putting this on rather sparingly.

The wings consist of two pieces of yellow goose or swan feather tied in the form of a strip wing, with a slightly upward tilt.

Next take two narrow strips of bronze mallard plumage and tie these in so that they slope downwards over the yellow wing feathers. No overlapping topping feather is necessary and all that remains is to finish off with a whip-knot and paint the fly's head with black celluloid varnish.

Use the recognized low water type of hook in sizes from 10 (roughly 11/16th of an inch) to 6 (about 1 inch).

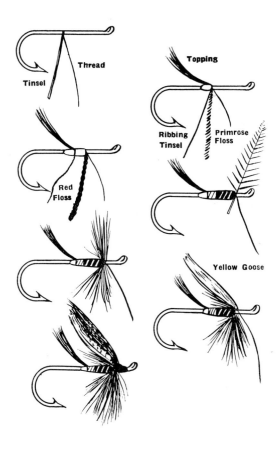

No. 29

Red
Legs

FLY FISHERS have at least four names for this large, glassy-winged and black-bodied insect, which invariably appears on the surface of the water about the beginning of August.

It is possibly better known as the Bloody Doctor or the Heather Fly, the latter being a name applied to it many years ago, in *Salmon and Trout Magazine*, by John Henderson, who suggested that the imitation of it should be dressed with a Coch-y-bondhu (ginger-tipped) hackle.

But, since the legs of the natural fly are nearer to scarlet—thus the name—a much more lifelike imitation can be achieved by using a black and white badger hackle dyed pillar-box red.

The Red Legs, to give the fly the name by which it is best known in the West of Scotland, where it is a favourite dry fly in the autumn, is about half-an-inch long. It is rather like a large edition of the angler's Blae and Black—except that it has comparatively thick red legs.

Like the Alder fly, for which it is often mistaken, although the wings of the Alder are noticeably duller and heavily veined, the Red Legs is a landborn insect, hatching out among trees or heather. It is either blown on to the water or falls on it in the course of flight. Where these flies are found fish rise to them with great gusto, giving them a reception similar to that accorded to the Red or Brown Ant, which incidentally, is very often found on the water at the same time as the Red Legs.

Quite the best of the dry fly imitations of the natural insect is the one provided by Duncan Macalpine, of Greenock and District Angling Club, who created the pattern whose dressing I am now supplying. Various methods have been tried in order to achieve the shiny black body, the best, up till now, being obtained with black ostrich herl, ribbed with fine, flat, silver tinsel.

The wing, which is folded and tied on flat, after the manner of of winging a sedge fly, is obtained from a young starling's outer coverts. I recommend the young bird because the blae feather is much paler than that of an older bird. Use the feather inside out to achieve a shiny effect.

Take the piece of feather and fold it over twice between the fingers and place it squarely on top of the ostrich herl, silver ribbed body. Then apply the pillar-box red hackle, which should not be too long in the fibre, but sufficiently thick to keep the fly afloat.

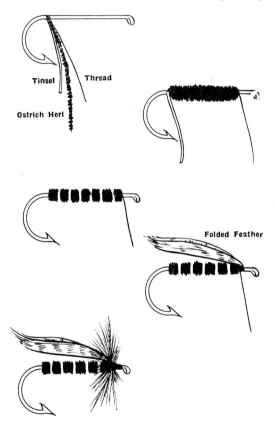

Since the natural insect is half-an-inch or thereabouts in length I usually dress the Red Legs on a size 11 or 12 (old numbers) light wire hook and fish it dry.

Merioneth angler and fly dresser Mr. Andrew Hughes tells me that over 30 years ago he evolved a pattern of the Heather Fly (or Bóngôch, as he named it in Welsh) and that when he first used it he got 17 fish out of 25 rises!

No. 30

Burleigh

CONTRARY to the widely-held belief this green-bodied, blae-winged fly, a favourite at Loch Leven, is not a recently invented pattern.

Mr. George Scott, the noted Dunfermline fly tier and an acknowledged authority on the fly life and other matters relating to this famous Scottish loch, tells me that he can remember the fly being used as far back as 40 to 50 years ago. It was then known as the Blae and Green, a name still given to the fly in other parts of the country.

The Burleigh, which differs from the normal tie of the Blae and Green by having a small gold tag or tip, was named after Burleigh Castle or the Burleigh Sands on the northern shore of Loch Leven, where is appears to fish best.

Yet the Burleigh's trout killing propensities are by no means confined to this productive area of Loch Leven. The fly has enjoyed a wide measure of success in many other waters, and, in fact, wherever green-bodied fly patterns are popular.

Mr. Scott first dressed the gold-tipped pattern some 30 years ago, and although he says with disarming modesty that his fly and the patterns popularly sold as Burleigh do equally well I must (having tried them all!) state a preference for the one that Mr. Scott ties and uses with marked success.

I normally use the pattern as a point fly or first or second dropper on a four-fly cast. If it happens to be killing fish I have no hesitation in putting on two—one on the tail and another on an intermediate place on the cast. The pattern is at its best from early June onwards.

The Burleigh has a fairly long tippet—two or three fibres from the Golden Pheasant's black-tipped orange neck feathers. The body is medium green, ribbed with the finest oval gold tinsel or wire. The hackle is light ginger and the wing, which can be made from starling or teal duck feather, is pale blae.

68

The fly is dressed on hook sizes ranging from 16s to 12s (either singles or doubles). These are old numbers.

To dress the Burleigh, tie in the tippet fibres, gold wire, and fine flat gold tinsel. Take a pinch of medium green wool, tease it with the fingernails, and then roll it into a taper between the palms of the hands. Work the thin end of the tapered wool on to the tying thread and wind the wool on to the shank of the hook. Then rib it with the oval tinsel or wire.

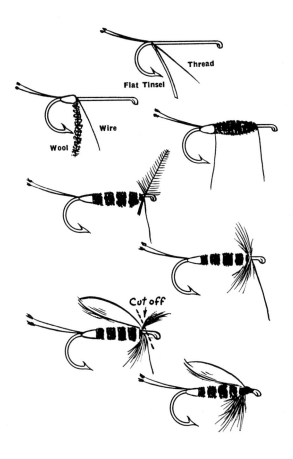

My diagrams show the whole process of tying in the materials, but I would advise the tier to use a pale green tying thread, and to remember that no more than two turns at most of flat gold tinsel are required for the tag or tip.

69

No. 31

Connemara Black

IRELAND, rightly or wrongly regarded as the birthplace of the fancy fly, has surely never produced a more popular pattern than this one.

Not only is it a first-class wet fly for trout fishing in lakes or rivers; it kills many sea trout, and takes its quota of salmon every season.

Perhaps my most interesting association with this pattern springs from a meeting I had with an angler on the River Don, in Aberdeenshire, several years ago. Looking through the contents of my flybox he took a fancy to the Connemara Black. I presented it to him and he caught seven trout with it.

Since then he has never tired of singing the praises of this fly—and now that he spends a great deal of his time in pursuit of sea trout in the rivers of Western Ireland I receive an unfailing request from him at the beginning of each new fishing season for a supply of "CB's"!

I dress the fly in three sizes—12s, 10s, and 6s—which are all suitable for the taking of trout, sea trout and the possible salmon.

The pattern is not a difficult one to dress. For the body one has the option of using black wool or seal's fur. I prefer the latter because wool, in my opinion, has a "dead" appearance when wet. At times, when I have been without seal's fur I have used black ostrich herl without detracting from the attractiveness of the fly.

The method of dressing the fly is as follows:—Tie in a small Golden Pheasant topping for the tail; a piece of swan feather dyed yellow will do at a pinch.

Then tie in the round or oval silver tinsel to be used for ribbing the fly's body. Take a small pinch of seal's fur and tease and break it into small lengths with the finger nails. Rub it between the palms of both hands to taper it and tie in the pointed end close to the ribbing tinsel. Roll the remaining fur round the tie-silk, which should be of any dark colour.

Wind the fur towards the head of the fly and tie down. Now rib the body with the tinsel in tight turns. Tie down the tinsel.

Tie in a black cock or hen hackle and when this has been wound on, tie in a throat hackle consisting of a piece of blue, barred jay feather—or, better still for manipulating purposes—a speckled guinea fowl hackle feather dyed bright blue.

The wings are from the bronze shoulder plumage of a mallard.

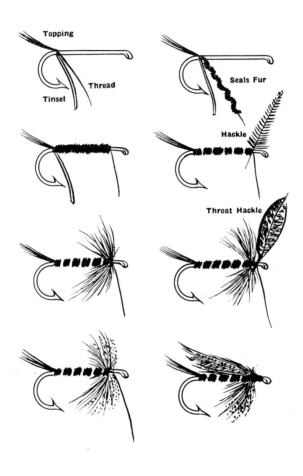

No. 32

Tup's Indispensable

NOW well over 50 years old, the Tup, to give it its usual abbreviation, is held in esteem by anglers all over the world as a fairly good representation of several duns and spinners. It is also fished very successfully as a nymph.

It was invented by the late R. S. Austin of Tiverton at the beginning of this century and quickly acquired a reputation for itself as a trout killer.

The Tup—or perhaps I should say my variation of it—has proved effective as a wet and dry pattern. I use it from mid-April to the end of the trout season and have had much success with it on river and loch. It is especially useful as a floater at dusk.

My dressing for the pattern is as follows: Tail—a few fibres of bright honey dun-cock; body—a mixture of tup's wool (thoroughly cleaned before use) with the merest suggestion of crimson seal's fur. The tag (at the end of the body) consists of two turns of bright yellow floss silk picked out with a pinpoint. The hackle is bright honey dun cock, which is recognizable by its golden-ginger points and a centre of pale grey or light (Andalusian) blue.

This is my usual dressing for the dry fly. For the wet or sunk pattern I replace the honey dun hackle with a small white, creamy-tipped hackle dyed pale blue dun.

The dyeing process brings out the hackle edges in a nice rusty shade. I dress the Tup in two sizes, 14 and 16 (old numbers).

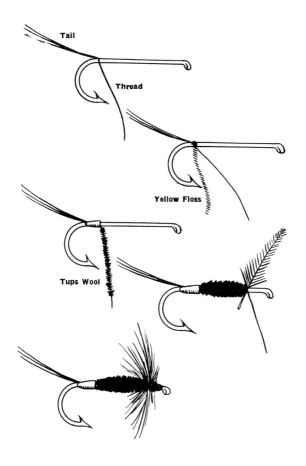

Tail

Thread

Yellow Floss

Tups Wool

73

No. 33

Grey

Squirrel

ANGLERS who prefer their salmon flies to be "thin on the wing" will like the Grey Squirrel, which already enjoys a very good reputation as a salmon killer on medium to small rivers.

It is especially popular with those who fish the River Annan in Scotland, but it will no doubt do good work on almost any river in the proper conditions.

This pattern is best for a clear, settled water. Fishing it on a small West Highland river last season a friend of mine took 11 salmon with it and killed 23 sea trout.

The beauty of the Grey Squirrel is that it is very easy to dress even by a novice in the art of fly tying. The materials, moreover, are likely to be found in almost every fly dresser's kit.

The squirrel-hair wing is somewhat similar in appearance to white-tipped turkey, but being more fibrous has a great deal more "play" in the water than the latter.

Dress the pattern on sizes 6 to 2 low water irons and do not be tempted to make the fly in any way bulky. Slimness is its killing attribute.

First step in dressing the pattern is to put on a flat gold tinsel tag (no more than two turns). Then add a Golden Pheasant topping as a tail and a black ostrich herl butt.

The body consists of black floss silk ribbed with fine flat gold tinsel. The hackle is pale blue (as in Teal and Blue) and the wing is a small bunch of grey squirrel hair, long enough in the fibre to reach the end of the hook.

Be rather sparing with the squirrel hair. In fact, it has been known for a pattern which had killed a great many fish and had only about half a dozen hairs left as a wing to keep on killing salmon.

If you find any difficulty in putting on the hair wing dip the ends which are to be tied in in celluloid varnish and allow this to harden before putting on the wing.

See that the hair wing lies down over the back of the fly's body.
The same fly can be dressed (with shorter hair fibres, of course)
on a size 10 (old number) hook for sea trout.

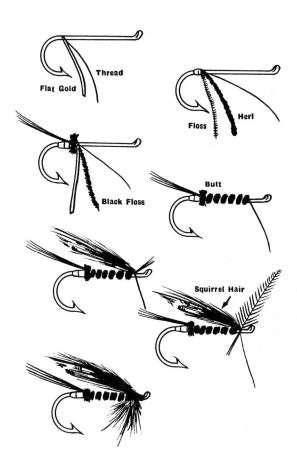

No. 34

Cinnamon and Gold

THERE is no doubt that this pattern derives from the age-old Cinnamon Fly—and as a trout and sea trout killer is clearly its superior.

It is particularly good as a lake pattern and fished in small sizes (14s or 15s, singles and doubles) it takes many a fish from waters like Loch Awe and Loch Leven every season.

The Cinnamon and Gold is especially useful when trout are rising but apparently are not keen on taking the artificial fly.

Some anglers maintain that the Cinnamon and Gold fishes best late in the season but it has been known to kill well as early as April. It is certainly a worthwhile fly to have on the wet or sunk cast when one is in doubt about what fly to put on the central position of a three-fly cast.

The wing, hackle, and even the tail of this fly are subject to variation in the hands of different fly dressers, but the most common materials are dark brown hen for the wings, a dark ginger hen hackle for the legs, and a few Golden Pheasant tippet fibres for the tail.

Some anglers prefer the wings to be made from dark brown owl, the cinnamon feather from a partridge's tail, or even corresponding pieces from reddish-brown corncrake quills.

A piece of red ibis or suitably dyed feather can be substituted for the tippet fibres in making the tail and a light ginger hen hackle may be used for the legs instead of the more usual dark one.

Tie in the tippet fibres or red feather first. Then fix in a piece of flat gold tinsel and wind this on in close, tight turns along the hook stem.

Now tie in the ginger hackle and wind it on. Then place the corresponding pieces of brown hen feather over the back of the hook and tie down. Cut off the surplus and finish off with a whip-knot.

For sea trout flies dress the pattern on sizes 10 to 6 (old numbers). The sketch shows the style of dressing to try to achieve.

76

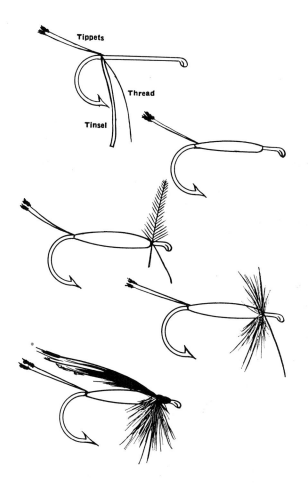

Tippets

Thread

Tinsel

No. 35

Blue
Dun

BEING such an old pattern—it was used by Charles Cotton 300 years ago—the Blue Dun has most certainly run the gauntlet of variation.

There are so many different dressings of the fly—each a favourite in its own locality—that it is difficult to decide on a standard style to suit the tastes of anglers everywhere.

My choice is one of the oldest dressings, the one used almost exclusively by professional fly tiers.

This pattern has dark starling or snipe wings, a yellow silk body lightly dubbed with mole's fur, a pale blue hen hackle, and whisks from the same source.

It is one of my spring time favourites—a fly to be fished sunk from late March until early June, and one which is particularly useful when Dark Olives or Iron Blues are hatching.

In the case of the dry fly I use a small bunch of fibres from a waterhen's breast feather to imitate the wings. These are tied on to the hook as shown in the sketch, then pulled into an upright position with the tying thread.

When the shiny blue dun cock hackle is put on the waterhen fibres are shown in silhouette or impressionist form through the hackle, and if teased out with a pinpoint are much less opaque than the normal starling wing feather.

I might also mention that when dressing the wet pattern I frequently use a pale Greenwell type of hackle—light brown with honey tips—in place of the blue hen one, and find it equally satisfactory.

Dressing the wet fly is a pretty straightforward process so I will confine instructions to the tying of the floating pattern.

First make the wing. Take a small bunch of fibres from a piece of waterhen's breast plumage and shape them into a small wad between the fingers.

Now tie in two or three fibres taken from a blue hen hackle to represent the setae or whisks. Tease out a pinch of mole's fur (water

78

rat or blue cat fur will also serve) and roll this on to the yellow tying silk.

Wind the mole's fur along the hook stem towards the "eye" and tie down. Take care that you don't overclothe the yellow silk with the dubbing material; you merely want to veil the tying silk so that the yellow silk "shines" through.

Now tie in the bunched waterhen fibres. Then tie in a blue hen cock hackle and wind it in front of and behind the wing fibres.

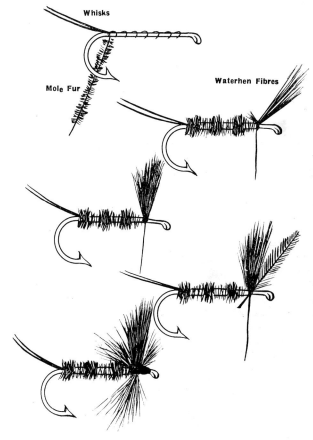

You can add a second hackle for extra buoyancy but remember that you are dressing a pattern to imitate a dun—a very delicate creature, and don't make the mistake of giving the fly a bulky appearance.

Hook sizes range from 16s to 14s, but you might care to tie a few patterns on size 12 hooks for use on a fast stream or a heavily-waved loch.

No. 36

Invicta

THIS is a most dependable fly for lake fishing and enjoys a considerable reputation as a trout killer on big waters like Chew Valley and the lochs of Scotland.

It can be especially useful as a bait fly on a spring cast when, if it is fished deep, it will often put a few trout in the bag. It also accounts for many fish on summer evenings when it is possibly mistaken by the trout for a large sedge fly.

The writer has fished it singly as a floating fly when large caddis flies were cruising about on summer nights and has found it just as effective as any wake fly. This is not surprising when it is remembered that the Invicta—or the Victor, as it is sometimes called—was invented by the late James Ogden, of Cheltenham, as an imitation of a dark sedge.

In small sizes (14s to 12s, old numbers) one can use yellow wool or floss silk teased out for the body, but yellow seal's fur makes a more suitable body for the larger sizes of flies.

The yellow body is ribbed with oval gold tinsel or gold wire (for small sizes) and the red cock hackle is carried down the body in palmer style.

A further red cock hackle can be added at the shoulder before the throat hackle, which is of blue jay or speckled guinea fowl dyed pale blue, is tied in.

The wing is made from corresponding pieces of the central feather of the hen pheasant's tail and a small golden pheasant topping or crest feather serves as a tail for the fly.

Some fly dressers tie the body hackle by the tip at the tail and wind it up the body but it is easier, in my opinion, to tie the hackle in by the ordinary method—that is by the root—at the throat of the hook and wind it down the body. The tip can then be secured with the tinsel and the surplus hackle fibres cut off.

This fly should never be overdressed, so it is advisable to keep the materials to a minimum. The body hackle should do no more than slightly veil the yellow wool or seal's fur.

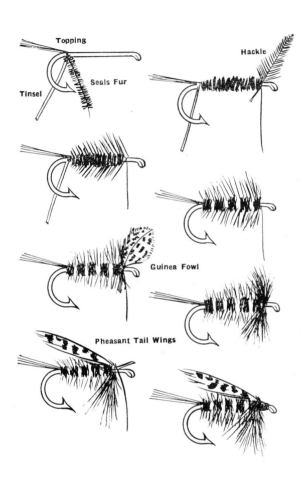

No. 37

Loch
Ordie

PROBABLY best known as a dapping fly, the Loch Ordie can be used to imitate the large caddis flies or moths that enliven the waterside scene on summer nights.

Chiefly composed of hackles put on in palmer style, it consists of two hooks tied closely together in tandem, with a small treble hook attached to a piece of gut tied in at the head.

The body hackles are brown, but an additional white cock or hen hackle is frequently wound in at the throat, though this isn't strictly necessary.

The Loch Ordie is especially useful as a dapping fly in the remote waters of the Scottish Highlands, but it has also been known to do well in the larger lakes of England and Wales and in the loughs of Ireland.

Fished in ordinary dry fly fashion (without the aid of the blow line essential to its efficacy as a dapping fly) its deadliness as a wake fly for bustard fishing is without doubt. Used as a bob fly for loch fishing on rough days it kills many big trout and sea trout every season.

When used as an ordinary dry fly, to be brought skimming across the surface in quick, erratic fashion, it does not require the flying treble. And, indeed, like myself, many anglers dispense with the treble when tying the fly even for dapping purposes.

If the treble is employed care should be taken that its hooks do not extend more than threequarters of the length of the entire fly. The treble hooks can be as small as 14s (old style) and they can be set to trail on either side of the fly.

The main hooks of the Loch Ordie are joined in tandem with a piece of strong gut or wire. After the hooks are linked together exert a strong pull to make sure they will not come apart.

Tie in the first brown cock hackle, as shown in the sketch, and wind it up the body until all the fibres are exhausted. Now tie in the second hackle and repeat the winding process until both hook stems and the intervening piece of gut or wire have been covered with hackles.

Remember to leave sufficient room at the head of the fly for the attachment of the treble and the additional white hackle. The treble appendage is put on last.

This is the normal dressing of the Loch Ordie, but variations can be achieved with different colours of hackle.

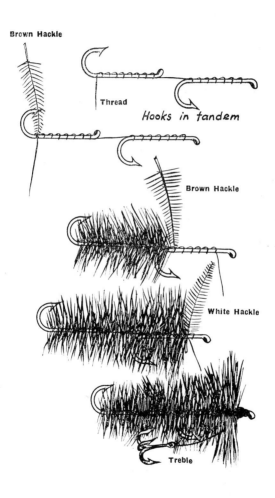

Brown Hackle

Thread

Hooks in tandem

Brown Hackle

White Hackle

Treble

No. 38

Shrimp Fly

IN some of the smaller rivers where I fish the pattern that kills most of the salmon is the Shrimp Fly—and the most popular version of it is Curry's Red.

The inventor, Pat Curry, of Coleraine, Northern Ireland, did a big service for salmon fishers when he produced this pattern, though it has been subjected—such is the inventiveness of anglers—to a host of variations.

All kinds of so-called Shrimp Flies kill many salmon every season but I would go so far as to say that Curry's Red takes a large percentage of them. I could enumerate several Shrimp Fly dressings but Curry's pattern is my personal choice.

Tie in a flat silver tag. Then tie in and wind on a piece of scarlet Golden Pheasant breast feather as a hackle. It should be long enough in the fibres to extend beyond the end of the hook.

The tail half of the body is red floss ribbed with oval silver tinsel, while the second half is of black floss ribbed with slightly thicker oval silver tinsel.

Both halves are veiled above and below with Indian Crow for which pieces of pale gold Golden Pheasant back feathers or small pieces of white feather dyed hot orange make suitable substitutes.

The centre hackle is badger (black and white) while the wings are two pieces of Jungle Cock cheek feathers tied back to back—and long enough to extend to the end of the body.

The front hackle is also badger and should be slightly longer in the fibres than the centre one.

The original pattern had its head varnished red but this is a refinement that can be done without.

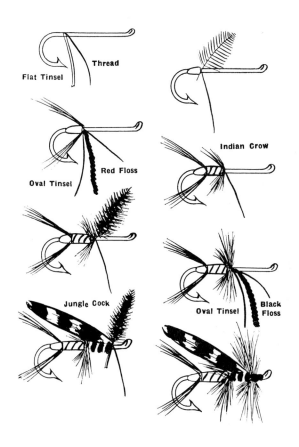

Flat Tinsel

Thread

Oval Tinsel

Red Floss

Indian Crow

Jungle Cock

Oval Tinsel

Black Floss

85

No. 39

Snipe and Purple

M ANY anglers regard this spider-type fly as indispensable on the early-season wet fly cast. It is particularly useful in late March and all through April, but it has also been known to take well during cold, blustery days in summer and autumn, especially when the diminutive Iron Blue Dun, which it is said to imitate, was hatching.

The success in Scotland of the Snipe and Purple is principally related to loch and reservoir fishing though it can also be a very good fly for fast or rough stream angling.

In some parts of northern England—especially in Yorkshire—it is a first-rate fly for river fishing and seldom fails to take its quota of trout.

Good results are achieved with this fly on overcast days when the water is well ruffled. Two flies are used—one on the tail or point of the cast and another on the bob or top dropper position—and each kill trout equally well.

Some anglers even go so far as to use three of these Snipe and Purples on their wet fly casts at the same time and do great execution with them when Iron Blue Duns are floating downstream in numbers.

The Snipe and Purple is a dark fly, even more sombre-looking when wet. It is ostensibly mistaken for the nymph of the Iron Blue Dun.

It is quite easily dressed with a purple floss silk or thread body and a dark, almost black, feather from the outside of a jack snipe's wing. The right feather is obtained from the knuckle of the wing near its junction with the bird's body. No other feather does quite so well, but some fly dressers use coot, jackdaw, waterhen, or blackbird plumage as substitutes for the snipe.

The Snipe and Purple is sparsely dressed on a small (size 14, old number) hook for the perfectly obvious reason that it represents such a minute form of insect life.

In loch fishing it invariably pays to fish the fly well sunk when trout are not moving on the surface and to quicken the pace of recovery when the fish are rising to natural Iron Blues.

When dressing the fly strive for a slim, slightly-tapered body with a minimum of hackle. Only short-fibred hackles should be used and these should be given a twist or two of tying silk behind them to make them incline backwards towards the eye of the hook.

The purpose of this is to ensure that when the fly is being retrieved the hackle fibres will be activated by the water in a lifelike manner.

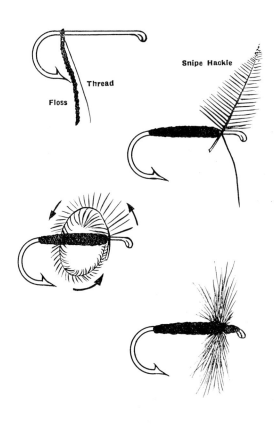

No. 40

Ian Wood

THIS notable fly, which owes its origin to Ian Wood, former editor of *Trout and Salmon,* was used by him on Loch Lomond and on many other waters with success for years before his record Loch Lomond catches were made.

On June 5th, 1952, Mr. Wood was fishing Millarochy Bay and he landed five salmon weighing 67½ lb. This catch broke the record for a single day's fishing—which had stood since 1919—of five fish weighing 60 lb.

On June 12th of the same year he broke his own lately established record by landing seven salmon weighing 77½ lb.

In thirteen days' fishing Mr. Wood that year took 33 salmon from the loch, and every fish was caught on his turkey-winged, gold-bodied fly. He uses two of these flies on his loch cast and confesses that he gets most of his salmon by careful working of the bob fly.

Although this fly was dressed in the first place as a salmon fly it has proved excellent for sea trout and brown trout when dressed in smaller sizes. It was first dressed by Miss Doris Cruize, a professional fly tier employed by Robertson of Glasgow.

After the record catches Glasgow tackle shops were besieged for copies of the killing pattern!

The Ian Wood, as dressed by Miss Cruize, has a small Golden Pheasant topping (taken from the crest of the bird) for a tippet, a flat gold body ribbed with fine oval gold, a black and white turkey wing and a ginger hackle.

Very often Mr. Wood took salmon on a hackle-less version of the fly, and he always makes a point of splitting the wing fibres of a new fly with a pin because he believes that the turkey feather, so treated, works better in the water—has more "play" in other words.

The accompanying sketch shows how the fly is dressed. Hook sizes are 4 to 6, singles or doubles.

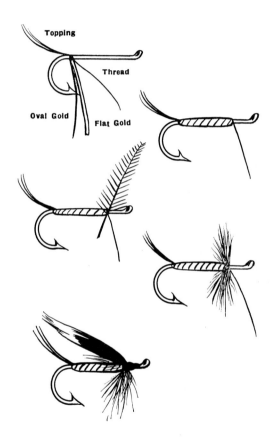

Topping

Thread

Oval Gold   Flat Gold

89

No. 41

Woodcock and Harelug

IN northern lakes and rivers there are few wet flies to beat this one for springtime fishing, yet, apart from a touch of gold on its tip, it is a sombre-looking pattern, constructed entirely of natural undyed materials.

No season ever passes without this fly taking its quota of trout from river and loch.

It is particularly useful in late April, but it has been known to take fish at almost any time in the angler's year. It is regarded as a variation of the Blue Dun and while it may not bear any real likeness to the natural insect it certainly kills well when that fly is on the water.

In some parts of the country it goes by the simple names of Hare's Ear or Hare's Fleck and it is subjected to quite a number of variations in its dressing.

The name it is given at the head of this article is the Scots one and the dressing is fairly representative of all the others.

It was James Ogden, the noted Cheltenham fly dresser and inventor of the Invicta (which also happens to be a favourite fly in Scotland), who supplied the original dressing.

His tie lacked the gold tag which is given to the fly by most professional fly tiers today and it did not have the pinch of pale olive green wool or seal's fur mixed with the hare's ear body which many anglers deem essential to the fly's success nowadays.

The normal Scots dressing is: Body—Darkest fur from hare's ear dubbed on yellow silk, with the fur fibres well picked out nearest the head to resemble the fly's legs; Wings—Woodcock, with the inside of the feather outward ; Tail—two or three strands of Mallard bronze feather; and Tag—two turns of flat gold tinsel.

The fly is usually fished on an intermediate place on the wet fly cast and since dropper flies of a killing description are not particularly easy to find it enjoys a considerable degree of popularity as a centrally-placed companion to established favourites like the Greenwell's Glory and Silver Butcher.

In normal practice the Woodcock and Hare's Lug is dressed on hook sizes ranging from size 14 to 12 (old numbers).

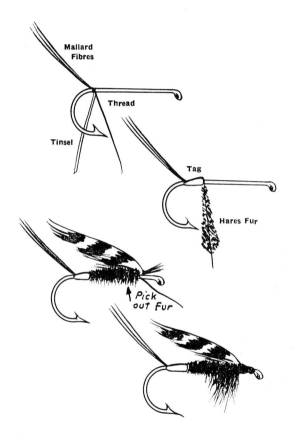

No. 42

Heckham
Peckham

IT is as a sea trout fly that I like the Heckham Peckham, but I can recall the time when it enjoyed a considerable reputation as a trout killer at Loch Leven. Why it ever fell out of esteem there will always be a source of wonder to me.

Originator of this fly, which can be dressed with a red, green, yellow, claret, blue, and even a silver or gold body, was a very successful Aberdeen angler, William Murdoch, who first used the fly for sea trout. As its fame spread it was tied in smaller sizes and the green and red-bodied versions of it became brown trout favourites.

In the small rivers where I fish, the Heckham Peckham series of flies take more than 60 per cent of the sea trout and whitling caught with the fly each season. The most popular pattern is the red-bodied one.

There are several variations of this fly. Some fly dressers match the red body with a red or flame hackle, others rib the fly with gold tinsel, while others, like myself, prefer flat silver ribbing and a Cambridge blue hackle. I have always found that blue-hackled flies exercise a big appeal on sea trout and whitling.

The wings for the Heckham Peckham flies are obtained from the white-tipped outer coverts of the mallard drake. They are the tips of the feathers that are popularly used for the wings of various Butchers.

To tie the fly, fix in a small Golden Pheasant topping with the tying silk, then the flat silver tinsel, which should have a breadth corresponding to the size of the fly being tied.

Then tease out some red wool, seal's fur, or mohair, and work this on to the tying thread so that it tapers as shown in the sketch.

Wrap the wool or fur round the hook shank towards the eye of the fly, tie in at the throat, and start winding the tinsel in ribbing fashion over the body material. My own method is to put in a silver tip, similar to that used for the Peter Ross, and then to rib the body as usual.

I like my sea trout flies to have a nice shiny hackle so I use a henny-cock white hackle dyed Cambridge blue.

To make the perfect wing one must take a piece from corresponding quills of the white-tipped feather.

The fly may be tied in 14 to 10 size hooks for brown trout and the same sizes and up to 6s and 7s for sea trout and whitling.

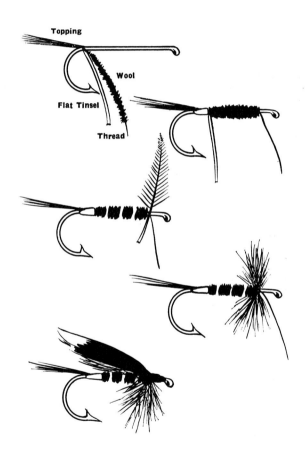

No. 43

Yellow Torrish

IF beauty means anything in a salmon fly the Yellow Torrish is a winner all the way. Colour and tinsel make it radiate with attractiveness. Anglers in some northern rivers hold it in such esteem that they are loth to be without it on their cast.

Because of its bright appearance it is a particularly useful fly when the water is rising darkly—before the first earthy stain is apparent. And again—when the stream is settling after a spate.

Old fly dressers will tell you that once you can dress a Yellow Torrish you are capable of tackling almost any salmon fly.

The fly dresser would be well advised to ignore the more exotic feathers once regarded as essential for the make-up of a Yellow Torrish. Feathers such as bustard, summer duck, and Indian Crow have suitable substitutes in mottled oak turkey, barred teal duck, and the amber-coloured back feathers from a Golden Pheasant.

First step in dressing the Yellow Torrish is to tie in a piece of flat silver tinsel, following this with gold floss silk. Then tie in a small topping with a piece of red feather (ibis) on top.

Now tie in a piece of black ostrich herl as a butt and follow this with oval silver tinsel. After the butt has been wound on wind the tinsel half-way up the body in close turns and tie down. Now tie in the amber Golden Pheasant plumage points as veiling feathers— one on top and one below. Then tie in another piece of ostrich herl for a second butt.

Cover the remainder of the body with the oval tinsel and put on a lemon-yellow hackle.

The next step is building the wings, but first take two matching strips of dark, white-tipped turkey tail feather and tie these in as a base. On top of these but not completely obscuring them, put the "married" feathers (folded in the rotation shown in the sketch) and sheath the turkey feathers with these.

The sheath feathers comprise strips of the following feathers:—mottled oak turkey, barred teal duck, bronze mallard, and yellow, red and blue swan.

When the wing has been completed, tie in two pieces of Jungle Cock feathers as cheeks. Dress the fly on $1\frac{1}{4}$ to 2-inch irons.

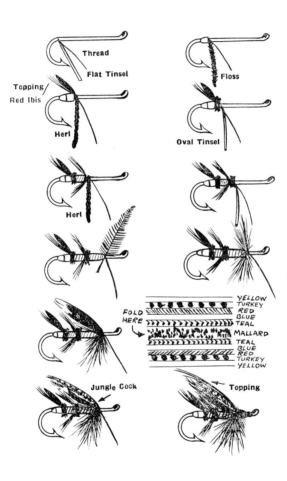

No. 44

Blae and Black

THIS well-known fly, of which there are several variations,
imitates a Chironomid (*C. niger*) though this is of less importance to the angler than the fact that the artificial fly is a very deadly
one to have on the wet fly cast.

In the main, the Blae and Black, or Duck Fly, as it is known in
some quarters, is a brown trout fly, but, dressed in bigger sizes, it
takes its quota of sea trout.

A few seasons ago, during correspondence with a reader in Wales,
I gave him the dressing of the Blae and Black in regular use in my
part of the country—and in a subsequent letter he told me that he
had taken 15 trout with it on a very dour day on Bala Lake.

This may not prove the efficacy of the fly everywhere, but it suggests at least that its powers as a trout killer are not confined to
Northern waters.

The pattern I like best has a red tail—not because the chironomid it imitates is so adorned but simply for the reason that I have
a weakness for putting a red tail on many of the wet flies I use.

I dress the Blae and Black on hooks ranging from size 15 to 12
for trout and 12s to 8s for sea trout.

The method of dressing is as follows: Tie in a small piece of
white feather dyed pillar-box red. Then tie in either flat or oval
silver tinsel, and follow that by tying in a short length of black
floss silk (black wool or black seal's fur may also be used).

Wind the silk or wool up the hook stem in the direction of the
eye, thickening the material as you near the neck of the hook to
give the fly a nicely tapered body. Tie down the end of the silk or
wool at the throat of the hook and snip off the waste material.

Now start ribbing the body with the tinsel. Do this in evenly-
spaced, tight turns. Cut off the surplus tinsel and put on the hackle.

The hackle is black hen, but if you are dressing very small flies
—anything from 15 to 16—there is no harm in using a very tiny

cock hackle which can be manipulated much better than a hen one of the same size. Two turns of hackle are all that is required.

Having trimmed off the surplus hackle fibres, put on the wings, which can be either of medium starling or the blae part of a jay's wing. Take corresponding pieces from right and left quills and make certain that they sit properly on the neck of the hook before tying them in.

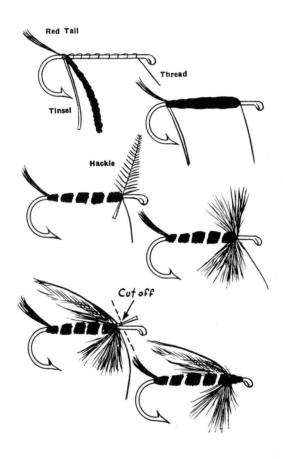

No. 45

Lunn's Particular

THE late W. J. Lunn's contribution to fish and fly life conservation will never be forgotten by chalk stream anglers.

Neither will the flies he so meticulously copied from the natural insects with which he had become so familiar in over 40 years' close contact with the River Test.

Notable among the various flies Lunn created were the Houghton Ruby, his own dressing of the Sherry Spinner, and the winged Yellow Boy.

Many of his flies were dressed in the "spent" style—that is, they had their wings tied in flat and projecting on each side of the body.

He was probably one of the first fly dressers to realize the value of hackle tips for imitating the wings of spent flies. He liked the blue dun (cock or hen) hackles for this purpose because of their shiny translucency and similarity to the wings of the natural insect.

An equally good effect, however, is achieved by winding on a blue dun hackle and shaping it with criss-crossings of the tie silk to provide a wing on each side of the fly's body. Some fly dressers, on the other hand, snip off the hackle fibres above and below the fly's body.

Dressing a Lunn's Particular is a fairly easy operation. And it is noticeable in this pattern, as in most of the flies that Lunn dressed, that the materials are not very difficult to obtain. He believed in simplicity.

The tail consists of several fibres of natural red cock hackle, while the body is made from the stalk of a similar hackle with the fibres removed.

Two medium blue dun cock hackles are tied in flat, projecting on each side of the body, for the wings, while the hackle is again natural red cock. The tying silk is crimson.

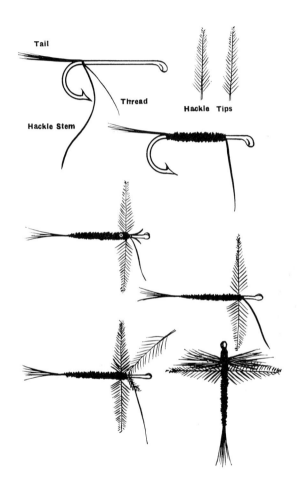

No. 46

Red Palmer

APART, perhaps, from the Black Palmer, or its near relative the Black Zulu, I do not suppose any fly kills more trout in the remote lochs of the Scottish Highlands than does the Red Palmer.

It is particularly good when fished as a bob fly in a big wave, when it should be made to skim across the surface; but I have found it equally useful as a tail fly. I have also taken many trout with it, fishing it as a floater at dusk when large caddis flies and sedge flies were capering on calm water. It is a deadly sea trout pattern.

The suggestion that the Red Palmer is taken by the fish for a woolly caterpillar can be safely discounted as the number of these creatures which reach the water is very small indeed. It is more probable that the Red Palmer, when fished wet, is accepted as a nymph of some sort. When operated on the surface it is a "buzz" fly representing a struggling insect.

There are various dressings of the fly. Some tie it with a red wool or seal's fur body, ribbed with flat or oval gold tinsel. Others, like myself, prefer it with a bronze peacock herl body, also ribbed with gold tinsel which is wound over the top of the palmer-tied hackle to protect the body and hackle from the ravages of the fish's attack.

The fly is easily dressed and offers the novice a good starting point for the dressing of fully-hackled patterns.

Tie in the gold tinsel and one or two strands of peacock herl. Wind the herl up the hook shank towards the eye and tie it down.

Fix in the hackle by the stem—using a red-brown hackle for the wet fly or a similar cock hackle for the floating pattern.

Some fly dressers prefer to tie in the hackle by the tip and wind it upwards towards the head, but my own method is to tie in the hackle tip with the tinsel after winding the hackle in the opposite direction—i.e., towards the tail.

Try to achieve a nicely tapered effect by using a hackle that is fairly short in the fibres at the tip.

Dress the fly on size 14 to 10 hooks for trout and sizes 8 to 6 for sea trout. If fishing it as a floater at dusk use a reasonably big pattern—say, size 6. These are old numbers.

By the simple addition of a red wool tail (tied in when the herl and ribbing tinsel are being put on) the fly becomes a Soldier Palmer, another very useful pattern for trout and sea trout.

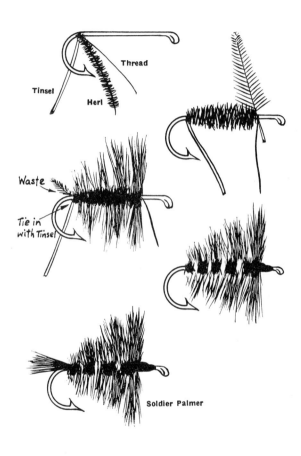

Soldier Palmer

No. 47

Brown Turkey

AROUND the western rivers of Scotland few salmon flies enjoy so large a measure of popularity as this one. It scores over the general run of salmon patterns in that it is so easily dressed and does not involve the use of expensive materials.

Nowadays, unfortunately, the brown or cinnamon turkey feather with which the fly should be winged is not so easily obtained as it used to be and so the fly dresser has to fall back on grey goose feather as a substitute. In very small sizes, of course, it is also possible to use brown hen feather for the wings.

Apart from its paleness the goose feather comes reasonably close in appearance to the turkey one and it has that mealy or whitish tip to it which many salmon fishers find so desirable in the wings of their Brown Turkeys.

Variations in the composition of this fly are by no means confined to the wings. It can be dressed with a yellow, red, and black wool or seal's fur body (these colours being in rotation from the tail) or a yellow, red, and pale blue body.

The tail feather can either be Golden Pheasant topping or tippet fibres, while you may use a Cambridge blue, turquoise, or black hackle at the throat.

Fly sizes vary from one to two-inch irons and the fly can be dressed on single or double hooks. Some anglers prefer the long-shanked low water type hooks, but this is purely a matter of taste.

To dress the fly, tie in the topping or tippet fibres and a piece of flat silver tinsel. Then dub the body with yellow, red, and blue wool or seal's fur, and rib the wool with the tinsel in tight evenly-spaced turns. Tie down the tinsel.

Now put on the hackle, as shown in sketch, using a blue one preferably, and once it has been wound on and tied in lay the two pieces of winging feather along the back of the fly. The length of the wing should correspond roughly to the extreme point of the tippets or topping.

This fly takes well in a settled water, but may also be used with success when a river is rising and has not yet taken on the red or yellow earthy stain that comes with a flood.

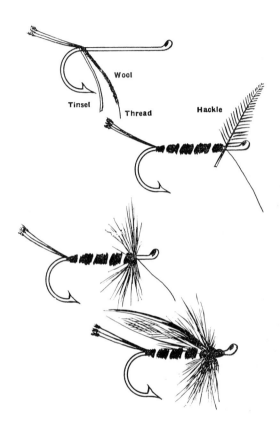

No. 48

Jock
Scott

THE Jock Scott first found fame on the River Tweed, the date of its birth being 1850. At that time the Makerstoun stretch of the river was rented by Lord John Scott and it was while he was serving Lord Scott as a gamekeeper that Jock Scott devised the fly that was to win repute not only on the Tweed, but throughout the salmon angling world. From that day till this the Jock Scott has been a killing pattern and probably our most widely used and best known salmon fly.

In the hands of the beginner the Jock Scott is not an easy pattern to dress, but once the novice has got over the difficulties of building the wings he should be capable of tackling the most ornate salmon patterns.

Here are the requirements:—

Tag—silver tinsel and yellow floss silk; butt—black ostrich herl, wool, or seal's fur; tail—topping from Indian crow.

Body—first half (nearest tail) yellow floss ribbed with silver oval tinsel; central butt—yellow toucan and black herl.

Body (second half)—black floss with a black cock hackle over all and ribbed with silver oval tinsel in palmer style; throat hackle—speckled guinea fowl.

Wings (mixed)—dark turkey with strips from the Golden Pheasant's tail, bustard, grey mallard, two strands of peacock herl, strips of swan feather dyed blue, red and yellow.

Cheeks—jungle cock and kingfisher; topping—from Golden Pheasant crest and smoothed to lie flush with the top outside of the winging feathers; horns—blue macaw; and head—black herl.

These would appear to be the materials required for the original dressing, but many amateur fly dressers, faced with the expense and difficulty of obtaining certain of the feathers mentioned, either omit them or improvise with others.

Indeed some leave out almost half of the winging feathers without, apparently, impairing the fly's usefulness!

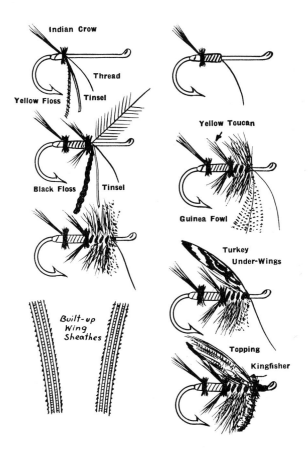

Indian Crow

Thread

Yellow Floss

Tinsel

Black Floss

Tinsel

Built-up
Wing
Sheathes

Yellow Toucan

Guinea Fowl

Turkey
Under-Wings

Topping

Kingfisher

No. 49

March Brown

FEW lake fishers, especially in the northern parts of Britain, would care to be without a March Brown, in its winged or hackled form, on their wet fly casts in the early months of any trout fishing season.

This is odd in the sense that the natural fly (*Rhithrogena haarup*) is seldom, if ever, found on still water, but appears to hatch out, exclusively, on faster-flowing streams.

It is equally peculiar that this pattern should include the third month of the year in its name since the efficacy of the artificial is by no stretch of the imagination confined to that month.

If one is to differentiate between the males and females of the natural fly it will generally be conceded by the regular March Brown fisher on lakes that the male, the darker pattern, is the better of the artificials.

There are a great many variations of the artificial March Brown and I can do no more than plump for the one that has served me best.

It is a simply dressed pattern, consisting of: Tail—few fibres of bronze mallard; body—any dark silk dubbed with the darkest, withered fur from the edge of a hare's ear, ribbed with oval or fine flat gold tinsel; hackle—dark partridge; wing—either hen pheasant tail (inside out) or speckled partridge tail.

I do not suggest that this pattern bears more than a remote resemblance to the natural insect, but it kills fish, which is the important thing.

Like the March Brown Spider, which is similarly dressed (without the wing) and is one of the best nymph-suggesting patterns that I know, the winged March Brown should be sparsely dressed. It seems to kill best when it is reduced to a tattered ruin of its former self.

106

One cannot leave the March Brown without mentioning the silver and gold-bodied variations of it. They are worthwhile lake trout flies, and will take their quota of sea trout as well.

For ordinary brown trout the fly or its variations can be dressed in size 10 to 14 (old number) hooks and for sea trout from 10 to 6.

It can be fished with equal success on the tail or as a dropper on the wet fly cast.

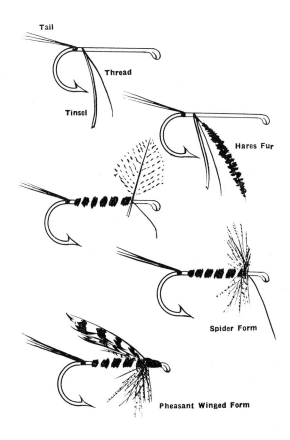

Tail

Thread

Tinsel

Hares Fur

Spider Form

Pheasant Winged Form

No. 50

Hardy's Favourite

INVENTED by the late J. J. Hardy, this fly is the standby of many loch fishers in early summer. It is a fancy fly and is particularly useful fished on the tail of the wet fly cast. When it has been taking fish I have known anglers to put another on the bob or top-dropper place on the cast with equally good results.

The writer has found it a thoroughly reliable pattern on a rough day at Loch Awe and other northern waters.

Some anglers find it successful as a sea trout fly but it has never served me very well in this respect and I prefer it for loch fishing rather than on rivers.

The original pattern had a dark brown turkey wing but there have been variations on the theme and my own choice is a well-marked woodcock wing and golden pheasant tippets in place of the original brown mallard fibres.

In view of the red silk used in the fly's body I suppose the use of the woodcock wing brings my pattern closer to the Woodcock and Red than a Hardy's Favourite but I am not so much a stickler for original fly dressings that I would let that worry me.

My only excuse for using the woodcock wing and golden pheasant tippet fibres is that I have had more trout with this variation than with the original, but I am prepared to concede that Hardy's pattern may be suitable enough for certain districts. The original version, after all, has stood the test of time.

For the purposes of this article I am giving the original dressing, but I would suggest that the reader makes a few dressings on the lines of my choice—to ascertain which of the patterns suits him better.

To dress the fly, tie in the brown mallard fibres—two or three, to choice—then tie in a piece of red floss silk and a strand of bronze peacock herl. Wind on the peacock herl to form the fly's body and rib it with the red silk.

108

Now tie in and wind on a small dark partridge hackle and add the dark brown turkey wing. Dress the fly in sizes ranging from 12 to 14 (old numbers).

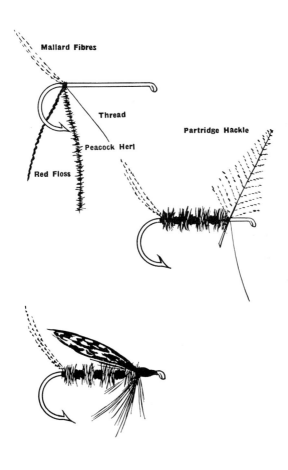

Mallard Fibres

Thread

Partridge Hackle

Peacock Herl

Red Floss

BOOK TWO

No. 1

Watson's Fancy

W HEN the usual run of loch-fishing wet flies has failed it is very often good practice to try an attractor fly such as Watson's Fancy.

Watson's Fancy is normally fished on the tail of the wet fly cast. It can be particularly deadly on a rough day when there is little evidence of fish feeding on the surface.

It is not known what its inventor, Mr. Donald Watson, of Inverness, had in mind when he dressed it. Most certainly it was not a copy of any natural insect. It is essentially a fancy fly—one of those patterns that fly dressers dream up often with the most unexpected results.

I have found the Watson's Fancy to be especially useful at Loch Awe and Loch Ard in Scotland and I have been told that it has taken many fish from Blagdon and Chew Valley as well as from Bala Lake in Wales.

Moreover, it is a first-class sea trout fly for a slightly coloured water, the jungle cock cheeks showing up well when the water is dark or stained.

It is dressed on hook sizes ranging from 14s to 8s (old numbers) and, on occasion, has killed salmon when the angler was fishing for trout or sea trout.

To begin dressing the fly, tie in a short golden pheasant topping as a tail, then fasten in the round or oval silver tinsel which will be used to rib the body.

The body consists of equal parts of red and black wool or seal's fur (with the red half nearest the tail). Dub on the wool or fur with the tying thread and rib the entire body with the silver tinsel.

Now fasten in a black hen hackle and wind on a couple of turns at the neck of the fly.

The wings are from dark but not shiny crow quills and each has a small jungle cock "eye" feather on each side.

Watson's Fancy is a most attractive-looking fly and is certainly a pattern to keep in the fly box for bringing out when the fish are hard to catch.

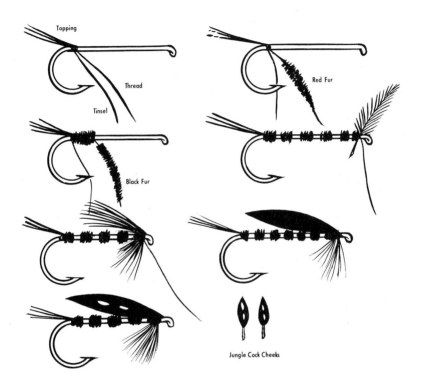

No. 2

Akroyd

ALTHOUGH this fly is best known as an early-season strip-wing salmon pattern for the Aberdeenshire Dee its popularity has spread in various other directions.

It was invented by Charles H. Akroyd in 1875 and was an immediate success.

In more recent times it has been tied in much smaller sizes than Akroyd and his contemporaries used and it has even been modified to suit greased-line fishing in low summer waters.

Akroyd used a golden pheasant crest feather or topping instead of the dyed yellow hackle now employed by the modern fly dresser. He maintained that the natural feather from the golden pheasant had a more glittering effect, which is certainly true.

Today's dressing of the Akroyd, which is also known as the Brown Wings (as it was tied by Dr. T. E. Pryce Tennat) is: Tag—silver tinsel; tail—topping and tippet (from golden pheasant in each case) in strands; body—first half, light orange seal's fur with lemon hackle over and ribbed with flat silver (or oval) tinsel; second half, black floss (ribbed, as before), with black heron's crest hackle over the black floss; throat hackle—teal plumage; wings—a pair of cinnamon turkey tail strips (sometimes white turkey is used, in which case the fly is known as the White Winged Akroyd); cheeks—jungle cock (set to droop alongside the hackles).

Hook sizes are up to three inches for early, big-river fishing and down to one inch for greased-line, low water fishing.

My diagram shows how to dress the Akroyd but I would finally point out that the wings should be set (tie them in on each side of the body) to slant slightly outward so that when the fly is drawn through the water they open and close most attractively.

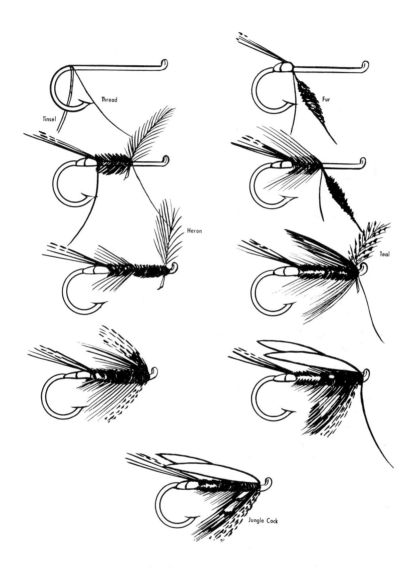

Thread

Tinsel

Fur

Heron

Teal

Jungle Cock

115

No. 3

Black
Goldfinch

AN Irish pattern, this salmon fly enjoys a fair measure of popularity on the rivers where it is fished.

In some respects it corresponds to the perhaps better-known Garry or Yellow Dog, beloved of Tweed and other salmon fishers, but only in the basic wing and body colours and the hackle at the throat.

It is regarded as a first-class fly for a dark or slightly coloured water. In small sizes it is a capital sea trout fly for late evening fishing.

One of its principal virtues is that it is a fairly easy fly to dress. The materials as a whole are easily come by. It should be tied on one-inch and up to two-inch irons.

In the first instance, tie in a piece of round silver tinsel for the first part of the tag. Wind this on and then tie in a piece of deep yellow or orange floss silk to complete the tag.

The tail normally consists of a golden pheasant topping with a small piece of Indian crow (hot orange feather) on top, but the Indian crow can be omitted without spoiling the fly's efficiency.

Now tie in a piece of black ostrich herl or rough black wool for the butt. When this has been wound round the hook, tie in a short length of oval gold tinsel. This will be used to rib the body which consists of black floss silk.

After tying in the black body floss and winding it on towards the neck of the hook, tie in the body hackle, a henny-cock one dyed claret, at the throat and wind this down the body in evenly spaced turns.

Now take the end of the oval gold tinsel in the hackle tweezers and, after tying down the pointed end of the hackle with the tinsel, wind the rest of the tinsel in ribbing fashion over the wound hackle and body silk tightly and with even spacing.

You will now be ready to put on the throat hackle which may be either blue-barred jay or guinea fowl dyed blue.

The wings consist of a few golden pheasant tippet strands surmounted by strips of yellow and red swan set upright. Some fly dressers, it may be pointed out, use an orange feather in its entirety for the wing.

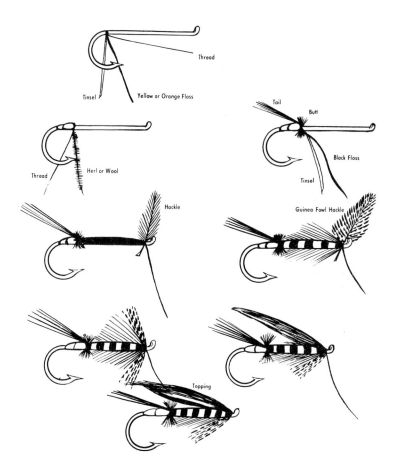

All you have to do now is to add cheeks of Indian crow (swan feather or goose feather dyed hot orange will do) and tie in two or three golden pheasant toppings overall.

You may also add horns of blue and yellow macaw but these are not deemed strictly necessary by many fly tiers—and the fish don't appear to mind whether they are included or not!

No. 4

Col. Downman

MANY anglers who fish for lake trout find this fly a very useful one to have on the cast when the trout are not responding very well to anything else.

Although it may be described as an attractor type of fly in much the same way as the Dunkeld is, the Colonel Downman, if deprived of its jungle cock cheeks, is close in resemblance to such well-known artificial flies as the Blae and Black and the Lord Saltoun.

As an attractor fly it has no set season and can therefore be used at any time in the trout angler's year. It appears to do best when fished in a fairly rough water and I have found it to be particularly useful in the spring as the tail fly on the well sunk cast.

I have also used it for sea trout fishing and have enjoyed some measure of success with it. It is mainly employed, however, for brown trout and rainbow, and is extremely popular among anglers who fish Scottish lochs.

Like so many flies, the Colonel Downman has been subjected to variations. I have seen it with teal fibres used for its tail and with the blue-barred feather from the jay as its wing. There are also dressings of it which are ribbed with oval gold and others which have a dark Coch-y-bondhu hackle.

The usual tie, however, is: Tail—a few dyed red hackle fibres; body—black floss silk or thread ribbed with fine oval silver tinsel; hackle—black hen; wing—the blae feather from the jay with small pieces of jungle cock eye feather on each side of the wing as cheeks.

Sometimes, in the absence of the blae jay feather, corresponding pieces of light starling are used for the wing.

The fly is normally dressed on size 14 to 12 hooks (old numbers) for brown trout and up to 10s for sea trout.

118

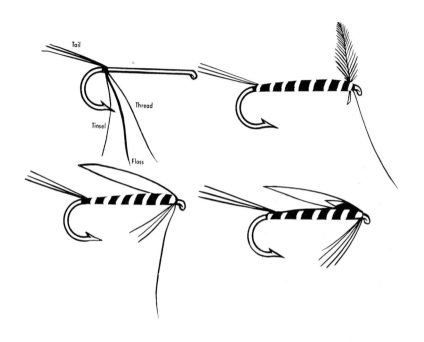

No. 5

Waterhen Bloa

IN springtime, when the dark olives are hatching or on those days when iron blue duns are on the water the Waterhen Bloa is a very useful fly to have on the sunk cast.

It is, perhaps, most favoured on the streams of Yorkshire, but it is becoming increasingly popular as a loch fly in Scotland, especially for early and late season fishing.

On the underside of the waterhen's wings there are several feathers, spear-shaped, blae in colour, and glossy on one side. One of these, stripped down to the size required for the hook on which the fly is to be dressed, is the feather with which to hackle the Waterhen Bloa.

It is also possible to use other feathers, including pieces from under the wings of a hen blackbird or a darkish starling, but these are poor substitutes for the waterhen or moorhen feathers.

The body of the fly is formed of bright, thinly waxed, yellow tying silk, very sparsely dubbed with fur from a water shrew or a young mole which has a brownish tinge to its blue-grey fur.

No more than a tiny pinch of fur is required for dubbing the yellow silk body. The fur should be well broken up, teased out with the finger nails and then very sparingly applied, so that the yellow shines through the thin film of fur. When done correctly the body should have a faintly ribbed appearance.

The Waterhen Bloa can be fished anywhere on a wet fly cast. It has proved its worth as a point fly when it has apparently been taken for a nymph, but it has also been known to do well as a bob fly when iron blues were on the water.

Normally the writer accords it the middle position of his three-fly wet cast for loch and stream fishing.

Usually the Waterhen Bloa is fished more often as a sunk fly than a floater but it will also serve as a dry fly when iron blues or dark olives are hatching.

Dress it on size 14 (old number) hooks and avoid at all times giving it a bushy appearance. Its body should be slim and its hackle sparse.

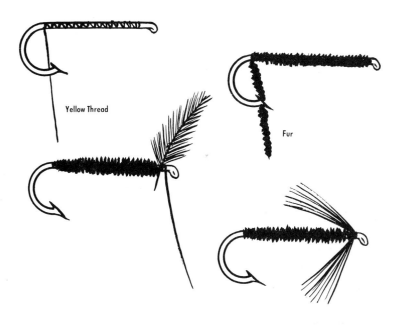

Yellow Thread

Fur

No. 6

Jimmie

H ERE is a first-class salmon fly whether it is used as an ordinary sunk pattern or for the purposes of greased-line fishing.

It is one of my favourites for fishing on small rivers. I am inclined to suppose that it owes a great deal of its appeal to the contrast afforded by the bright orange silk imposed against the black silk of its body.

Flies with yellow or orange in their make-up are nearly always attractive to salmon, especially in certain naturally dark waters fed by streams running through peaty ground or in rivers that are well shaded by trees.

The Jimmie is one of the easiest types of salmon fly to dress. To begin with tie in and wind on a short flat silver tag. Add a small golden pheasant topping as a tail. Then fix in a piece of oval silver tinsel with which to rib the body.

The tail half of the body is bright orange floss and the second half black floss. Do not make the body too bulky, but strive, rather, to make it taper from head to tail.

When the floss has been wound on and ribbed with the oval tinsel, add a black henny-cock hackle and fix in two strips of dark mottled turkey tail feather for the wings.

On each side of the wing tie in a piece of jungle cock as a cheek and finish the fly's head with the usual whip knot and varnish. Tie this fly on hook irons measuring from three-quarters-of-an-inch to about one and one-eighth.

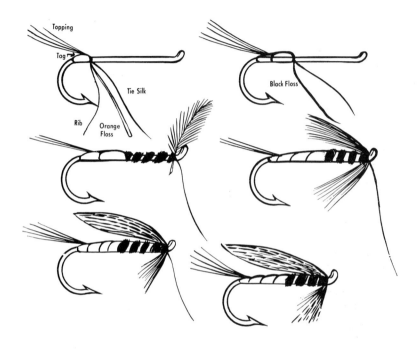

No. 7

Gravel Bed

A NGLERS who happen to be at certain waters in late April or early May are likely to encounter the naturals of the Gravel Bed or Sandfly, as it is sometimes called, in their thousands.

The insect is well named, for it is generally to be found crawling about on the gravel or sand when it is not capering along the surface of the water or indulging in its swift aerial acrobatics.

Trout seem to go mad when it is on the water. They gulp the tiny insects in their hundreds so that the surface is peppered with their rises.

Some angling writers insist that the killing powers of the artificial Gravel Bed or Sandfly have been greatly exaggerated. They claim that it is practically impossible to imitate the nature insect because of the speed at which it invariably darts about.

But fly fishers on the Clyde, in Scotland, do not contribute to either of these views. In their experience the Sandfly, as they describe it, is a very killing pattern—and apart from the fact that fly dressers among them may have their own pet versions of the fly, most of them pin their faith on patterns of the following dressing.

It is dressed on small hooks, from 14s to 16s (old numbers) and is generally fished as a top dropper or bob fly in imitation of the natural insect racing along the surface of the water.

Like all Clyde-style flies it is very sparsely dressed. Give it a slim black silk body ribbed with bright blue silk, a wing of speckled hen pheasant tail, and a shiny black cock hackle, long in the fibre, but very sparingly put on.

Many fly dressers put the hen pheasant tail feather in a small bunch of fibres tied flat over the back of the fly's body in the style of dressing a sedge fly.

I have also seen wingless dressings of the Sandfly. In these a dark partridge hackle was wound on in semblance of the wing and the black cock hackle added afterwards.

Alfred Ronalds, in his *Fly Fishers' Entomology,* gives a dressing of the fly which is quite different from the one given above.

Ronalds' tie was: Body—Lead-coloured silk; wing—from the under covert feather of a woodcock's wing; hackle—rather long black cock's, two turns.

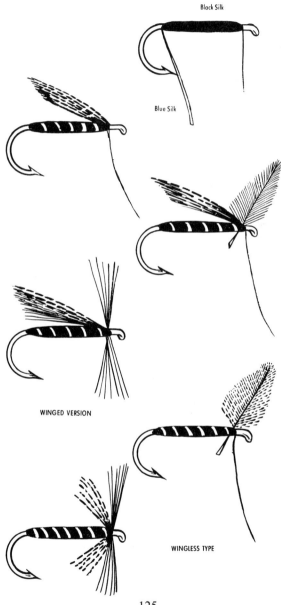

Black Silk

Blue Silk

WINGED VERSION

WINGLESS TYPE

No. 8

Black Silk

GREATLY popularized by Ernest Crosfield, this salmon fly has for long been a favourite pattern. It is especially useful in a water which is in the process of fining down and it enjoys a considerable reputation in greased-line fishing.

Slenderness is only part of its attractiveness. The inclusion of such materials as golden pheasant topping fibres in its wings and silver ribbing over its black silk body give it the flash which many anglers think is essential to success.

Crosfield dressed his flies in such a way that every individual winging fibre showed itself, an effect which he achieved by tying in the wing materials in a series of small bunches.

In these days some of us who tie flies are somewhat less meticulous than Crosfield was and are more inclined to follow the so-called modern style of dressing the Black Silk. In the interests of simplicity this is the one I am giving here.

Start off by making about three turns of flat or round silver tinsel as a tag and follow this up with a small butt of yellow floss silk.

Now tie in a golden pheasant topping as a tail and then a piece of flat or oval silver tinsel for ribbing the body.

Next tie in the black floss silk and wind this up the hook stem tightly so as to form a slim, slightly tapered body.

Tie in a bright, shiny claret cock hackle and wind this down the body from the throat to a point opposite the barb and bind in the end of the hackle with the ribbing tinsel. Cut off the surplus hackle tip.

Now wind the ribbing tinsel up over the claret hackle and black silk body in evenly spaced turns and tie down the end.

Next tie in a throat hackle of bright blue cock, barred blue jay, or speckled guinea fowl dyed blue.

The under wing of the fly is composed of golden pheasant toppings fibres tied in a bunch. The overwing consists of married strands of red, yellow, and blue swan and speckled turkey in that order from the bottom, with narrow strands of Lady Amherst pheasant tail feather tied in on each side of the wing.

Strands of speckled guinea fowl tail or grey mottled turkey tail are sometimes substituted for the Lady Amherst tail feather and seem to serve their purpose quite well.

This fly is normally dressed in hook sizes 4 (15/16ths.-inch) to 3/0 (1¾-inch). If dressed on low water irons, the sizes may be 6 (1-inch) up to 2 (1½-inch).

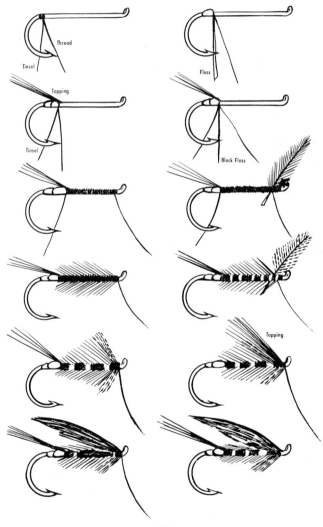

No. 9

Cinnamon Sedge

A NGLERS fishing rivers and lakes from late May onwards are likely to see a lot of sedge flies fluttering over the water or zig-zagging across the surface like miniature speedboats.

One of the most common of these is the species known to anglers as the Cinnamon Sedge, which can be used very successfully in its artificial form as a dry or wet fly.

There are various dressings of this sedge fly, all of which have their adherents, but the one I like best is constituted as follows:

Body—a single strand from a cinnamon turkey tail feather with the hackle (ginger or light brown) tied down the body in palmer fashion and ribbed with fine gilt wire or oval gold tinsel.

Wing—Light brown hen or corncrake (if obtainable). The accompanying sketch shows how the fly should be built up.

This makes a very good wet or dry fly, but if extra buoyancy is required an additional hackle (ginger cock) should be added in front of the wings.

Sedge flies, when resting or moving about on the surface of the water, have their wings closed or folded over their back. You may either tie a small wad of the winged feather flat over the body (for the dry fly) or place the corresponding pieces of wing together as in normal wet fly dressing.

Another very good wet fly dressing consists of a harelug body with brown hen wing and dark brown hackle.

When fishing the Cinnamon Sedge as a floater bring it skimming across the surface in erratic fashion, altering its course by twitching the line—or manipulating the rod point.

When you are using it wet make it a dropper, preferably as a bob fly, in imitation of the hatching insect coming to the surface or about to make its landward journey across the water.

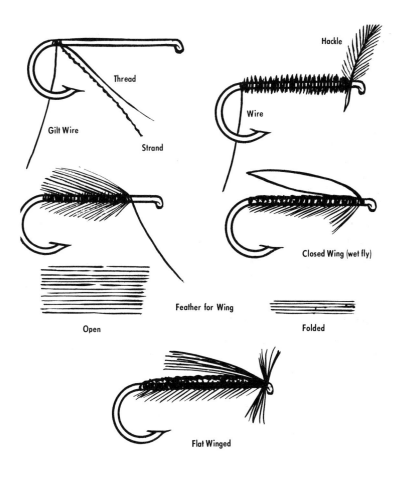

Thread

Gilt Wire

Strand

Hackle

Wire

Closed Wing (wet fly)

Feather for Wing

Open

Folded

Flat Winged

No. 10

Golden Olive

THIS is a favourite Irish salmon fly and, like so many of the patterns that had their origin in that country, its popularity has spread far beyond the Emerald Isle.

One should not be put off by the multiplicity of materials included in the original pattern. Some of these, notably summer duck, florican and bustard, can very well be omitted or represented by more easily acquired substitutes.

Tie in a tag of two or three turns of round silver tinsel, followed by several turns of golden yellow floss. Add a tail consisting of a golden pheasant topping with a few strands of golden pheasant tippet on top.

Old dressings of the fly omit the ostrich herl butt and unless you are a perfectionist you may very well leave it out.

Now tie in a length of oval gold tinsel, later to be used to rib the body, which consists of four equal parts of seal's fur in this order from the tail to the head: light orange, bright orange, fiery brown and olive brown.

Tie in the hackle, which is golden olive, and wind it down the body from head to tail. Fix the end down with the oval gold tinsel and rib the body materials and hackle in even turns towards the head.

Before proceeding to build and tie in the wings add a throat hackle of either blue-barred jay or a guinea fowl hackle dyed blue.

Build the mixed wing in four stages. In the first place tie in an underwing of golden pheasant tippet strands. Next add "married" strands of red, blue, yellow, orange and green swan, surmounted by strips of brown (oak) speckled turkey (a substitute for the bustard). You can omit the florican and, indeed, the golden pheasant tail feather strips.

Follow these with narrow strips of barred teal (omitting the summer duck) and, finally, top-veil all of these winging materials with broader strips of bronze mallard.

Horns of blue and yellow macaw can be added if you wish. The head is black and the fly is usually dressed in sizes ranging from one-inch to an inch-and-a-half.

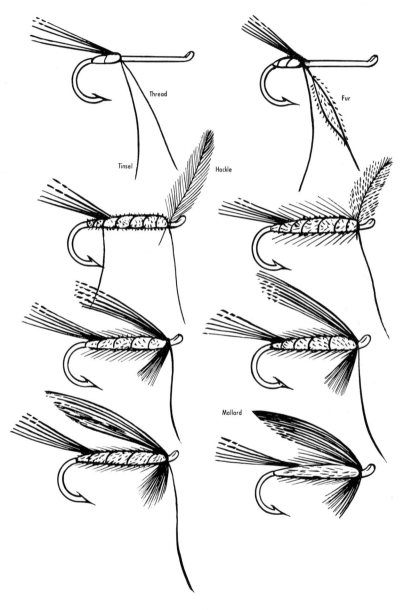

No. 11

Haslam

IN the estimation of the late Captain Jack Hughes Parry, with whom I had some correspondence about this pattern some months before his death, the Haslam was one of the best salmon flies ever invented. He had good cause to know its worth, for he fished it almost exclusively on his beloved Welsh Dee.

The Haslam was first dressed by the late Peter Vaughan, a veteran Dovey angler—I believe that it is still tied locally and a great favourite with anglers who fish that river.

The fame of the Haslam, which Hughes Parry considered bore some resemblance to a small shrimp, has spread far beyond the place of its origin. Only a season or two ago, while fishing the River Stinchar, in Ayrshire, I met a friendly angler who gave me a copy of the Haslam and told me that he had achieved marked success with the pattern on his native Wigtownshire rivers.

The dressing of the fly given me by Captain Hughes Parry corresponds in every detail with the fly passed on to me by that angler. The tie is as follows:

Tag—flat silver tinsel; butt—white wool or floss silk; tail—golden pheasant topping (small); body—flat silver tinsel, ribbed with oval silver; hackle (at throat only)—barred blue jay (or speckled guinea fowl, dyed bright blue); wing—hen pheasant tail (slim); horns—blue macaw, for which fibres of dyed blue swan feather can be used as a substitute.

Hughes Parry had a theory about the horns. He insisted that they should be tied in and set so that they curved along the sides of the wings and the tips crossed each other, as shown in the sketch.

It was his considered opinion that the horn points crossed and re-crossed each other when the fly was drawn through the water and that this invested the fly with a lively, attractive action. This sounds good, but I have never put it to the test.

You can dress the Haslam on 1-inch and 1½-inch irons for normal fly fishing or on hooks as small as 10 (old number) for fishing low water. Fished in small sizes it will also kill sea trout.

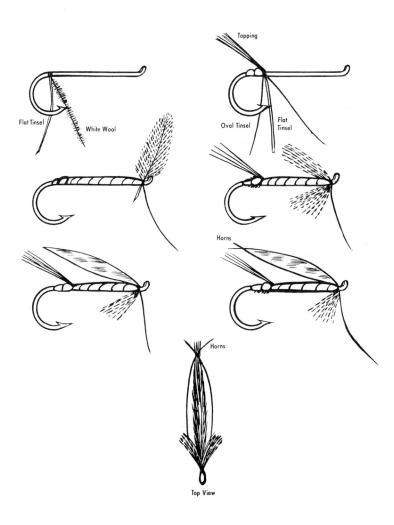

133

No. 12

Baigent's Brown

THE creator of this very popular pattern, Dr. William Baigent, of Northallerton in Yorkshire, did not apparently design this fly in imitation of any particular insect, but rather as a representation of several.

By arrangement with Messrs. Hardy, the Alnwick tackle makers, the fly, along with a number of others which are equally familiar, was put on the market and won immediate praise from all who used it.

Baigent's Brown, like the entire series of "Refracta" flies designed by the doctor, fishes best when dressed with the long-fibred, often natural, gamecock hackles upon which he insisted. They are most life-like, sitting high-cocked on the water.

Unfortunately, hackles such as Dr. Baigent used are much more rare today than they were when the doctor, who had his own special birds, was recommending their use. Unless, therefore, one has a good source of stiff, long-fibred hackles, it is necessary to obtain the best possible substitutes.

Dr. Baigent recommended the use of a pale furnace cock's hackle with very stiff fibres. The body is of yellow floss, made reasonably thin, and the wings, dressed split and upright, of pale, almost unmarked, hen pheasant wing quill strips.

The fly should be dressed on size 14 to 12 hooks (old numbers).

Originally, this and so many of Dr. Baigent's other flies, were intended for use on rivers, but nowadays, with the growing cult of using the dry fly on lakes and reservoirs, especially during rises to natural flies, it can be a very deadly pattern on still water.

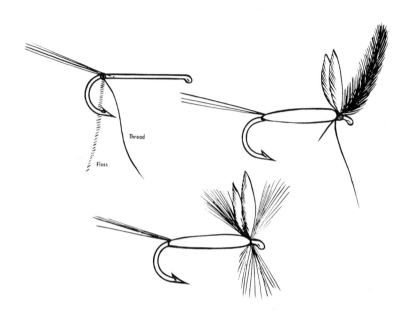

Thread

Floss

No. 13

Broughton's Point

IT is fairly safe to assume that this fly had its baptism on Ulls-
water, in the Lake District, since it owes its origin to a Penrith
shoemaker who fished that lovely water about 137 years ago.

Today the Broughton's Point is a great favourite with North of
England anglers but it is also popular with a small number of loch
fishers who have come to know its worth for stillwater fishing.

As its name might suggest this fly is normally fished on the point
of the wet fly cast both for trout and grayling.

In its earliest days the "Point" had a light blue silk body but in
these days it is most often given a reddish-purple silk body, and
F. E. Tudor, in his *Trout in Troubled Waters,* suggests an alternative body dressing of dark claret silk.

The wings of the fly are of medium blae starling and the hackle
is black hen, with a few fibres of white hen dyed scarlet intermingled
with the black ones.

One method of doing this is to put on a black hackle in the
ordinary way and then tie in a few red hackle fibres in a tiny bunch
below the black ones and mix them by rolling them between the
fingers.

I have also seen a so-called Broughton's Point which was dressed
with two full hackles—a black one succeeded by one dyed pillar-
box red, and even with a piece of dyed red swan set between the
blae wings.

This variation, according to the loch fisher who used it, was a
very killing fly, but I have not tried to confirm this, being content
to use the normal dressing.

Tie the Broughton's Point on hook sizes ranging from 14s to 12s
(old numbers).

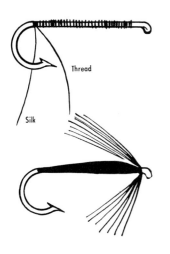

Thread

Silk

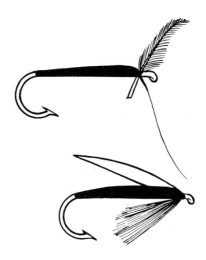

137

No. 14

Dusty Miller

THIS is a built-wing salmon fly and because I believe that too much dressing in such flies tends to make them too heavy I am giving a dressing for the Dusty Miller without those materials which I do not consider are essential to the fly's success.

For instance, I am omitting the overwing of bustard, florican, and golden pheasant tail. And for the summer duck, often incorporated in the wings, I am substituting strips of barred teal plumage married to the uppermost edge of the yellow, scarlet, and orange swan sheaths.

Like many other salmon fishers I have used Dusty Millers shorn of these adornments for a number of years.

In my sketch showing the process of dressing the Dusty Miller I have tied in three turns of oval silver tinsel and three turns of gold floss silk, followed by a small golden pheasant topping, with a small sliver of scarlet feather (substitute for Indian crow) on top, then a butt of black ostrich herl (black wool is just as good).

The first two thirds of the body is supposed to be of embossed silver tinsel, but flat tinsel, ribbed with oval tinsel or left unribbed, is equally good. The other third is of orange floss ribbed with oval silver.

Sometimes a golden olive hackle is put over the orange floss, but this, too, can be safely omitted. The throat hackle is speckled guinea fowl, undyed.

The underwing consists of two strips of the black, white-tipped feathers from a turkey's tail. Use only the slenderest of strips and tie them down near the back of the fly. Over these, but not completely hiding them, place the married strips of yellow, scarlet, and orange swan, and teal, in that order from the bottom and (if you like) you can add strips of speckled oak turkey in substitution for the bustard.

138

Then shield these feathers with narrow sheaths of brown speckled mallard plumage. Add jungle cock cheeks to the sides of the composite wings, and put a golden pheasant topping over all. Forget about the macaw horns; they are not strictly essential. Dress the fly on 1-inch to 2½-inch irons.

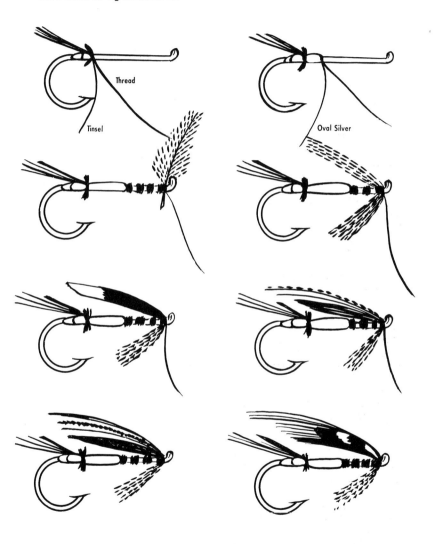

No. 15

Claret Alder

SALMON, although they normally do not feed in fresh water, have a confoundingly bad habit of taking flies that are fairly reasonable copies of natural insects!

They have been known to rise to and be caught on a floating Greenwell's Glory (trout size) which is credited with being a close enough imitation of the natural Olive.

Equally, they no doubt accept the Claret Alder because of its obvious resemblance to the Alder fly which is common to most of the rivers in this country where salmon run.

The Claret Alder, as used in salmon fishing, differs very slightly from the ordinary Alder fly imitation used in trout fishing. The difference is that the salmon fly has a silver tag and yellow tip with a tuft of claret wool as a tail.

The tag (flat silver) tip (yellow floss) and the tail tuft are tied in first. Next comes the fine oval gold tinsel for ribbing the herl body.

Then tie in and whip on two or three strands of bronze peacock herl. You can also thicken the body by putting on a core of fine brown wool or silk before winding on the herl.

Add a shiny dark claret hackle and put on the wings, which consist of two strips of bronze speckled mallard plumage, with a slightly horizontal set.

The Claret Alder should be dressed on hooks ranging from about three-quarters-of-an-inch to an inch-and-a-quarter.

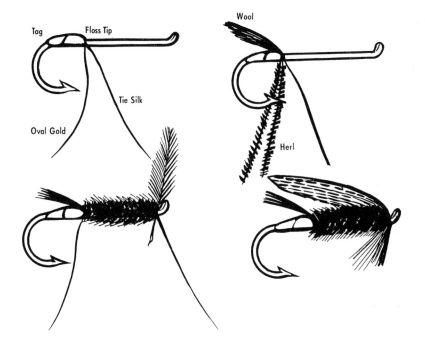

No. 16

Grey Hen and Rusty

THIS is an extremely popular fly on the Clyde and Tweed. It is chiefly used as a floater and bears a close resemblance to the Pheasant Tail, of which it is possibly a variation.

The description Grey Hen is, perhaps, slightly misleading, for the hackle, which is greyish-blue, is usually taken from a cock bird. The shinier it is the better.

The hackling is done by the orthodox method of winding it round the neck of the hook, but some fly dressers prefer the so-called "Parachute" method, made famous by Alexander Martin's, the Glasgow tackle dealers.

In putting on the Parachute hackle it is wound round a hackle stem, a short piece of stout gut, or a bit of springy wire, on top of the body.

The rusty body consists of at least two strands taken from a cock pheasant's central tail feather, ensuring that the fine point of the strand is tied in first because it has the necessary rusty colour.

Some fly dressers prefer, as in the case of the Pheasant Tail, to wind a very fine piece of wire round the herl body to protect it from the trout's teeth and general wear and tear, but this is not strictly essential.

Indeed, it has been found that the fly often becomes more attractive to the trout, though perhaps not in the angler's eyes, when it has been chewed up a bit by the fish.

It is a very easy fly to dress. Simply tie in the strands of herl, wind them up the body in close turns, thickening the body nearest the head. Then tie in the hackle by the ordinary method. Normal hook size (old numbers) are 14s to 12s.

142

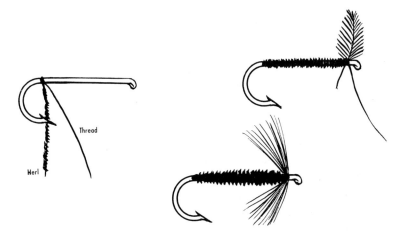

Herl

Thread

No. 17

Murray

A LTHOUGH it is not quite so well known today as it used to be, this salmon fly still kills many fish every season on west of Scotland rivers.

It was once a popular fly on the River Stinchar in Ayrshire and on the Tay in Perthshire. The pattern for the latter was dressed with two sets of wings—the first set being tied in half way up the body.

This was to overcome the difficulty, when using extra large irons, of finding a feather which was long enough in the web to reach from the shoulder to the bend of the hook.

The late Eric Taverner had a name for this method of winging; he called it the "four-in-hand", after, I suppose, that old form of transport—a carriage drawn by four horses.

In its single-winged form the Murray, as it was used on the Stinchar, had thin strips of speckled grey dun turkey for its wings. The tail was a tuft of yellow pig's wool; the butt—black ostrich herl; the body—darkish-red claret mohair, ribbed with oval silver tinsel; the body hackle—darkish-red claret similar to the body material; and the throat hackle—guinea fowl (undyed).

Such a fly will still kill salmon on the Stinchar and various other rivers where it is used, but like so many of our older salmon patterns the Murray has undergone certain variations.

The pig's wool tuft, for instance, has been replaced by a small golden pheasant topping and the addition of a golden yellow floss silk tip immediately after the flat or oval silver tag.

This addiction to yellow is of some importance on the Stinchar. The river draws water from peaty streams which give it a brown ale appearance in which the colour yellow shows up well. This is borne out by the fact that such flies as Yellow Dog and Yellow Torrish are counted among the deadliest salmon flies on that river.

Today, too, the claret body hackle is often omitted without, apparently, spoiling the fly. Also, I know fly dressers who supplant the guinea fowl hackle with nothing more than a black or reddish-brown hen hackle. And it does no harm to leave out the black ostrich herl butt.

The wing remains constant. The turkey strips should be tied in one at a time on each side of the hook's shoulder so as to keep them

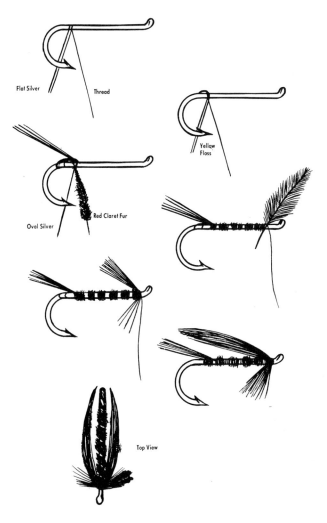

Flat Silver

Thread

Yellow
Floss

Red Claret Fur

Oval Silver

Top View

slightly split. This ensures that when the fly is swimming, the winging feathers open and close in an attractive manner.

Dress the Murray on two-inch and one-inch irons, and always strive for a slim effect.

No. 18

Dunkeld

THIS is one of those so-called attractor flies which trout fishers normally introduce when the fish need something to quicken their interest.

On such occasions it can be a very deadly pattern, but there are many lake fishers who put such dependence on the Dunkeld that they seldom have it off their wet fly casts.

It is one of the fancier patterns, probably deriving its name from the salmon fly, but, of course, its dressing is considerably modified.

Normally, the Dunkeld is fished on the tail of the cast so that it swims well under the surface. It bears a passing resemblance to a small fish and since trout are predatory in their habits they will often seize it quite boldly.

On the other hand, the Dunkeld's attractive colours, accentuated by the jungle cock cheeks, seem to entice fish not only to the fly itself but to other flies on the cast, so that it serves a two-fold purpose.

To dress the trout pattern tie in a very small golden pheasant topping as a tail, then a piece of finest gilt wire and follow that with a piece of flat gold tinsel.

Wind the flat tinsel tightly on to the hook shank, then tie in a hot-orange, henny-cock hackle at the throat. Wind this hackle down the tinselled body towards the tail and tie down its end with the gilt wire which is then used to rib the tinsel body and hackle.

In small sizes of flies it is not strictly necessary to carry the hackle down the body; a hen hackle tied in and wound on in the ordinary way is quite sufficient.

Now tie in strips of brown mallard speckled plumage and face these on each side of the wing with jungle cock cheeks.

Dress the fly in various sizes—14s and 12s for brown trout and 10s to 6s for sea trout. These are old numbers.

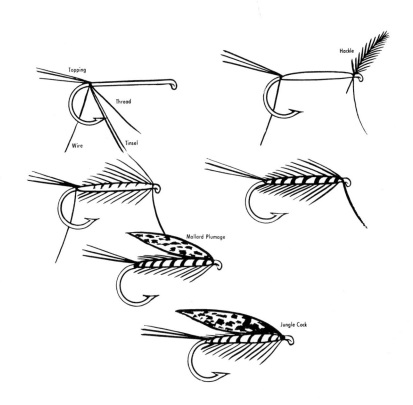

No. 19

The Priest

IT should be explained at the outset that this does not refer to the grayling fly of the same name. That has a badger (white and black) hackle as distinct from the all-black one of the Priest I am now describing.

This pattern is variously known as the Butcher Spider, the Red-tailed Silver Spider and the Silver Zulu. It is extremely popular for lake and river fishing.

Most fly fishers use it as a top dropper or bob fly and it can be a very deadly one, fished like the ordinary Zulu that is, tripping across the wave tops.

It can also be fished very successfully as a tail fly on a dour day when no fish are rising—its silver body conveying the impression, in the water, of a beetle carrying an air bubble.

Without its red silk or feather tail it is, of course, the so-called Silver Spider, another attractive variation.

Although it is chiefly used as a stillwater fly, in small sizes ranging from 12s to 14s, the Priest also fishes well in rivers, either as a wet fly with a black hen hackle or as a floater, which should be dressed with a cock hackle.

Tie in a small piece of feather dyed pillar-box red. Then wind on a flat silver tinsel body and put on a sooty black hen or cock hackle at the neck.

The trout's teeth often tear off the flat tinsel, but you can strengthen the body by ribbing it with silver oval tinsel or wire.

As this can also be a very useful sea trout fly, dress a few copies of it on size 10 to 6 (old numbers) hooks.

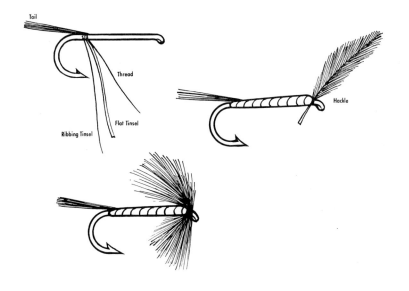

No. 20

Greentail

SOME time ago a reader of *Trout and Salmon* asked me to identify "small grey, moth-like insects", a fantastic hatch of which he had seen in the upper reaches of the River Spey.

From the information supplied I suggested that the flies might have been Grannoms, or Greentails as they are known in some parts of the country.

The angler who saw the insects hatching described them as pale grey in colour, and said they hatched out in "countless millions" every morning during the first week of May. I have seen similar hatches of the Greentail, and have fished an imitation of the insect during a rise to them, but not with very much success.

On the other hand, I have used a Greentail as the bob fly on a springtime wet cast on various rivers and have taken fish with it. I also know that it can be a very useful dry fly.

The natural insect hatches out in April or sometimes a little later. It is found on rivers rather than on lakes and has a greyish body with yellowish wings. Being a fairly small fly it is generally dressed on a size 14 (old number) hook.

The female insect is distinguishable by the bluish-green eggs attached to the end of its body. It is from this that the Grannom derives its alternative name, Greentail.

To dress the imitation, wind on two turns of green floss silk (or green sword peacock herl) to imitate the egg sac at the end of the body. Then spin on fur from a hare's mask for the body. The hackle is very pale ginger hen and the wing, applied pent fashion, is made from corresponding pieces of the palest feather from a partridge's wings.

If using the fly as a floater the wing can be rolled or folded over and over and put on as a small wad. The hackle, of light ginger cock, is wound on afterwards.

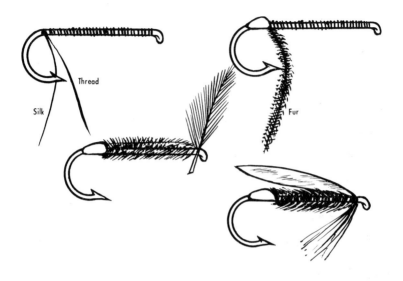

No. 21

Black Maria

I FIRST came across this hair-winged salmon fly during a visit to the Glasgow branch of Hardy's, the Alnwick tackle makers. It was here I learned that it was greatly favoured by Major F. G. S. Graham of Port of Menteith, Perthshire.

In subsequent correspondence with Major Graham I was told that he had so much confidence in the Black Maria that he never uses any other fly; in fact, he was so successful with it that he sold all his other salmon flies!

Major Graham informed me that the fly was first given to his father by Lieut.-Col. J. Hay Young of Bridge of Allan in 1954. On finding that it took salmon and sea trout from the Teith, even in low water, his father had it copied by Hardy's.

Col. Hay Young says that the fly was given to him in Ireland and he does not know how it got its name, but a few years ago Major Graham met an Irishman fishing on the Spey who produced a small fly of the same name which he said had been given to him by its inventor, Mrs. N. K. Robertson, of Slaney fame.

The Irishman's fly, however, which was dressed on a No. 10 hook, bore no resemblance to the Black Maria as Major Graham knows it. Could it be, then, that two different flies are similarly named?

Major Graham has caught fish on the Black Maria on the Teith, the Spey and the Deveron. He has been informed, moreover, that other anglers on the Spey have done very well with it. Five hundred out of six hundred fish taken at Knockando a few years ago succumbed to its attractiveness.

Major Graham fishes this fly on a greased line, preferring a double hook because it seems to swim better.

In very low water he uses a No. 8 (11/16th.-inch) and has had salmon and sea trout on that size, but he has fared much better in those conditions with a No. 4 (15/16th.-inch).

Here is the dressing of the fly: Tag—silver oval tinsel (fine); tail—small golden pheasant topping; body, tail half—yellow floss

152

silk, ribbed with fine silver oval tinsel; top half—black floss silk with black hackle over and ribbed with fine oval silver tinsel; wing—slender bunch of black bucktail or bear's hair. The black hair from a retriever's tail will also suffice.

Following publication of this article in *Trout and Salmon*, Lieut. Col. M. R. Braithwaite, of Norwich, in a letter to the editor of that journal stated : —

"Tom Stewart's dressing for the Black Maria is not very different from that given by Mrs. Robertson in her book *Further Thrifty Fishing*. Her Maria has a silk body, half yellow, half black, black throat hackle and black bucktail wing. The additions in this new dressing of Mr. Stewart's are the tail, silver tinsel ribbing and floss body.

"I have found the Maria a very useful pattern in the smaller sizes but have not done any good with it over size 6 or in peaty water. In the smaller sizes an all bucktail wing may be a little too stiff and I think it pays to mix the bucktail with something softer such as dyed black squirrel."

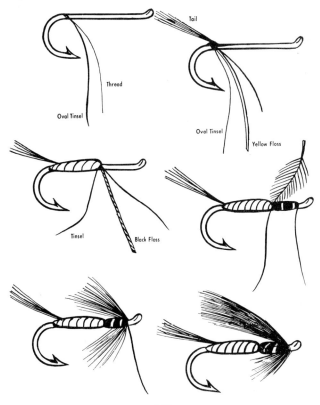

153

No. 22

August Dun

O N waters where it occurs in its natural form, floating imitations of the August Dun are taken well by trout.

It is a late-season fly, bearing a passing resemblance to a March Brown, but it does not usually make its appearance on the water until late July or August and may be seen as late as September.

Various writers have stated that the August Dun (*Ecdyrus longicanda*) only occurs on fast-running rivers. I cannot contribute to this view for I have seen hatches of the fly not only on smooth-flowing streams but even on Scottish lochs as far apart as Sutherland and Renfrewshire.

The natural August Dun is distinguishable from the March Brown because it is smaller. Its wings, too, are not quite so darkly mottled as those of the March Brown. They are normally imitated with the palest parts of the hen pheasant wing feather.

There are various dressings for the artificial fly but the one I like best is a slight variation of that ascribed to Francis Walbran.

He called it the August Brown, and used a cock pheasant wing feather for the fly's wing and two rabbit whisks for the tail. I prefer the paler hen pheasant wing and find that dark ginger hackle fibres are adequate for the tail.

Tie in the tail fibres first, then a piece of yellow cotton thread or gut dyed bright yellow for ribbing the body, which consists of light brown floss silk.

Now tie in the wings, which are set upright for the floating fly and at a rakish slope for the sunk pattern.

The hackle, like the tail fibres, is dark ginger, cock feather for the floater and hen, which is softer, for the wet fly. The hackle is put on before the wing in the case of the sunk fly.

You can use hooks in sizes from 14 to 12 (old numbers) and do not make the fly too bulky.

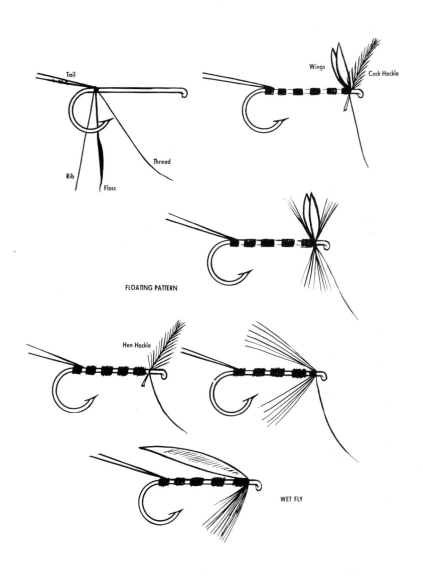

Tail

Thread

Rib

Floss

Wings

Cock Hackle

FLOATING PATTERN

Hen Hackle

WET FLY

No. 23

Yellow Owl

T HIS is a very popular fly at Loch Leven where it does great
execution every season.

I have seen natural flies very similar to the Yellow Owl flitting
about in their hundreds at Loch Leven and the fish making the water
positively boil as they rose to them.

Fished as a dropper fly during such rises the Yellow Owl is a
first-class fly. I particularly like it as a bob fly to be brought tripping
over rising trout.

My best catches with the Yellow Owl have been made on midsummer evenings when the natural flies were hatching. Before the
onset of darkness I use the fly dressed on a small double hook (size
15 or 14, old numbers) but in the dusk it is better to use a size 12
single hook.

Dress the Yellow Owl by tying in a few fibres of dark partridge
hackle as a tail. Then tie in a piece of black cotton thread (ordinary
tying silk is too fine) with which to rib the primrose yellow floss silk
body. Add a dark partridge hackle at the throat and corresponding
strips of pale hen pheasant wing feathers for the wing.

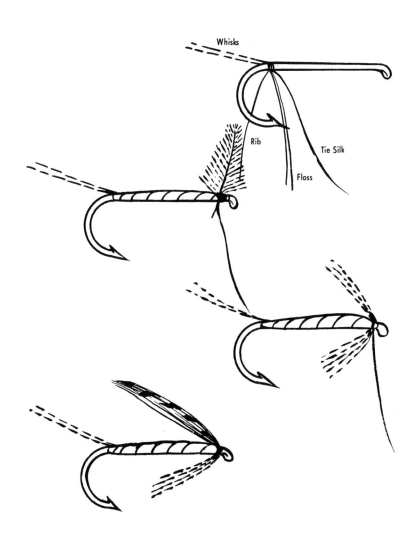

Whisks

Rib

Tie Silk

Floss

No. 24

Wormfly

THE late Courtney Williams gives the credit for the introduction of this extremely popular tandem fly (or lure) to William Black, the novelist.

But in the light of correspondence I have had with Mr. Thomas Clegg, the well-known Scottish fly dresser, I am inclined to believe that its true inventor was Black's close friend Donald Watson, who also gave his name to Watson's Fancy.

Mr. Clegg tells me that the Wormfly, which is, by no stretch of the imagination, anything like a worm in or out of the water, was first used for loch fishing in the Inverness area by Watson and his friend.

The tie-up between Watson and the Wormfly is confirmed by J. Reidpath, present manager of D. Watson and Co., of Inverness.

Fundamentally, the Wormfly is no more than two Red Tags tied in tandem, but over the years there have been some variations on the theme. Some anglers find that two Coch-y-bondhus or two Black or Blue Zulus tied in tandem give equally good results.

The Wormfly is normally fished well sunk and worked through the water so that it darts and hesitates. It can be used on its own or as the tailpiece to a wet fly cast but it has been known to do well when fished as a top dropper or bob fly on a wet fly cast in rough water.

First join two size 14 or 12 hooks (old numbers) with strong gut or wire, with the end one facing downwards (see sketch).

Now tie in a small piece of red silk or feather for the tail of the end fly. Wind on one or two strands of bronze peacock herl for the body and add a reddish-brown hackle. Do the same with the second hook but you can this time omit the feather or silk tail.

While the Wormfly is mainly fished in still water (lakes and reservoirs) it will also take trout and sea trout from rivers. It once took an 11 lb. salmon from Loch Ard.

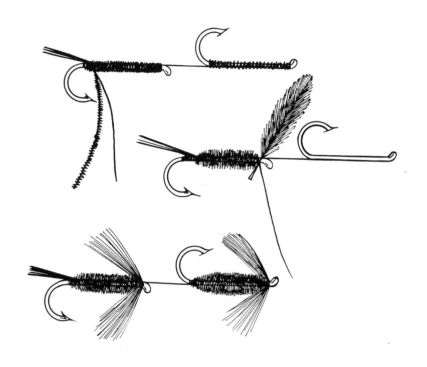

No. 25

Bloody Mary

THERE are several variations of this spider-type fancy fly, all of which have their adherents in the areas where they have become established.

The one probably most commonly used has a golden pheasant scarlet feather tail, a flat gold tinsel tag, a bronze peacock herl body, and a plymouth rock (white and black-barred) hen or cock hackle dyed blood red.

This has proved a worthwhile pattern, but, in my experience, the one referred to now is even more attractive to trout and sea trout and can be thoroughly recommended as a standby for lake and river fishing.

It was first introduced to me by Duncan Anderson, a West of Scotland amateur fly dresser. He learned of it from an elderly angler while fishing a Perthshire loch and has done so well with it that he is seldom without it on his wet fly cast.

I have also had marked success with it and so have others who have tried it.

In some respects it resembles the Poacher, referred to earlier in this series (see *Fifty Popular Flies, Vol. I*). If I receive as many letters from satisfied readers as I received when I gave the details of that fly I shall be very pleased.

First tie in a small piece of red feather (as in the Butcher) for the tail, then a strand of oval silver tinsel.

Now dub on a sufficiency of orange seal's fur to cover half the length of the fly's body.

Next wind on a strand of bronze peacock herl for the remainder of the body and rib seal's fur and herl with several turns of the silver tinsel.

There are two hackles. The first should be black and the second (nearest the eye of the hook) a very dark claret.

Fish this pattern on the tail of the cast for best results and tie it on hook sizes up to 10 (old number) for trout and sea trout.

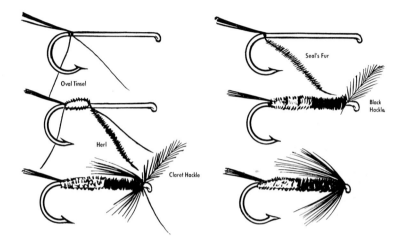

No. 26

Malloch's Favourite

THIS is acknowledged to be an imitation of certain types of Olives to be found on many waters throughout the angling year.

It owes its origin to the well-known Scottish tackle firm of Malloch in Perth and was used with great effect by the members of that noted angling family. Boatmen at Loch Leven still talk of the great catches the Mallochs made with this and other patterns.

There are, moreover, many anglers who have a particularly high regard for this fly for Loch Leven fishing, though its deadliness is by no means confined to that water.

It is not quite known why it was given a silver tag unless it was to increase a comparatively plain fly's attractiveness; quite a number of flies used in Scotland have similar tinsel adornments.

Usually I fish the Malloch's Favourite as the central fly on a three-fly cast but I don't suppose it matters which position it occupies. It kills anywhere.

The tippets, which are subjected to variations, usually consist of a few fibres of bronze mallard speckled plumage, tied in before the silver tag, which is followed by a quill body made from a peacock herl stripped of its fine flue.

Incidentally, it is the practice to use a fairly dark tie-silk so that the windings of the quill show up in distinct segments. And there are fly dressers who varnish the quill body with clear cellulose to preserve it to some extent from the teeth of the trout.

The hackle is now put on and consists of several turns of Andalusian (blue hen) feather.

Two corresponding strips of pale woodcock wing feather (inside out) are used for the wing and the fly is usually dressed on 14 to 12 hooks (old numbers).

162

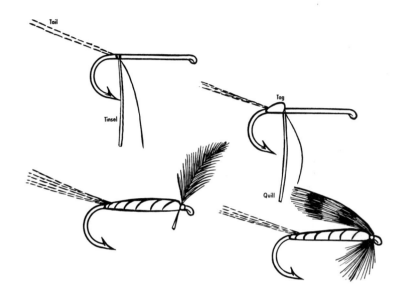

No. 27

Welsh
Partridge

WHEN it was introduced by the late Courtney Williams, this spider-type fly was so successful that he risked his very considerable reputation by describing it as an "infallible".

Like Mr. Williams I have often found that the label "infallible" has a habit of coming unstuck when related to fishing flies, but the Welsh Partridge is less liable to lose the qualifications than many other so-called fail-me-nevers.

Double hackled as it is, the Welsh Partridge can be used most successfully as a dry or floating fly for lake or river fishing. It has also proved to be a thoroughly dependable pattern for wet or sunk-fly angling.

It is a favourite for the trout in the lakes and tarns of Wales, but in recent years it has found adherents among anglers in Scotland.

Among the latter is Fred Irving, four times champion of Greenock and District Angling Club, who has good reason to sing the praises of this fly. He made most of his winning catches in club competitions with it, fishing it as the tail fly on his wet cast.

The Welsh Partridge is normally dressed on 14 to 12 (old number) hooks, but Mr. Irving was using a size 16 fly and found that the trout in Loch Thom, on the hills above Greenock, took it best when it was fished very deep in the cold months of the year and near the surface in warmer, almost calm conditions. Some of his catches with it went into double figures when other anglers were finding it difficult to catch a single fish.

The tail of the fly consists of a few fibres of dark partridge hackle (or three whisks from a piece of bronze mallard plumage).

Make the body of dark claret seal's fur ribbed with oval gold tinsel. Then tie in a dark claret hackle and wind on a slightly larger dark partridge hackle close up to it, nearest the eye of the hook.

Try the fly dressed on hooks ranging from 16s to 12s (old numbers), though in the light of Mr. Irving's experience and my own success I would suggest that you concentrate on the smallest size of fly. This I have found a good taker all through the season.

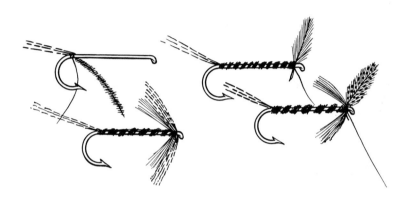

No. 28

Pheasant Tail

H ERE is an example of a fly, originally dressed for a given area—in this case Devonshire—which has gradually built up a reputation for itself in waters all over the country.

Payne Collier, its inventor about 50 years ago, never dreamed I suppose, that its fame and popularity would spread so far from his beloved West Country rivers.

Yet the Pheasant Tail is one of the best wet and dry flies for trout that any angler could use—and its usefulness is not confined to rivers.

It kills well as a lake fly and, indeed, on the small reservoirs in my part of the country it is a capital fly when Iron Blues are hatching.

I fish the fly on these reservoirs as a floater and can testify that whenever it has been put over a rising fish it has invariably earned an immediate response.

The pattern normally used by me is a slight variation from the original. Mine has a blue dun hackle and tail whisks instead of the honey dun preferred by Payne Collier, but in all other respects the dressing is the same.

The body consists of one or two fibres from the centre feather of the cock pheasant's tail with several turns of the finest oval gold tinsel or wire wound over it. The tail consists of several hackle fibres of the same type as the "legs".

Tie in the tail fibres first, then the gold tinsel, and after that a strand or two of the cock pheasant tail feather.

Wind the pheasant tail herl round the hook beginning at a point opposite the barb, then rib it with three or four turns of tinsel or wire.

Now put on the hackle, using a bright, shiny cock feather if you are tying a floater, and a soft hen hackle if you intend to fish the fly sunk.

If you are fishing the Pheasant Tail as a wet fly use it on the tail of the cast for it has a reasonable resemblance to a nymph.

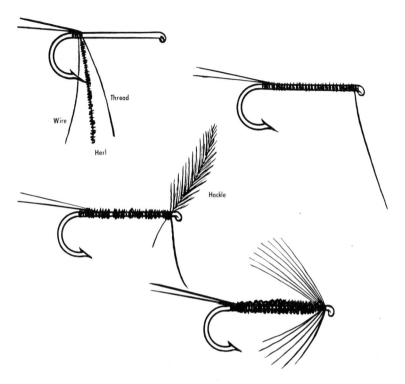

Tie the fly in small sizes, certainly never much bigger than a size 12 (old number) and preferably on a size 14 hook. Give it a nicely tapered appearance by thickening the herl closest to the fly's head.

No. 29

Black Gnat

I T is curious to note that this fly's body is not black at all; neither is the insect a gnat. The female has a dark olive-brown body; the male is darker still and as near to black as makes no difference.

These insects, which are prolific from late April till the end of the trout fishing season, are land-bred but spend the best part of their lives in the vicinity of ponds, streams, and lakes.

At times they will be seen in dense clouds over the water and fish will be rising madly to them. On such occasions a small Blae and Black, fished wet or dry, will take its quota of the rising trout.

The Knotted Midge, which is popularly regarded as an imitation of gnats in mating, will also often take a trick at such times.

I am convinced that many of the smallest black or dark-brown bodied flies used by wet and dry fly fishers are accepted by the trout because they are all near enough in appearance to the natural insect.

Most anglers fish the Black Gnat as a floater, but it has also proved itself to be a first-class wet fly, which when fished at a good depth, will often put a trout or two in the creel when nothing else will. It can also be used as a bob fly, when it should be made to dip and dance across the surface like the natural insect.

There are numerous dressings of the Black Gnat, all of which no doubt satisfy their users. After many years of experiment in which I have tried a multiplicity of patterns, based on the dressings supplied by some of our most noted fly tiers, I have come to the conclusion that the one suggested by E. M. Tod, author of *Wet Fly Fishing*, comes as near to meeting the trout's approval as any. It is, in effect, the pattern most often obtained from tackle shops.

Tod used black silk for the body, a small black hen hackle for the legs, and a pale starling wing. He also recommended black hen whisks, but these can be omitted without spoiling the fly's killing powers.

Tie in the strand of black floss or even silk tying thread and wind it tightly up the stem of the hook; then tie in the hackle, making no more than two turns. Now add the wings which should be quite short and set to lie like the wings of a house fly when it is resting. Use very small hooks, certainly never bigger than 14s (old numbers).

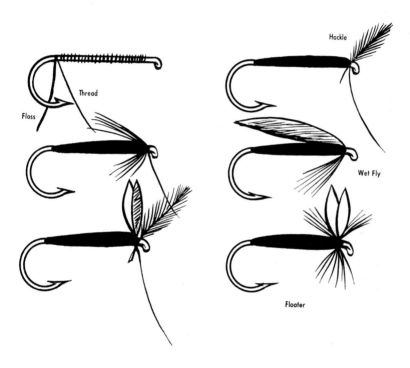

No. 30

Ke-He

ANGLERS who make the long pilgrimage to the Orkneys or even to the remote lochs of northern Scotland consider this peculiarly named fly something of a necessity on their wet fly cast.

I have often used it myself, but it was not until a reader of *Trout and Salmon,* R. Windwick of Orkney, wrote about it in a letter to the editor of that journal that I was made aware of how it got its name.

In the 1930's, according to Mr. Windwick, a certain David Kemp and his friend Bernard Heddle, who regularly fished Harray Loch in the Orkneys, noticed that when the wind was blowing freshly from the west an area of the loch was covered with great numbers of small, black bees.

At such times few other flies interested the fish, so Messrs. Kemp and Heddle contrived a pattern to match the bees, which had shiny black bodies and brownish wings. They named the pattern Ke-He (the first two letters of each of their names).

The bees no longer fall on Harray Loch but the Ke-He is still a killing fly fished in sizes 6 to 8 (old numbers). I have also used one dressed on a size 12 hook with remarkably good results.

There are actually two dressings of the fly and each has its advocates.

The original had a peacock herl body (fairly thick) with golden pheasant tippets and a Rhode Island Red cockerel hackle. In a later one a black rook hackle was substituted for the red and killed equally well.

Still later versions of the fly give it a tag of red wool or dyed feather under the tippets but when the fly is taking—and that is very often—this tag can be safely omitted. My sketch shows it with the tag.

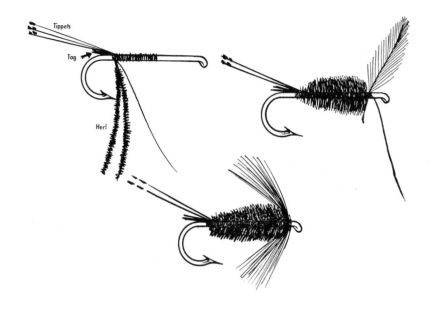

No. 31

Blue Upright

THIS well-known trout pattern, chiefly used as a dry fly, is generally accepted as representative, in its dark and light shades, of the Dark and Pale Olive. Certainly when either of these natural insects is on the water the Blue Upright can be expected to provide sport for the fly fisher.

It is said to be particularly useful for streamy rivers where the water is well broken, but in my experience it is also a first-class pattern for lake and reservoir fishing when it can be fished either sunk or as a floater.

Although some anglers like this fly to have wings (these can be of pale starling or snipe) this has always appeared to me to be like gilding the lily! I don't think the wings are necessary.

The late G. E. M. Skues provided a very good dressing of the pale version of the fly. He gave it an undyed peacock quill body, and a pale honey dun hackle, a few fibres of which were used as whisks or setae.

For the dark pattern, one cannot do better than use the dressing prescribed by the late R. S. Austin, who insisted, incidentally, that it was important to use the right colour of hackle.

The hackle in this case is steely blue, almost black, with a definite blue centre. If you use a good white cock hackle with shiny tips tinted in a fairly deep blue dun dye you will come near to the type of hackle required. The shiny tips will come out darker in the dyeing process.

The body of the fly should be of stripped peacock herl (taken from the eye feather, but not from the actual eye part itself). The late Courtney Williams suggested that when stripped of its flue this quill should be cinnamon-tipped.

Both light and dark patterns can be dressed in hook sizes ranging from 14 to 10 (old numbers).

Use hackles which are fairly long in the fibre, and make the tail from the same feather as the hackle.

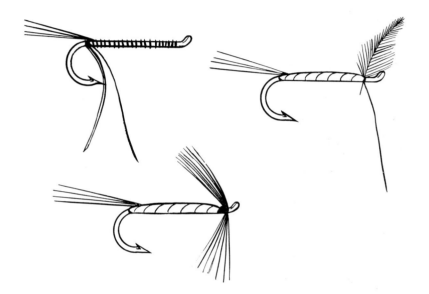

No. 32

Gold Sylph

IN conditions of low water, when a bright, slimly built pattern is required for salmon fishing, the Gold Sylph is well worth a trial.

Perhaps it is not so popular now as it used to be, but there was a time when it was regarded with the highest esteem for small-river fishing. Indeed, there are still many salmon fishers who carry it in their fly boxes in the full knowledge that it is also a very useful fly for sea trouting.

The beauty of the Gold Sylph, which falls into the category of simple strip-wing patterns, is that it is fairly easy to dress and requires the minimum of easily-obtained materials.

One can, of course, overlook the Cock o' the North feather tip, used along with a golden pheasant topping for the tail. A white cock hackle dyed dull orange is a good substitute for the former.

The body is flat gold tinsel, ribbed with fine oval silver tinsel. A lemon hackle of henny-cock texture is tied in at the throat and this is followed by the golden pheasant yellow breast feather.

Make the wings of bronze mallard strips, set in the accepted horizontal Spey fashion.

Use hook sizes ranging from three-quarters-of-an-inch to about one-and-an-eighth inch and try to create a fly that is light and slim, in keeping with its name.

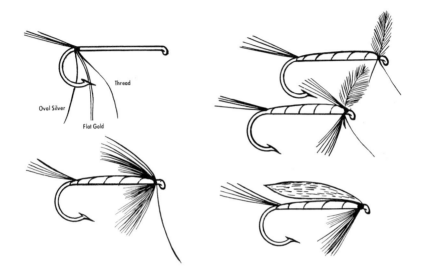

No. 33

Dogsbody

IT was the late Harry Powell, the so-called Wizard of the Usk and a very skilled fly dresser, who invented this comically named fly which became immediately popular.

As its name might imply, the first dressing of this fly had a body made from the hair of a dog. Some fly dressers still use combings from a camel-coloured dog's coat but it is the tendency nowadays to substitute wool or seal's fur of the appropriate colour.

The Dogsbody is a first-class floating fly for lake or river fishing and because of its near resemblance to a variety of natural flies it is seldom refused by rising fish. Grayling take it with the same eagerness as trout.

Dress this fly on small hooks ranging from 14s to 16s (old numbers) and use a minimum of materials to give it a delicate appearance.

First, tie in the whisks or setae, which consist of three strands at the most of the tail feather of a cock pheasant.

Now fix in the oval gold tinsel which is used to rib the dubbed wool or fur body.

The body consists of brown tying silk sparsely dubbed with camel-coloured seal's fur or wool of a fawn or golden-sand colour. The fur or wool should be picked out with a needle after the ribbing tinsel has been put on.

Next tie in a barred Plymouth Rock (in some cases called grizzle) cock hackle and after this has been wound on (not more than three turns) tie in another hackle (this time reddish-brown cock) in front of it.

176

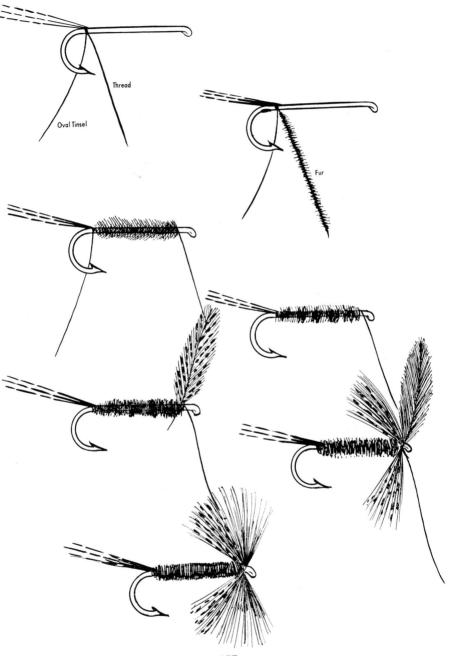

Thread

Oval Tinsel

Fur

No. 34

Stoat's Tail

O F all the hair-winged flies used in salmon fishing few enjoy the
measure of popularity that the Stoat's Tail does, whether it is
dressed in the conventional style on a single hook or in the more
sparsely-attired tube form.

Like so many other flies of similar type this one is subjected to a
host of variations, each of which appears to catch its quota of fish
and keeps its user happy.

For instance, in a round-up of the dressings used in various
localities, I find the fly being given a gold tip and gold ribbing in
one area, a silver tag and silver windings in another, and a solid
flat silver tinsel body in still another.

In all cases the wing remained uniformly of dyed black bucktail,
but in some of the flies, notably the gold-ribbed one, the hackle was
turquoise instead of the orthodox black

The most common of the dressings I found approximates to that
of the Black Pennell, and has a black silk body with an oval silver
tag and fine-oval silver tinsel ribbing.

This dressing has a short golden pheasant topping as a tail.

The hackle is black hen or henny-cock and the fly is dressed on
a size 4 (one inch) ordinary type of hook (double or single) or a
size 6 (also one inch) low water iron. The sizes are governed by the
waters where they are fished.

I suppose the Stoat's Tail derived its name from the fact that it
was first winged with the black tip of the stoat's tail. Nowadays it is
more often given a dyed bucktail or black squirrel wing—and the
salmon do not appear to notice the difference!

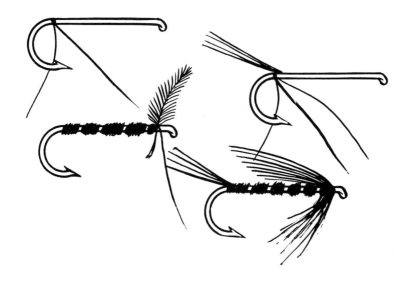

No. 35

Gold-Ribbed Hare's Ear

W ITHOUT wings this is one of the best nymph-suggesting patterns ever devised.

It is regarded in its wingless state as a very good imitation of the Lake Olive about to shake off its nymphal shuck, and for this reason it should be fished fairly close to the surface, especially when the fish are rising to the natural Olives.

Indeed, it will often be found, at such a time, that the nymph will kill better than a floating version of the hatching fly.

Tie the Gold-Ribbed Hare's Ear on size 14 to 16 (old number) hooks, using a few of the longest fibres of the dark fur from a hare's ear for the tail. Alternatively, you can use a few whisks of speckled bronze mallard plumage, or several fibres from a dark partridge hackle.

The body consists of dark fur from the root of a hare's ear, ribbed with fine flat gold tinsel. There is no hackle in the accepted sense, but the fur dubbed nearest to the neck of the hook is picked out with a needle to suggest the legs of the insect.

If one is dressing a winged version of the Gold-Ribbed Hare's Ear the best feather for the job is pale starling. This should be tied in to lie close-winged over the fly's body in the case of the wet or sunk fly, and doubled and slightly advanced towards the eye of the hook in the floating pattern.

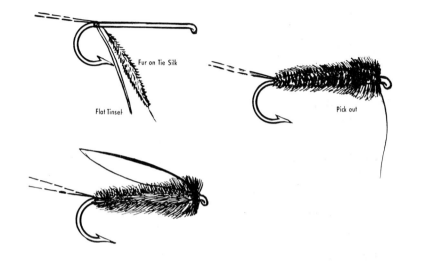

Fur on Tie Silk

Flat Tinsel

Pick out

No. 36

Mary Ann

STRICTLY speaking, this is not a fly but a lure. As such it bears a quite remarkable resemblance to a minnow in its spawning livery when it is drawn through the water.

Many lake fishing anglers regard it as a fail-me-never when the trout are not showing much interest in the ordinary run of wet flies.

It is particularly useful in large lakes, especially in those where minnows are plentiful. Yet it would be wrong to suppose that the Mary Ann's killing qualities are restricted to waters containing minnows. It has been known to kill fish in remote lochs in the Scottish Highlands where minnows are unknown.

It may be inferred, therefore, that the trout do not always take the Mary Ann for a minnow. They may be emboldened into seizing it because of its attractive colours, or its food-suggesting movement through the water.

The Mary Ann can be fished singly at the end of a six or seven-foot cast or as the tailpiece to a team of ordinary wet flies. In fact, it is by the latter means that many Scottish anglers use it very successfully on such waters as Loch Leven and Loch Awe.

It should be fished at varying depths. Keep it well sunk when no fish are showing, and near to the surface when they are.

Work it through the water so that it darts, hesitates, and glides, just like a natural minnow. Give it a little sideways jerk now and then to create that flashing movement which few fish can ignore.

Use flat gold tinsel for the bodies of the three "flies" of which the Mary Ann is composed. Then tie in a bright orange hackle on the hook which will be nearest the cast, and surmount the entire lure with a wing composed of seven or eight strands of green (sword) peacock herl.

Some anglers prefer these lures with red tails, as in the case of the Alexandra or Butcher, but these are not essential, nor is the golden pheasant topping which certain fly dressers place over the top of the peacock herl wing.

182

However, it seems to add to the Mary Ann's attractiveness if you add "cheeks" to each side of the wing. These may consist of red hackle points or pieces of swan or goose feather dyed red.

The complete lure should not exceed about $1\frac{1}{2}$ inches in length. The hooks should be 12s or 14s (old numbers).

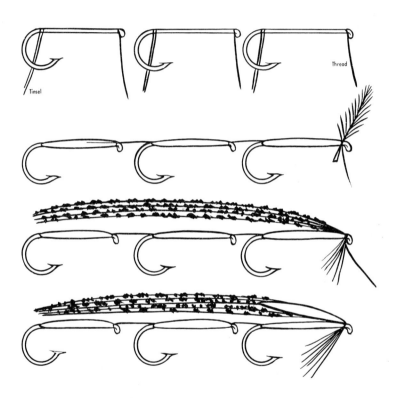

No. 37

Black Nymph

THIS was one of a series of nymph-type patterns evolved by the late R. C. Bridgett, who had probably a greater knowledge of loch fishing in theory and practice than any other angling writer of his time.

It is not clear what particular insect it was meant to represent in its nymphal state, but Mr. Bridgett suggested, and experience has proved the point, that it is a thoroughly good spider-type fly to use at the start of a trout fishing season in still water fishing.

Bridgett recommended its use as the tail or point fly on a wet cast and he tells in some of his writings about taking fish with it from Loch Awe and Loch Lubnaig, two of his favourite trouting waters.

The fly should be tied in sizes from 14s to 12s (old numbers) and dressed in the normal spider fashion.

Tie in a few fibres of a well marked guinea fowl feather for the tippets. Then fix in a piece of oval silver tinsel with which to rib the body, which consists of a strand of black ostrich herl, gradually tapered from head to tail.

The hackle is a speckled feather from a guinea fowl's plumage. It can be tied in either by the tip or by the stem.

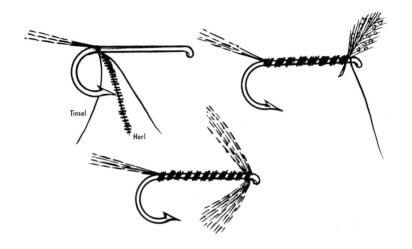

No. 38

Orange
Partridge

A S a nymph-suggesting trout fly for fast streams and even for lake fishing when there is a bit of a wave there are few spider-type patterns to equal this one. It is regarded as a fail-me-never by anglers up and down the country.

It is a particularly good fly on the Tweed and few anglers who fish the rivers of Yorkshire would care to be without it.

Although it is nymph-like and should therefore be fished fairly well sunk, I have known this fly to kill well when fished as a top dropper or bob. In this case, however, because of the softness of the dark brown partridge hackle, which causes the fly to sink quickly, it is essential to put on an additional hackle

The best one is dark ginger of a henny-cock type which should be put on in front (nearer the eye) of the partridge hackle.

In this guise it is known to many anglers who fish the Tweed as the "Paitrick" and is a very killing dry fly for fishing on the smooth glides and even in the rough and tumble of broken water.

Some anglers prefer the Orange Partridge to have a gold-ribbed body. Others give it an ordinary orange silk or wool body with a turn or two of gold tinsel as a tag or tip near the tail.

It can be fished with the double hackle on lakes as a floating fly and is particularly good during the rises at dusk.

The dressing I am giving here is the one in popular use by many anglers. It consists of a hot orange silk body with a brown partridge hackle tied in at the neck. The additional red-brown or ginger hackle can be tied in after that if the fly is to be used as a floater.

The Partridge and Yellow is a similar fly. It has a yellow silk body with pale partridge hackle and can have a pale ginger hackle added to give it extra buoyancy. Dress both patterns on hooks of size 14 to 12 (old numbers).

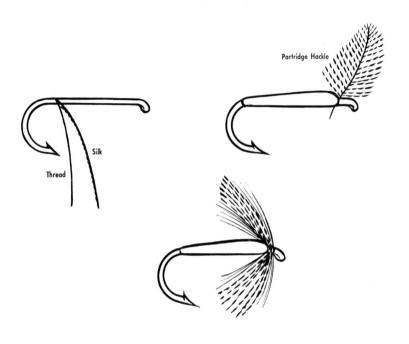

Thread

Silk

Partridge Hackle

No. 39

The Professor

NOT greatly dissimilar to the well known Teal and Yellow, a favourite fly for spring fishing for trout, the Professor takes its name from Professor John Wilson (Christopher North, the author).

Thomas Tod Stoddart, who, in his day, was one of Scotland's farthest-travelled anglers, mentions this fly in one of his books and describes it as being one of the patterns that killed well at Loch Awe. It still does so.

The dressing has changed very little since Stoddart's day, though it is no longer tied with the hackle running the full length of the body.

Dress the Professor with a bright primrose yellow silk body, ribbed with oval or flat gold tinsel and with wings of pale mottled grey mallard plumage, a dark ginger hackle and two or three fibres of red ibis (a dyed feather will do) for the tail.

I have used this fly very successfully for a great many years at Loch Awe and various other waters in Scotland. I can vouch for its trout killing powers, especially in late spring and sometimes again in the autumn. It is especially useful on rough days when used as a bob fly or top dropper, but I have also found it to be a capital fly for night fishing for trout and sea trout in high summer.

When you are using it for trout, tie it on hook sizes ranging from 14s to 10s (old numbers) and on 10s to 6s when you are fishing for sea trout at night.

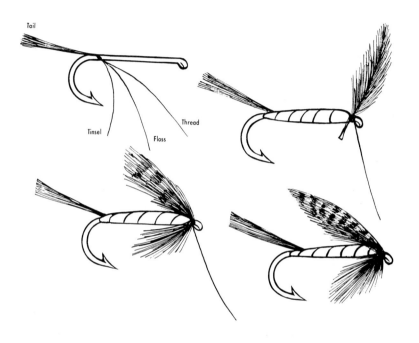

Tail

Tinsel

Floss

Thread

No. 40

Grey Turkey

THIS is a very old salmon fly, once a great favourite on the River Eden, and one of the few "old stagers" which escaped being completely ousted by the more gaudy patterns in the 19th century.

In those early days the Grey Turkey, which took its name from the winging feather, had a floss silk body of blue, violet, red or yellow. The grey turkey wing strips had a pair of jungle cock "cheek" feathers inserted between them and the colour of the hackle corresponded to that of the body with a throat hackle of undyed speckled guinea fowl or grey mallard plumage.

Since those days the Grey Turkey has undergone a number of changes. Only the winging feather remains constant and even the wing is altered by omission of the jungle cock feathers.

The floss silk bodies have been replaced by seal's fur, usually in mixed colours, one third (nearest the tail) being yellow, the middle third red, and the other (nearest the head) being black or dark blue, very much akin to the body of the Brown Turkey.

The whole body is ribbed with flat or oval silver or gold tinsel.

A golden pheasant topping or tippets from the neck feathers of the same bird can be used for the tail and the hackle can either be blue jay or dyed blue guinea fowl. In some cases the hackle is dark ginger, blue, or black to match the colour of the body nearest the throat.

The fly is busked on hook sizes ranging from 4s to 6s (old numbers) and should not be too heavily dressed.

190

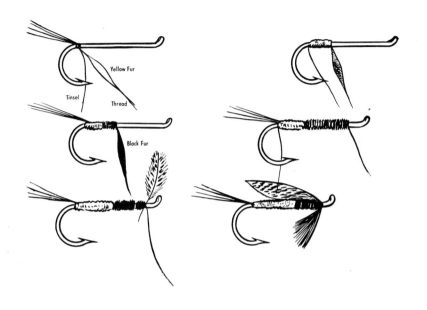

No. 41

Rough Olive

THAT noted Scottish angling writer the late R. C. Bridgett, once said that with a Rough Olive on his dry fly cast the angler had one of the finest imitations of the large Dark Olive of spring.

Bridgett was a noted angler and one of the earliest anglers to recognize the importance of the floating fly for loch fishing as well as river angling.

He sometimes used two floating flies on the one cast and very often one of them was a Rough Olive He killed many fish with this pattern on the River Clyde and on such waters as Loch Ard and Loch Awe.

The late G. E. M. Skues also considered the Rough Olive a first-class fly but his dressing was somewhat different from that of Bridgett's.

Bridgett dressed the fly with a body of swan herl dyed medium olive, ribbed with gold wire. He used an olive green hen hackle and fibres of the same for the tail or whisks, and he preferred snipe wings, rolled and tied back so that they pointed towards the eye of the hook in the so-called advanced fashion.

Skues, on the other hand, used heron's herl dyed brown olive for the body and ribbed it with gold wire. He used dark starling feathers for the wings, and a dirty brown olive hackle with dark centre and yellowish tips for the fly's legs.

Incidentally a very good hackle of this type can be obtained by dyeing creamy hen or cock hackle with shining points in this brown olive dye. The shiny points come out a yellowish olive colour.

Either of these patterns kills well, but if you are dressing one to be used as a bob fly on the wet fly cast I would recommend the Bridgett type. I have found it to be a very good imitation of the natural olive on the surface, and, correctly operated as a top dropper, it can be made to skip and skate across the surface in a very life-like manner.

Dress either pattern in hook sizes from 14s to 12s (old numbers).

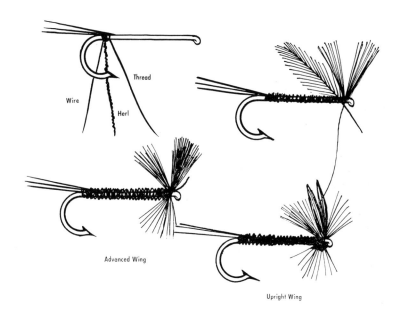

Thread

Wire

Herl

Advanced Wing

Upright Wing

No. 42

Grenadier

SOME years ago an enlightening article written by Col. Esmond Drury appeared in the *Fishing Gazette*.

It gave particulars of several nymph-type patterns which had been specially designed by Dr. Bell of Wrington for use on such stillwaters as Chew Valley and Blagdon.

Anglers who fish the lakes and reservoirs there took immediate notice and some of the patterns described have been markedly successful on these waters and elsewhere.

Among these is the Grenadier, a very lightly dressed, spider-type of fly, which the writer has been using by way of experiment and with some success on Scottish lochs and small reservoirs.

Presumably, Dr. Bell intended the Grenadier to be fished sunk, but it has been found, in practice, that it will also take fish when used as a floater.

I discovered this by accident while fishing a small West of Scotland loch. The Grenadier, on the tail of a three-fly cast, persisted in lying on the surface instead of sinking. It took five fish during a short-lived rise in near calm conditions.

The hook size recommended for this fly on the Chew Valley and Blagdon waters is 12 or 13 (old numbers), but I was fishing an even smaller size—15. I imagine that it was the cock hackle which kept it afloat.

The dressing mentioned by Col. Drury is hot orange seal's fur or floss of a similar colour. I used the floss and ribbed it with oval gold tinsel, as prescribed by the pattern's creator.

The hackle I used was light furnace cock (no more than a couple of turns), but I am assured that a pale ginger hackle makes an equally attractive fly.

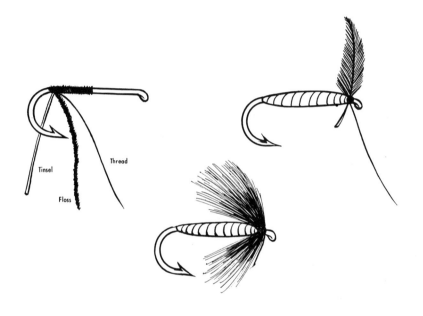

Tinsel

Thread

Floss

No. 43

Mar Lodge

ONCE, on the Spey, near Grantown, I watched an angler take four salmon from the same pool with a Mar Lodge and subsequent successes with it on a variety of rivers have convinced me further of its worth as a salmon fly.

A friend of mine, a gillie on a famous Scottish river, never tires of singing its praises and maintains that a very large percentage of the fish caught on the beat he looks after, succumb to its attractiveness.

It is, in all respects, a gaudy fly, what with its colourful "mixed" wings, tinselled body, and the use of jungle cock "cheeks".

The original dressing called for many more materials than are now deemed necessary. The strips of peacock wing feather used in the composition of the wings, for instance, can be omitted. So can the golden pheasant tail feather, while barred teal is rated a suitable substitute for summer duck.

It is not essential, either, to use embossed tinsel for the body; ordinary flat silver tinsel, ribbed with round or oval tinsel serves equally well.

The first step in dressing the Mar Lodge is to wind on three or four turns of fine, round or oval silver tinsel as a tag, following this with a similar number of turns of yellow or gold floss.

Now tie in a small golden pheasant topping with a tiny jungle cock feather tied down on top of it, the enamelled side uppermost. These make the fly's tail, which is separated from the three-part body by a turn or two of black ostrich herl as a butt.

Next tie in the ribbing tinsel, following this with the flat tinsel. One third of the body, nearest the tail, is composed of flat tinsel ribbed with oval or round tinsel. The next (or central part) is black floss silk, also ribbed with flat or oval tinsel, and the final part of the body is dressed the same as the part nearest the tail.

Add a finely speckled, undyed, guinea fowl hackle before putting on the wings.

By omitting the feathers mentioned earlier in this article it is possible to produce a not too bulkily dressed fly.

Build the wings all in one. Take suitably slender strips of yellow, red and blue-dyed swan or goose and "marry" these by stroking them between the thumb and forefinger so that the yellow strip is outermost in the composite wing on each side.

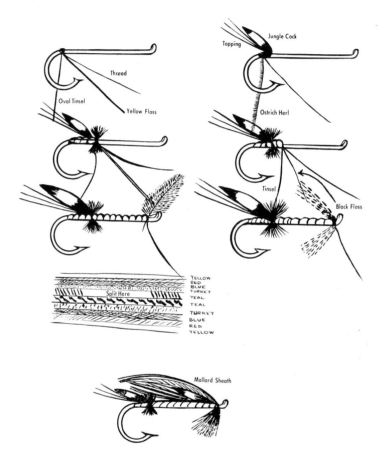

After the three colours of swan feather, add a strip of brown mottled turkey tail on each side and follow this with a broader strip of grey mallard or barred teal, which will be later folded so as to produce similar types of feather on each side of the wing.

Surmount this composite wing with strips of dark bronze mallard, add jungle cock cheeks to the sides of the wing, and then a golden pheasant topping, long enough to overlap the complete wing and almost join with the upturned topping used for the tail.

No. 44

Knotted Midge

F EW flies are so simply dressed as this one—yet it is one of the deadliest floating patterns that can be put over a trout.

It is supposed to represent the black gnat in the process of mating and, certainly, when these flies are hovering over the water and falling on to it the Knotted Midge does great execution.

Once, on the Clyde, at Abington, the writer watched a dry fly fisher take eight trout with this diminutive pattern in less than an hour during a flat calm—and they were all big fish.

Since the combined forms of the natural insects which the Knotted Midge is intended to represent are so small, one must use a reasonably tiny hook in dressing the artificial.

A size 14 (old number) is just about right and it is long enough in the shank, as a rule, to admit of the inclusion of the fore and aft hackles.

The smaller hackle is put on first, at the tail, after which the slim body should be formed of black tying silk. The slightly bigger hackle is added at the head.

There are two schools of thought in relation to the type of black hackle that should be used. Some fly dressers believe in the use of small hen hackles while others insist on hard, shiny cock hackles.

It is, of course, a matter of choice. The idea behind the use of the hen hackles is that they are soft enough to permit the fly to alight on the surface with the gentleness of the natural insects. Those who prefer cock hackles, however, claim that these hackles ensure that the fly rides high on the water without a great deal of oiling.

As the hatching of black gnats is by no means confined to rivers the Knotted Midge can be used on reservoirs and lakes with just as much success. Indeed, on small dams where black gnats hatch very plentifully it is a particularly good pattern to put over rising fish.

In some cases the black silk body is replaced with a quill body suitably dyed, but when the fish are taking the artificial they are not very particular about the type of body used.

No. 45

Black Pennell

THIS is only one of a whole series of flies invented by H. Chol-
mondely **Pennell,** author and sportsman. He insisted that they
should be dressed with thin, floss silk bodies, and long hackles very
sparsely put on.

They are essentially for trout and sea trout and are particularly
popular as bob and dapping flies, though, of course, for the latter it
is necessary, in the interests of buoyancy, to make the hackles
thicker than Pennell envisaged. When they are used as dapping
flies they are also tied on much bigger hooks than the 12s and 10s
(old numbers) invariably used in ordinary wet fly fishing for trout.

In the remoter waters of the Scottish Highlands, the Black and
Brown Pennells are extremely popular. The usual size of fly in use
is size 10, but in small reservoirs I have used a Black Pennell dressed
on a size 14 hook with equally satisfactory results.

It is a very good fly to have as the top dropper on the wet fly cast
when Black Gnats or the so-called Duck Flies are on the water.

Tie in a small silver tag (two or three turns). Then add golden
pheasant tippet fibres (three at the most) with a small topping from
the same bird's crest on top.

The body of a Black Pennell consists of black floss silk, very
thinly put on and ribbed with fine oval silver tinsel. A long-fibred
black cock hackle is wound round the neck of the hook.

There are, of course, variations on the theme. Alexander Martin,
the Glasgow tackle dealer, supplies a version of the fly which has a
red tail (as in the Silver Butcher) and a solid (flat) silver body, with
the hackle carried down the body from shoulder to tail. This pattern
does good work.

Best results are obtained with Pennell flies when they are kept
on or near the surface. They are especially deadly when the water
is rough and they are lightly bounced through the wave tops.

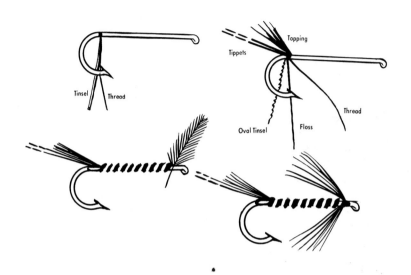

No. 46

The Hoolet

IN case you are wondering about the name of this fly, it might be as well to explain that it derives from the fact that it is winged with an owl feather—and "hoolet" is a Scots name for that nocturnal bird.

This is essentially a night-fishers' fly, to be fished at dusk and even into the hours of darkness in the manner of a large sedge.

The natural insect, an inch-long caddis fly, hatches out in certain parts of Britain about the end of May or the beginning of June. It has a thick brown body and veined cinnamon-coloured wings.

These big flies can be seen capering about the water for about a month. They skim across the surface like miniature motor boats, and it is usual to find trout slashing and dashing at them in the gloom.

In most respects the Hoolet is similar to a large version of the Coachman. It has the same bronze peacock herl body, and a dark ginger hackle, put on after the wing, which is tied down flat.

The wing can be from either the white or brown parts of a brown owl's wings. A very good wing can be made from a mixture of both.

This large fly, which is usually dressed on a size 6 (old number) light wire hook, but sometimes on a low water iron, is fished on the surface.

In those places where the natural insects occur, their arrival is acclaimed in much the same way as the Mayfly is on waters where it hatches.

The Hoolet is also a very good fly for daytime fishing on lochs and reservoirs when there is a good wave on the water. It has been known to kill many sea trout at Loch Eck in Scotland when it was used as a bob fly.

In fishing this fly at night on lakes it is a good idea to use two on a 6 ft. cast. Have the uppermost or dropper fly near the cast's junction with the line so that you can keep it tripping enticingly along the surface. You will generally find that most of the fish you catch are attracted to this bob fly.

A few words of instruction to those who propose to dress this big fly; don't make the mistake of making the head hackle too bushy. If you do, you will find that rising trout will merely nose the fly out of the water because of its over buoyancy, and you will miss more fish than you hook.

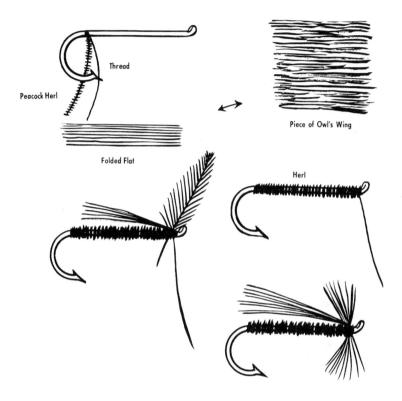

It is best to use a tapered line and to grease it with a floatant preparation. The fly should also be oiled and dried before use.

No. 47

Jeannie

THE low water version of a very good salmon fly, this one is regarded by some anglers as one of the best that can be fished through the faster runs of a river at reduced level in high summer. It is also worth a trial when the water is fining down after a freshet.

Fish it on a greased line so that it swims just under the surface and mend the line periodically to keep the fly travelling at an even pace and depth.

Use a size of fly corresponding to the depth of water being fished, going as small as a low water size 9 (three-quarters-of-an-inch) when the water is very thin or clear. Raise the size if the water is fairly deep or running fast over a rough bottom, going up the scale, say, to a low water size 5 (one-and-an-eighth-inch). If you are "missing" fish go up rather than down.

The Jeannie is a very attractive-looking fly, its special features being the distinctive lemon floss end to the otherwise black floss body, and the jungle cock cheeks.

Tie in four turns of round or oval silver tinsel as a tag. Then add a small golden pheasant topping for the tail and follow that with a piece of oval silver tinsel with which to rib the body.

The posterior third of the body is lemon floss silk and the remainder black floss, with the ribbing over. The hackle, sparingly put at the throat only, is natural black of a henny-cock description.

In the low water fly start the dressing about halfway up the hook shank, using the minimum of materials to achieve a lightly dressed fly.

The bronze mallard wing, put on in the simple strip-wing principle, is given a slightly upright set and the jungle cock cheeks are added to each side.

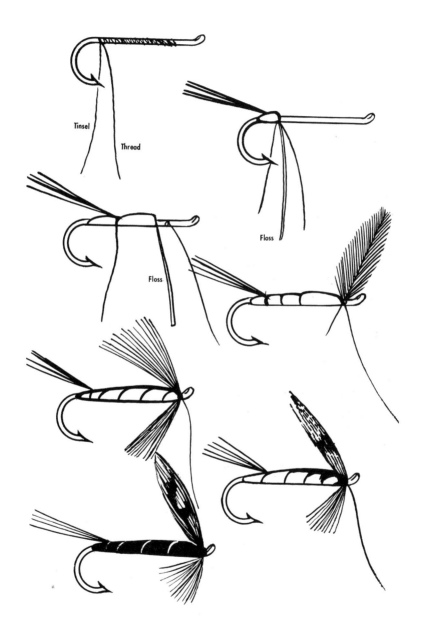

Tinsel

Thread

Floss

Floss

No. 48

Corixa

OVER the past few years quite a number of so-called Corixa have come on the market. Many have no resemblance to the natural Water Boatman, being, in fact, mere figments of the fly dresser's imagination.

Yet, as so often happens, these variations take trout, and since the purpose of all artificial lures is to catch fish we can have no quarrel with them.

Corixids are common to most still waters, and they will also be found in the quieter parts of streams. Often they may be seen in their passage to and from the surface where they collect air. They are indentifiable by the air bubble they carry, which gives them a silvery appearance as they move about in the water.

The natural corixa I examined had a dingy cream or buff-coloured body with dark brown elytra or wing cases. It had three pairs of legs, the so-called paddles, which enable this beetle to swim so quickly, being of a greyish-brown colour and the others more of a gingery hue. The head, too, was brownish.

It will be understood, of course, that there are different forms of corixids, but a fair imitation of the above one can be achieved with a pattern which A. J. Pridmore, of Market Harborough has very kindly sent to me as representative of the type which kill trout at Chew Valley.

It is dressed on a No. 10 (old number) hook, has a pale straw-coloured silk body, ribbed with fine oval silver tinsel, and it has a small silver tag. The wing cases are formed of a dark woodcock feather and the head hackle is medium ginger hen.

I do not suppose this pattern can be described as more than an approximation to the natural corixa but I prefer it to the more elaborate dressings, near to life-like as some of them appear to be, which several prominent angling writers have recently recommended.

At the same time I am intrigued by another pattern, this time with a white or cream marabou silk body, sent to me by W. E. Rylands, of Wirral, Cheshire. This tagless one has more silver about it than Mr. Pridmore's pattern, but it corresponds in most other particulars.

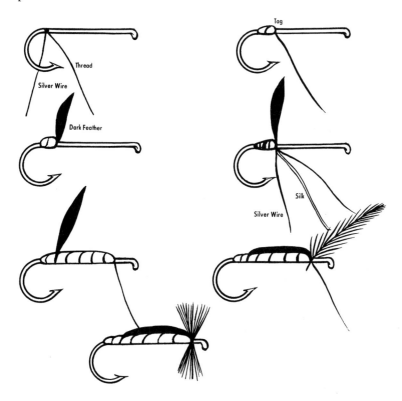

My sketches show the method of dressing the type of corixa supplied by Mr. Pridmore, but I would suggest that it might be worth while tying a few with the body described by Mr. Rylands; it has no fewer than five turns of oval silver tinsel.

Indeed, it might be a good plan to use cream-coloured fur for the body, since fur gives a more glistening effect than silk in the water, and abetted by the silver, might create something nearer to a semblance of the air bubble which the natural corixa carries.

No. 49

Red Ant

THIS fly only assumes the mantle of popularity at certain times in the angling year, mainly in late August or September. It is then that the natural ants, equipped with wings for migration purposes, are most likely to fall on to the surfaces of rivers and lakes.

When these falls of ants occur they come like manna from heaven to the trout, which rise to them to the exclusion of almost everything else. I have seen a near-calm lake suddenly become a place of boiling activity as trout of all sizes rose and splashed after the diminutive creatures, and I have at times deplored the fact that I did not posses a suitable imitation of the ant to float among the rising fish.

One such experience is usually sufficient to warn the angler never to be without a red ant imitation in his fly box, ready to be fastened to a dry fly cast at a moment's notice whenever a fall of these ants occurs.

Sometimes, of course, an ordinary red spider will serve to take a few trout during one of these phenomenal rises to the natural ants, but the popular dressing of the imitation is so easy to achieve that it is preferable to rely on it.

Tie in a small frond of bronze peacock herl to make a butt at a point opposite the hook's barb.

Then, when the herl has been wound round, tie in a short length of bright red floss silk and wind this round the body so that it is put on thick at the end, slender (or narrow-waisted) in the middle, and slightly thicker nearest the wing and hackle.

The hackle is dark ginger cock and very small. No more than a couple of turns are necessary and the wing can either be slips from corresponding starling wing feathers of very shiny cock hackle points dyed pale blue dun shade.

The wing should be quite short and, since the natural ant is such a tiny creature, the fly itself should be dressed on a size 15 or 16 hook (old numbers).

Take care that you do not make the body of the imitation too bulky.

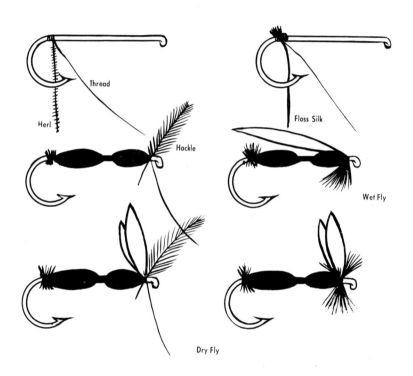

No. 50

Black Dose

O NE of the most successful salmon flies used on the Tweed, this pattern's popularity is by no means confined to that great river. It is one of the duller flies which invariably does well in a dark water and is fished in sizes ranging from $\frac{1}{4}$-inch to two inches.

Tie in a piece of flat silver tinsel for the tag, following this up with several turns of bright orange floss silk.

Now tie in the tail, consisting of a short golden pheasant topping, obtainable from that bird's crest with married strips of barred teal plumage and scarlet swan on top.

The body of the fly comprises three turns of blue seal's fur and the remainder black seal's fur, which should not be teased out but left reasonably smooth. The entire body is veiled by a shiny black henny-cock hackle, and ribbed with oval silver tinsel. A fiery brown or pale claret hackle is wound on at the throat.

The wings of the fly are not particularly difficult to prepare, though it takes a little practice to wed certain strips of feather properly. They consist of a pair of whole golden pheasant tippet feathers tied back to back and surmounted by married strands of dyed scarlet and green swan or goose feather, light brown turkey, and golden pheasant tail. The entire wing is overlapped by a golden pheasant topping.

No attempt should be made to hide the underwing. Strive to let the golden pheasant tippet feather shine through the veiling feathers.

The original pattern had peacock herl strands superimposed on the wing sheaths but these are inclined to make the wing rather bulky and can be omitted safely.

Horns of blue and yellow macaw can also be left out, but many salmon fishers maintain that bright blue cheeks on each side of the winging feathers add to the fly's attractiveness.

It should be noted that the golden pheasant tippet feathers used as an underwing in this fly should not be too broad. Strip off some of the fibres to achieve the slim effect shown in the sketch.

In marrying the various feathers take slender strips from both sides of the plumage required and smooth them together by drawing them between the forefinger and thumb.

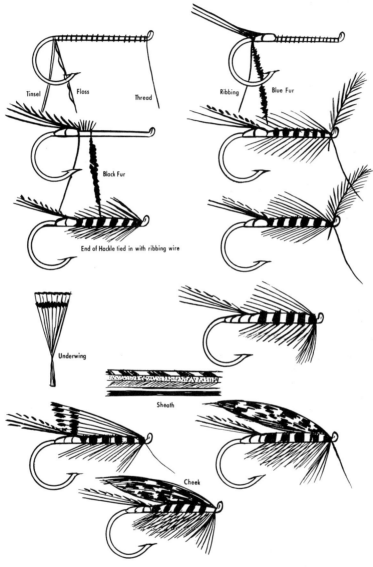

The veiling sheaths should be built on to the wing in one piece (for each side) in the following order, starting from the bottom: —
scarlet swan, green swan, light brown turkey, golden pheasant tail.

BOOK THREE

No. 1

Thunder
Stoat

INVARIABLY when a fly becomes an established favourite it is subjected to variations by fly dressers hoping to make a good fly a better one.

That wonderful hair-winged salmon fly, the Stoat's Tail, is one of them.

By the very simple addition of jungle-cock cheeks it becomes the Thunder Stoat.

The contrast created by the jungle-cock feathers against the black hair of the wing makes this a very fine pattern for a rising water, or one that is just beginning to run off after a spate.

The full dressing of this fly is as follows: Tie in a tag of three turns of fine oval silver tinsel, then fix in a small golden-pheasant crest feather or topping.

Now wind on a slender butt of black ostrich herl or wool, though the butt can be safely omitted. Tie in a piece of oval silver tinsel with which to rib the body, which is black floss silk.

Add a short blue or black henny-cock hackle at the throat, and tie in the black squirrel-tail wing, adding a jungle-cock eye feather to each side of the wing.

There is a variation of this fly which has a good reputation for evening fishing for salmon. The tail is the same, but the black floss silk body is ribbed with oval gold tinsel instead of silver, and the hackle, put on as a beard rather than wound round the hook stem, is of hot orange henny-cock fibres.

The wing is red squirrel, with jungle-cock cheeks added, as before. The hackle in each case should be short and sparse.

Normal sizes of both these flies, are 10s to 6s (old numbers), dressed either on Limerick singles or low-water doubles. The winging hair should not be carried beyond the bend of the hook.

To put on the beard hackle I reverse the hook in the vice and tie in a small bunch of hackle fibres. This helps to give a neater head to the fly.

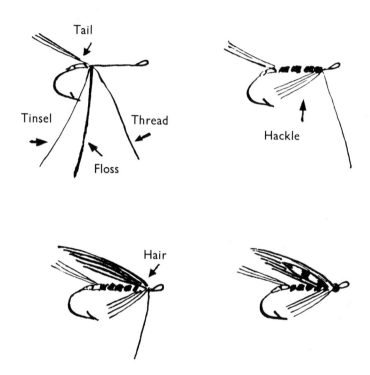

No. 2

Kate MacLaren

DURING a visit to my friend Angus Robertson, of the Glasgow firm of fishing-tackle dealers, I learned about this fly which was first dressed by his father, the late William J. Robertson.

The Kate MacLaren had its baptism in Loch Maree in Wester Ross and apparently did well as a variation of the Black Pennell for sea-trout fishing in that water.

That was as long ago as 1934, but the fly has maintained its popularity all those years in the north.

To dress the Kate MacLaren, tie in a small golden pheasant topping as a tail. Then make a fairly thick body of black seal's fur over which you wind a small fibred black cock hackle from head to tail in palmer fashion. Now rib both the body and the hackle with oval silver tinsel in evenly-spaced turns.

Finish off the fly with a red-brown cock hackle at the throat, putting on about four or five turns so that it has a quite bushy appearance.

Dress the Kate MacLaren in hook sizes ranging from 10s to 8s (old numbers).

It can be fished with success as a tail fly but is probably better as a bob fly or top dropper.

If you wish you can fish this fly along with the Black Pennell, both of them being highly-favoured flies in these north of Scotland waters where the trout and sea trout often run to big proportions.

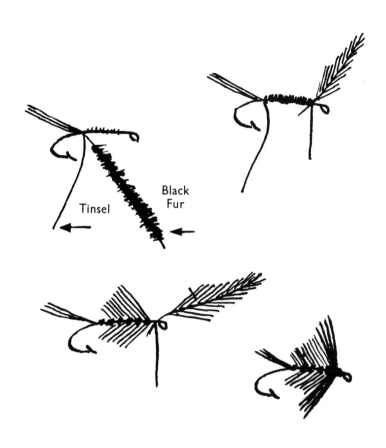

Tinsel

Black
Fur

No. 3

Blue
Doctor

EXCEPT for the purposes of exhibition and fly dressing on a competitive basis it is not essential to incorporate all the winging materials mentioned in the original dressings when tying salmon flies.

For example, when dressing a Blue Doctor it is possible to omit quite a number of the ingredient feathers which were once deemed necessary to the fly's success—and the salmon do not seem to mind in the least!

Begin the dressing by tying in a tag of silver tinsel (flat or round) and follow this up with a few turns of golden yellow floss.

Then tie in a golden pheasant topping and tippet in strands and wind on a butt of scarlet wool or ostrich herl.

The body of the fly consists of pale blue floss silk with a paler blue hackle over and ribbed with oval silver tinsel.

Use a blue-barred jay hackle or a suitably dyed piece of spotted guinea fowl plumage for the throat hackle.

As the base for the wings tie in a few strands of golden pheasant tippets and strips of feather from the same bird's tail. Over these put "married" strands of scarlet, blue, and yellow swan with light mottled turkey and narrow strips of barred teal.

This makes a perfectly simple wing and you can safely leave out florican bustard, peacock wing, and barred summer duck feathers.

Place narrow strips of bronze mallard plumage over the top of the wing sheaths without completely veiling them and tie in a topping extending from the neck of the fly to meet the point of the uptilted tail.

The head can be of red wool, ostrich herl or red cellulose paint.

Dress the fly on 1-inch to 1½-inch irons, or even bigger, dependent on the river to be fished.

218

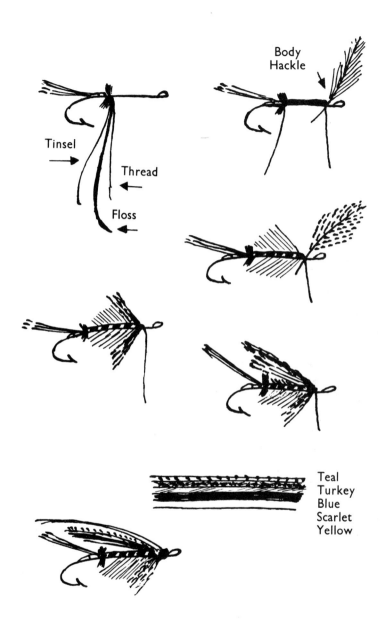

Tinsel

Thread

Floss

Body Hackle

Teal
Turkey
Blue
Scarlet
Yellow

219

No. 4

Golden
Demon

THIS pattern, which I have used most successfully for sea trout, had its origin, I believe, in America. It is mentioned by that very able writer and fly dresser, J. Edson Leonard, in his dictionary of flies.

But the dressing given by Mr. Leonard differs in certain details from the hair-winged pattern I am about to describe.

Mr. Leonard gives the dressing as: Tail, golden pheasant crest (or topping); body, flat gold tinsel, ribbed with round gold wire; hackle, orange; wing, hen pheasant; shoulder, jungle-cock eye feathers; topping (over wing), golden pheasant crest.

I understand that Mr. Leonard intended this for a salmon fly. To my mind, the following, which is, as I have said, for sea-trout fishing, is a simpler dressing.

In these days, when so many fly dressers are going in for the use of hair wings to their flies, I think this one will prove popular.

The tail consists of a few fibres of dyed yellow cock hackle. Flat gold tinsel is used for the body, this being ribbed with oval gold tinsel.

The hackle is hot orange cock, put on as a beard (that is, below the fly only). Brown bucktail or brown squirrel is used for the wing, on both sides of which a jungle-cock eye feather is placed.

I have found this fly to do especially well in the evenings when fishing for sea trout, and a companion angler swears by it for angling during the hours of darkness. He takes many big sea trout with it.

The Golden Demon, as I have described it, is usually dressed on size 8 to 10 (old number) Limerick hooks, but it could be dressed on low-water irons for greased-line fishing for salmon. Indeed, during a recent angling holiday in the north of Scotland, I was intrigued to discover that the Golden Demon is such a prime favourite for salmon fishing on the River Thurso.

220

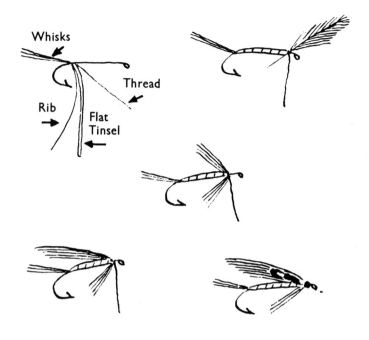

No. 5

Ramsbottom's
Favourite

THIS is essentially a sea-trout fly though it has been used with some success for lake trout, but it has never aspired to the favouritism among anglers that its inventor, the late Robert Ramsbottom of Clitheroe, in Lancashire, accorded it.

The possibility is that Ramsbottom, who did much of his fishing in Wales and Scotland, first tried it out when fishing for sea trout in these countries and that its use as a lake pattern came later. Many of our best lake flies of the fancy category derived from sea-trout flies being dressed in miniature.

The body of the fly consists of yellow seal's fur, ribbed with oval, gold tinsel; or even fine, flat, gold tinsel, which is regarded by some fly dressers as being better.

A piece of red ibis or suitably-dyed feather is used for the tail, and the hackle is red-black or coch-y-bonddu.

The wing can be tied by mixing the component feathers in a small bunch and tying them down along the back of the fly's body.

But the accepted method is to tie in two thin corresponding strips of mallard bronze plumage as an underwing and to "marry" slender strands of red, yellow and blue swan or goose feathers into sheaths for placing over the mallard feather without actually concealing it.

It appears that Ramsbottom preferred the mallard feather to show through the dyed swan or goose feathers. He dressed the fly in hook sizes ranging from 6 to 12 (old numbers).

222

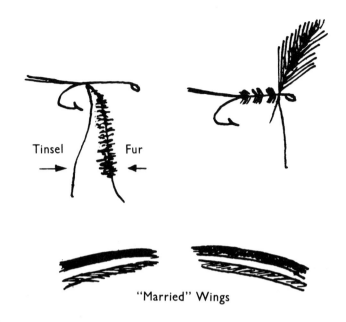

Tinsel →   ← Fur

"Married" Wings

No. 6

Sir
Richard

A SURVIVAL of the days when salmon-fly dressers went to special pains to produce highly-decorative patterns, this fly still enjoys a considerable reputation on big rivers like the Tay and Tweed despite the inroads made by hair-winged and tube flies.

It is one of those patterns which, when fully dressed by the expert, can be made to look like a piece of jewellery. But, as I have said in the case of other ornate flies, it is not essential to incorporate all the exotic materials that were once deemed necessary for such mixed-wing dressings.

For instance, you can omit the blue and yellow macaw horns without spoiling the fly's efficiency and you can substitute the tips of a dyed-blue hackle for the blue chatterer cheeks.

The Sir Richard is usually dressed on hook sizes ranging from $1\frac{1}{4}$ to 3 inches.

Begin with the tag, which consists of several turns of round or oval silver tinsel, followed by a few turns of dark orange floss.

Then tie in a small golden pheasant topping, with a piece of Indian crow (dyed red feather) on top to form the tail, and add a butt of black ostrich herl or wool.

The body is made of black floss, ribbed with flat silver and oval silver tinsel wound close up to each other on top of the black hen (or heron in the larger sizes) hackle, which runs the length of the body.

When the body has been completed add a guinea fowl speckled hackle at the throat.

The mixed wing consists of "married" strands of red, orange and blue swan (in that order from the bottom), with oak-speckled turkey next to them, a strip of golden pheasant tail after that, and a slender strip of speckled guinea fowl wing over. The last-mentioned is often omitted, as are such feathers as Florican and mottled grey turkey.

Cheeks of blue-dyed hackle tips are then added and the macaw horns if you deem them necessary.

Finish off the dressing with a golden pheasant topping.

Although the size of fly is given as up to three inches it is only in exceptional circumstances that such a big iron is now used. Normally, a fly of about 2 inches is considered adequate, even for a big water.

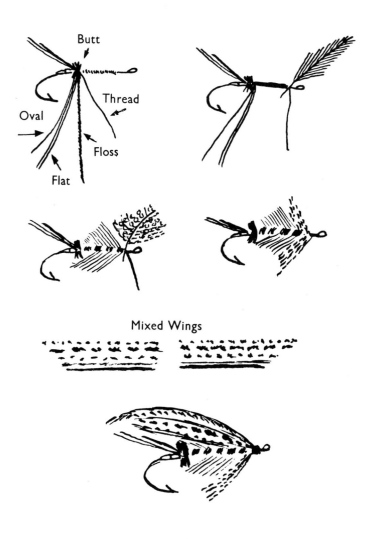

Mixed Wings

No. 7

Dotterel
Dun

REGARDED as a fairly reasonable copy of the Pale Watery Dun, this fly, which takes its name from the bird a feather from which is used for its hackle, is particularly useful from late spring onwards.

It is reckoned to have had its origin in Cumberland, where the pattern has always been held in the highest esteem, though, of course, it has its adherents among anglers in many other parts of the country who value its use when the Pale Watery Dun is in evidence.

The Dotterel Dun can be fished wet or as a floater, but if you are using it for the purposes of dry-fly fishing I would suggest that an additional cock hackle (preferably dyed a slate colour to match the dotterel hackle) be tied in and wound on before or after the latter. This counteracts the lack of buoyancy in the dotterel feather or substitute.

On the other hand, some anglers prefer the soft dotterel hackle even for their dry flies, presumably because it lies so close to the surface.

It seems unnecessary to mention that the dotterel feather is not very easy to obtain. And so a substitute is often used.

This is usually a piece of the bluish-grey feather from the inside of an old cock starling's wing, which seems to make a very good and easily-obtained substitute for the real thing—a feather from the outside of a male dotterel's wing.

The body consists of fur from the mask or face of the hare, lightly dubbed on straw-coloured silk.

There is an old Yorkshire dressing which dispenses with the hare's fur and has a straw-coloured silk body. The hackle is the same as in the other pattern.

Both are tied on hook sizes ranging from 16 to 14 (old numbers).

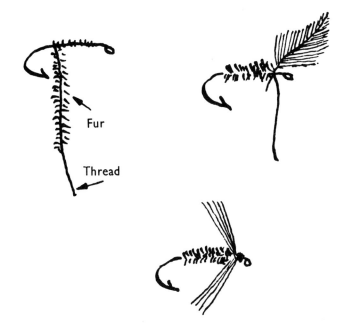

Fur

Thread

No. 8

Benchill

HERE is a salmon fly which is very popular on the Tay in Scotland, where it takes its quota of fish season after season. It is in the category of whole-feather winged flies though the main feathers—a pair of golden pheasant tippets tied in back to back—are veiled with certain other plumage.

It is a highly-coloured pattern and although it is essentially a big-river fly it can be used to good effect in its smaller sizes for small-river fishing.

Begin by tying in a tag of several turns of round or oval gold tinsel. Then tie in a tail consisting of a small golden pheasant topping with the tip of a golden pheasant breast feather (port-wine red) on top, and add a butt of black ostrich herl or wool.

You are now ready to tie in the flat and oval silver tinsels which are wound on close to each other to rib the seal's fur or wool body, consisting of equal sections of orange, scarlet, claret, and pale blue.

The throat hackle is pale, powder blue.

Now tie in the under-wings—the two tippet feathers tied back to back—and veil these with "married" strands of peacock wing, scarlet and blue swan, golden pheasant tail and bustard (or oak-speckled turkey, which is an excellent substitute), in that order from the bottom of the veiling wing.

Cheeks of the fly consist of strips of speckled guinea fowl with jungle cock over. A golden pheasant topping extending the length of the wing completes the dressing.

This fly is dressed on hook irons ranging from $1\frac{1}{4}$ to 3 inches.

Do not make the seal's fur body too thick or you will upset the balance of the fly by pushing the wing feathers out of their proper alignment. But use a needle to pick out the fur fibres on the underside of the body.

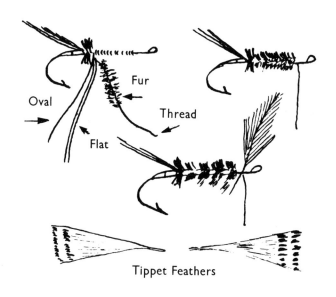

Oval

Fur

Thread

Flat

Tippet Feathers

Wing Sheaths

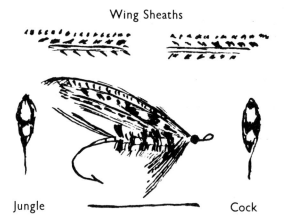

Jungle

Cock

No. 9

Arndilly
Fancy

I SUSPECT that this will be a new pattern for many anglers. I first heard of it during a visit to the Brora district of Sutherland, where I had the pleasure of meeting Miss Megan Boyd of Kintradwell, one of Scotland's leading fly-tying professionals. She was kind enough to give me the details for dressing this hair-winged salmon fly.

The Arndilly Fancy is a most attractive-looking pattern for use in sunk or greased-line fishing.

According to Miss Boyd, it has already established a good reputation for itself in the Morayshire area of Scotland.

Several anglers I have met since my meeting with Miss Boyd have informed me that they have had marked success with this fly on the Spey. They used it dressed on sizes ranging from 7 to 10 low-water doubles.

The dressing of the Arndilly Fancy presents no great problems. First tie in and wind on a short piece of fine oval silver tinsel as a tag. Then tie in the tail, consisting of a small golden pheasant topping.

The next step is to fix in the ribbing tinsel, which is oval silver, and a strand of pale yellow floss silk. Wind on the yellow floss and rib it with evenly-spaced turns of the oval silver tinsel.

Reverse the hook in the vice and tie in a slim bunch of bright blue cock hackle fibres, beneath the hook only, in beard fashion. Secure with a half hitch. Then restore the hook to the normal position in the vice and take the appropriate quantity of black squirrel tail hair (or bucktail dyed black for the larger sizes) and tie in as a wing.

All that remains now is to fix in a jungle cock "eye" on each side of the hair wing, and after applying black varnish for the head, ring this, nearest the wing, with red cellire.

Alternatively, as I have done, you can tie in a piece of wool or dyed red ostrich herl for the red part of the head.

Since this dressing was published in *Trout and Salmon* I have learned from Mr. Robert McOwan, of Menstrie, Clackmananshire, that the Arndilly Fancy was originally dressed by an amateur fly tier, an exciseman from Rothes.

The fly came into the possession of John Macdonald, a Spey expert and a gamekeeper for the Menzies of Menzies, who resided at Arndilly House.

I understand that the pattern was meant as a variation of the Stoat's Tail.

Mr. McOwan tells me he used this pattern on the Spey some ten years ago.

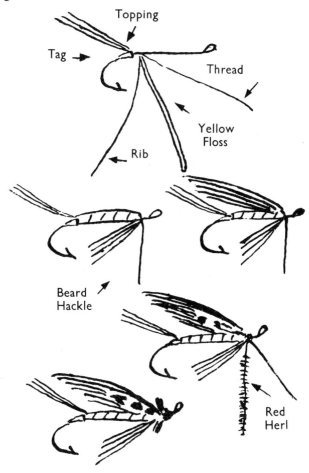

No. 10

Childers

THIS is another of those almost gem-like, mixed-wing salmon flies that our fly-tying ancestors went to such pains to perfect. And, like so many of the confections of fur, feather and tinsel that they invented, it has stood the test of time and is likely to retain its popularity for years to come.

Start the dressing by tying in a tag of round or oval silver tinsel, following this with a few turns of pale blue, floss silk. Then add a tail comprising a small golden pheasant topping with a piece of Indian crow (or red feather substitute) on top.

Separate the tag from the main body dressing by tying in a butt of black ostrich herl or wool.

Now tie in the flat silver and oval silver tinsel which will be wound on close together to rib the floss and fur body.

The body consists of three equal sections of golden-yellow, floss silk (at the tail), followed by orange and fiery-brown seal's fur, the whole body being veiled by a badger hackle dyed lemon, which is held in place by the ribbing tinsels.

There are two throat hackles. The first is of golden-pheasant breast plumage (a port-wine red colour), and the second of widgeon or pale, barred teal plumage. The under-wing consists of two golden-pheasant breast feathers (port-wine colour) tied in back to back. Veiling these, but not quite hiding them, are "married" strands of red, blue, orange and yellow swan, followed by bustard (or oak-speckled turkey), golden-pheasant tail, cinnamon and mottled, grey, turkey tail.

I have included all these winging materials for the benefit of those who like to be perfectionists in their fly dressing, but I can assure you that the cinnamon turkey and the grey turkey can be safely left out.

The sides of the fly are formed from barred summer duck strips, but if you cannot get these use jungle cock "cheeks" partly veiled by barred widgeon or teal plumage.

Blue chatterer is used for the cheeks but as these feathers are extremely difficult to obtain you would be advised to make do with dyed-blue hackle tips.

Add the golden-pheasant topping, which should run the whole length of the wing and, if you like, add the blue and yellow macaw horns, but, again, these are not strictly essential.

This fly is dressed on hook sizes ranging from one to two inches or slightly larger.

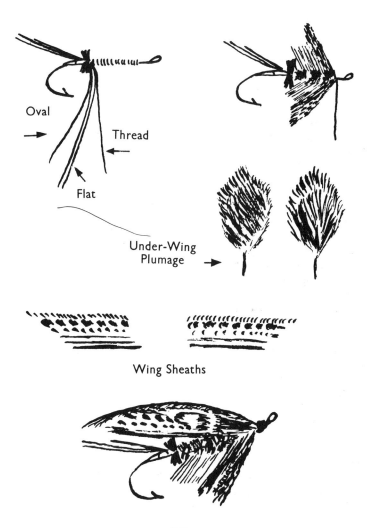

Oval

Thread

Flat

Under-Wing Plumage

Wing Sheaths

No. 11

Red Sedge

DURING the hours of darkness on summer nights, when sedge flies are capering about the surface of lakes and reservoirs, you can mount almost any bushily-dressed, well-hackled fly to your cast, fish it on the surface, and catch trout with it.

This is a kind of "wake-fly" fishing. The fish are attracted to the fly, in the first instance, by the wake-like disturbance it causes on the water as it is pulled across the surface.

One of the best patterns for this style of fishing is the Red Sedge. It can be dressed in the range from, say, size 12 (old number) to size 8 light-wire hooks.

You oil and dry this kind of fly and cast it out into the areas where fish are rising to natural sedges. Then you bring the fly towards you by coiling in line on the rod-free hand so that the artificial insect skates about on the surface.

Sometimes the fish will follow the sedge fly quite close to the bank before it makes its pounce. So don't be too quick in your line recovery.

I have taken quite a number of fish on the smaller sizes of the Red Sedge just before dusk, and then have changed to a bigger pattern when darkness came down. I did this not because I felt that the fish could not see the smaller one, which they could, but because I thought I had a better chance of hooking them with the bigger hook.

The Red Sedge is very easy to dress. Tie in a short length of gold wire, then dub on dark red wool for the body and wind a red cock hackle from head to tail, binding in the end of the hackle with the gold wire.

Now rib the body and hackle with the gold wire and tie in the wings, which are of plain brown hen wing, tied close together as in normal wet-fly practice. Or you can fold them over and over in the shape of a

234

small wad of feather which is tied in to lie over the back of the fly's body.

Then put on another red cock hackle slightly longer in the fibres than the body hackle. This additional hackle gives the fly the necessary buoyancy to keep it afloat. Don't make it too bushy or you are likely to find that the fish will only succeed in "nosing" the fly out of the water when they rise to it.

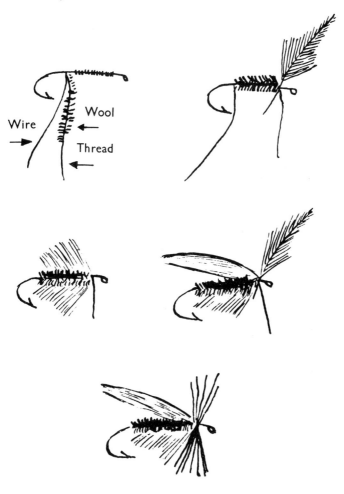

No. 12

Grey Monkey

MY INTRODUCTION to this pattern was at Loch Leven, where a friend of mine, fishing a Grey Monkey on his wet-fly cast, took nearly a score of trout with it during an evening's angling. He presented me with a copy of it—and since then I have fished it with considerable success for brown trout.

I have not been able to ascertain who invented this fly but, like many other anglers, I have good cause to know its capabilities as a sea-trout pattern on certain Ayrshire rivers, where it kills a lot of migratory fish every season and is particularly good as a night-fishing fly.

The original dressing, given here, has been subjected to a number of variations, especially in relation to the materials used.

For instance, some anglers prefer the bluish feathers of the wood pigeon for the wings instead of the pale starling or widgeon secondary feathers used in the original. Others use combings from a blue rabbit or cat's fur for the body instead of the grey monkey fur or grey wool.

Some fly dressers too, incline not to bother about the third-part gold wool or floss silk nearest the tail of the fly's body. But all these dressings produce a fly which performs just as effectively as the original pattern.

Tie in a few fibres of barred teal for the tail. Then tie in a piece of fine oval gold or silver tinsel which will be used to rib the body. The first third of the body consists of gold-coloured wool or floss silk and the remainder of grey monkey fur, seal's fur, or just plain grey wool. It has also been known for fly dressers to mix a pinch of yellow wool with the grey wool or blue rabbit combings used in the body.

The hackle is light grey dun hen, though some anglers prefer what is known as a Scots Grey (Plymouth Rock grizzle) hackle, which is a sort of off white with grey markings on it. Both serve equally well.

Wing the fly in its smallest sizes with pale starling and with the widgeon secondary feathers or wood pigeon strips in the case of the bigger flies, which require a feather which is longer in the web. Add small Jungle Cock cheeks.

The Grey Monkey can be dressed in hook sizes ranging from old number 14s to 10s, singles and doubles, for brown trout and up to 6s for sea trout.

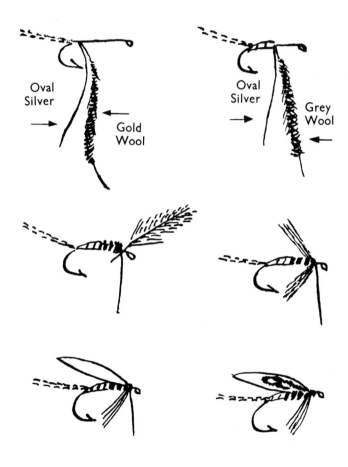

No. 13

Black Bomber

HAIR-WINGED flies for salmon fishing are now almost as popular (or even more so) than the old and well-tried, feather-winged patterns. And some of them which have done well in America and Canada are now proving their worth in the rivers of this country.

It was a certain Joe Aucion of New Waterford, Nova Scotia, I believe, who was responsible for the Bomber series of salmon flies in which the wings are either composed exclusively of hair, or have jungle-cock cheeks and toppings added.

One of the best known of these patterns is the Black Bomber, which has been tried out very successfully in north of Scotland waters both as an ordinary sunk pattern and as a low-water fly.

The tail of the Black Bomber consists of a small golden pheasant topping or crest feather. The tag is oval silver or wire, followed by a tip of yellow floss.

Use black wool or seal's fur for the body and rib it evenly with oval silver tinsel. Then tie in and wind on a black henny-cock hackle and add the wing, which is made of hair from a black squirrel's tail.

Along the sides of the hair wing, tie in the jungle-cock cheeks and over the top of the wing mount a golden pheasant topping.

Tie this fly on ordinary forged salmon hooks ranging in size from 10s to 2s and on low-water salmon hooks from 10s to 4s. You can also dress it on larger hooks according to the water you are fishing.

Hair-winged salmon flies have a most enticing movement in the water. They have a sort of breathing action in the wing that is lacking to some extent in many feather-winged flies.

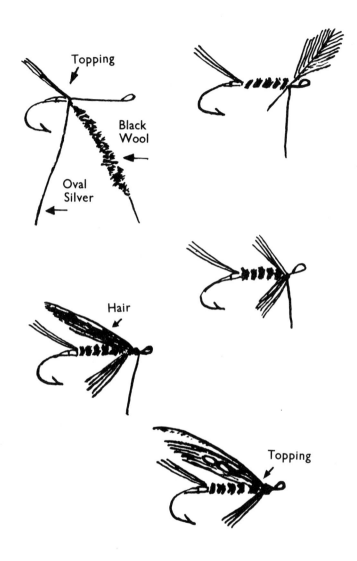

Topping

Black
Wool

Oval
Silver

Hair

Topping

239

No. 14

Kenny's Killer

WHILE on a fishing holiday in Sutherland I chanced to call in on my friend Robert Wilson, the Brora rod-maker and tackle-dealer, who showed me a number of flies which have been very successful in the Rivers Brora and Helmsdale.

One of these was a hair-winged, sea-trout fly which had been invented by a friend of his, Ken Burns of Gordonbush, Brora.

Mr. Wilson told me that each season Ken Burns has enormous catches of sea trout with this particular pattern, and I must confess that, in my rather limited use of it on the estuary waters of the River Brora, I was delighted with the catches of both sea trout and finnock it produced. I found it especially effective early in the morning and at dusk.

Ken dresses the fly on a size 12 (old number) hook, but I have since used it in bigger sizes (up to No. 6) on other rivers and have found that it will even take salmon. This is probably due to its resemblance to a silver-bodied Stoat's Tail, though I have yet to find a dressing of that fly with a yellow hackle!

The tail of Kenny's Killer consists of a few fibres of golden pheasant tippet (neck feathers) and the body is flat silver tinsel with round or oval silver tinsel as ribbing.

After these have been put on tie in a soft cock hackle dyed bright yellow, snipping off the uppermost points of this hackle where the hair wing will lie along the back of the hook. The hackle can also be tied-in beard fashion.

Wing the fly with black squirrel tail or with a slender bunch of glossy black dog's hair from a retriever's tail.

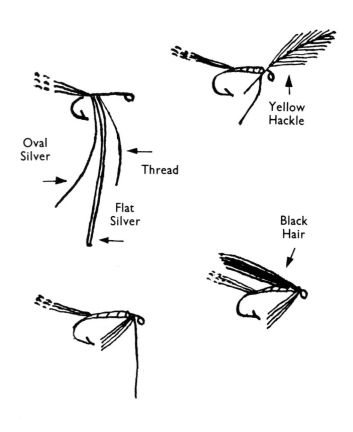

Oval
Silver

Thread

Flat
Silver

Yellow
Hackle

Black
Hair

No. 15

Black and Orange

MY FIRST acquaintance with this fly was the result of correspon-dence with an Irish angler whom I contacted prior to a fishing holiday in northern Donegal. He told me that it was a particularly good fly for sea-trout fishing and everything he said in its favour was proved before my holiday had ended.

The river I was fishing is a small one by Irish standards and it has a good run of sea trout. When I arrived for my holiday the weather was hot and sunny and remained so for most of my stay. This meant of course, that while there were plenty of sea trout in the pools, the river level was very low and apparently too clear for successful fishing.

In this respect I was agreeably surprised, therefore, when I found the sea trout taking the Black and Orange, dressed on a size 12 (old number) hook, with great gusto.

On my first visit to the river this fly accounted for eight of the ten fish I caught. Day after day I returned from the water with equally good catches of sea trout weighing up to 4 lb., and, in the main, it was the Black and Orange which was the killing fly.

Since then I have used this pattern on the Brora and Helmsdale rivers during a north of Scotland fishing tour and here, too, the fly lived up to the fine reputation my Irish friend had given it.

The beauty of it is that the Black and Orange is a very easy pattern to dress. The tail consists of several strands of golden pheasant tippet fibres (i.e. the orange, black-barred feathers). The body is of orange floss, unribbed. The hackle is black hen and the wing any really black feather.

In the original pattern the wing was made from strips from a black cock's tail, but rook or crow do just as well.

Tie in the tippet fibres, then wind on the orange floss silk and tie in a black hen hackle. Wind on the hackle, giving it several turns, and put on the two strips of wings.

You can dress this fly in hook sizes ranging from 12s to 6s (old numbers) but, in my experience, the smallest sizes do best.

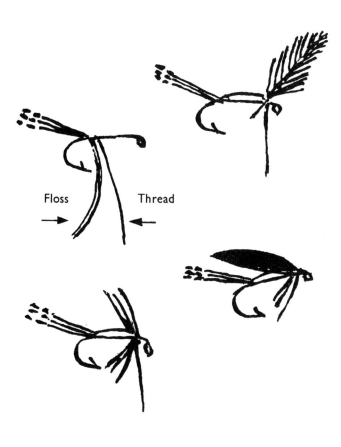

Floss   Thread

No. 16

Orange
Quill

IT WAS that reputable fly fisher, the late G. E. M. Skues, who first realized that the Orange Quill was a particularly deadly fly when the Blue-Winged Olive was on the water although, of course, he did not invent the pattern.

For many years anglers had watched trout rising greedily to the Blue-Winged Olive without any clear-cut ideas of what to offer the fish by way of imitation. Many different patterns were devised, but it was not until Skues discovered the efficacy of the Orange Quill during hatches of the Blue-Winged Olive that the Quill's reputation as a first-class dry fly was firmly established.

The Blue-Winged Olives normally appear on the water towards the end of June though sometimes they occur a little earlier in some rivers. They are upright-winged flies, the wings being a dark bluish-grey and the body something between a green olive and brown.

While the B.W.O. is hatching on summer nights the Orange Quill does great execution, so it is an artificial fly that anglers should always have in their fly boxes—especially anglers who fish the chalk streams.

Use orange thread during the dressing process. Tie in several fibres from a fairly stiff, bright-red cock hackle as the tail or setae. Then wind on a piece of condor or peacock herl quill stripped of its flue and dyed hot orange (you can obtain the appropriate dye for this from dealers in fly-tying materials).

The wings consist of strips of pale starling and should be put on fairly large. Then wind on a bright red cock hackle, taking its turns behind, between and in front of the winging feathers.

Dress the Orange Quill on size 13 and 14 (old number) light wire hooks and always fish it dry.

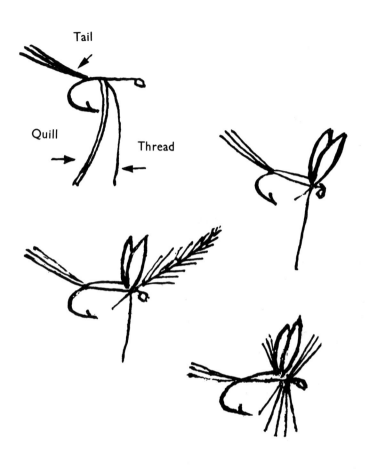

No. 17

Stuart's Killer

THIS attractive sea trout and salmon fly was invented by the late Mr. Angus Stuart, of Grantown-on-Spey.

It was first brought to my notice by Mr. James Wood, of Elgin, a well-known angling writer. He told me that since he first mentioned the killing properties of this pattern in fishing articles and in one of his books, he had so many requests for the dressing that he could not find the time to replenish his personal stocks of this particular fly!

According to Mr. Wood, Stuart's Killer is a firm favourite on the Spey for finnock, sea trout and salmon.

Until his stocks of the pattern were denuded by giving away copies of the fly to so many interested correspondents, he had it in all sizes ranging from 12 to 6 (old numbers).

He informed me, too, that at least 50 per cent of all the migratory fish which he caught in a season were taken on this pattern.

For sea trout and finnock, Mr. Wood dresses the Stuart Killer on small doubles but for his larger dressings of the fly he uses single irons of fairly fine wire and busks the fly as slimly as possible. He finds that the thinly-dressed fly seems to kill better than a heavily-dressed one when he is fishing for salmon.

To dress Stuart's Killer tie in several fibres from a red hen hackle as the tail. The body is flat silver tinsel, ribbed with oval gold tinsel, and the hackle is the same as the tail.

The wing consists of strands of golden pheasant tippets, veiled or overlaid with strips of bronze mallard plumage, and on each side of the wing there is a jungle-cock eye. This eye feather should be fairly large for, according to Mr. Wood, a fly dressed with small jungle-cock cheeks is not nearly so deadly.

Since I received Mr. Wood's letter and a copy of the Stuart's Killer, I have learned that in some cases the fly is dressed with a black squirrel wing. But this would appear to be a departure from the original pattern.

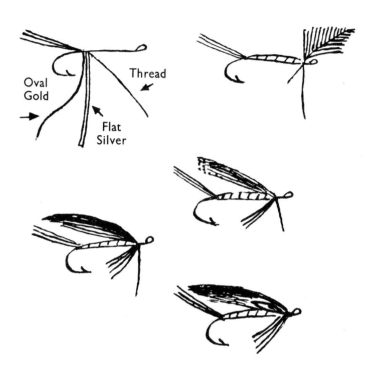

No. 18

Usk Grub

I HAVE to confess that I have never used this particular salmon pattern, which is so close in its resemblance to the type of Shrimp fly which I invariably use that I have never really found the necessity for doing so.

This is not said in disparagement of the Usk Grub, which appears to have been a great favourite of that very knowledgeable salmon angler, Captain Coombe Richards.

It is to Captain Richards that I am indebted in the first place for this abbreviated and simplified dressing of the pattern.

In reply to a reader of *Trout and Salmon* some years ago he defined the type of Usk Grub that he used himself and I can merely say in giving it here that if it was good enough for Captain Richards it is good enough for any salmon angler.

He confessed that he omitted such luxuries in the dressing as toucan feathers at butt and throat and I agree with him in this respect, for I am inclined to think that many salmon flies are over-dressed with materials which are not strictly necessary. We have yet to find the salmon that can tell the difference between a fly dressed with toucan feathers and one that isn't.

Coombe Richards, moreover, dressed his Usk Grub on light irons for low water and even made them very slim. He believed, as I do that the jungle-cock feathers used as the wings are necessary since they are part of the fly's attraction. But, as in the case of the Shrimp fly which I use, the jungle-cock feathers in the Usk Grub are tied in small.

The dressing is as follows: Tie in a few turns of fine round or flat tinsel as a tag. Then put on a tail consisting of a few fibres of golden pheasant red plumage.

The body is made in two equal parts; the tail end is of dull orange wool and the upper half of black wool. The two halves are ribbed with oval silver tinsel and they are butted in the centre with two hackles—white superimposed by hot orange. Now tie in one or two (if necessary) coch-y-bonddu hackles and finish off with a pair of small jungle-cock feathers tied high.

Captain Richards preferred a red-varnished head to the Usk Grub and liked to tie the fly well back from the eye of the hook.

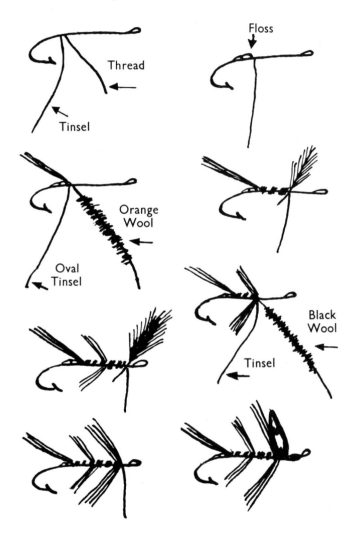

No. 19

Paddy's Fancy

THIS was one of the late Roger Woolley's great favourites and it is much used in Scotland by anglers who are familiar with its worth as a trout killer from April onwards.

It seems to be at its best during the early part of the season and again at the back-end.

Some time ago this particular fly featured in readers' correspondence in *Trout and Salmon*.

A reader asked for a dressing of Paddy's Fancy and another reader replied, mistakenly giving the dressing for a fly known as Erin's Pride—which is little more than a variation of the Alexandra, with an orange hackle, a gold body, a green peacock herl wing, and a piece of orange feather as a tail.

The correct dressing of Paddy's Fancy was finally given in another letter by Hugh Blair, of Largs, in Ayrshire, one of a family of anglers which has fished this particular fly for many seasons with considerable success.

Paddy's Fancy is dressed as a palmer-style spider. Use olive tying silk for the body, then tie the hackle which can be red-black (Furnace) or what is known as a Greenwell hackle, or simply a plain red-brown hackle the full length of the hook stem (stopping at the bend). Body and hackle are then ribbed with flat gold tinsel (or oval gold tinsel).

Some fly dressers tie in the hackle by the tip and work up the turns to the head but I prefer to tie the hackle in at the head and to use the ribbing tinsel to hold its pointed end in place, cutting off the surplus fibres from the tail end of the fly.

Paddy's Fancy can be dressed in hook sizes ranging from 15s to 12s (old numbers) in singles and doubles.

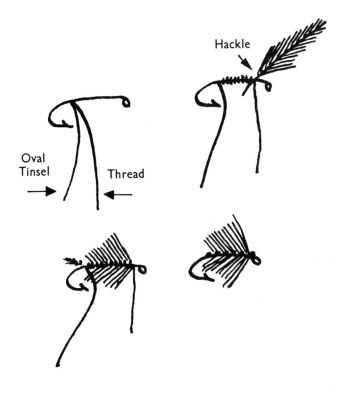

No. 20

Parmacheene Belle

ONCE at Loch Leven, a visitor to that well-loved trouting water shocked his boatmen by producing a large red-and-white-winged fly which he duly mounted to the tail of his wet-fly cast.

It had been one of those fishless days when the trout were apparently lying on the bottom of the loch feeding on snails. Other boats had come in quite clean. So the two boatmen, quietly eyeing each other up, declared in unison: "Och, well, anything's worth a trial."

The fly the angler had put on his cast was a Parmacheene Belle, which is in considerable favour in America and Canada, but is little known and almost unused as a trout fly in this country.

Yet, at the end of the day, it was one of the few flies to kill fish. To the lasting surprise of the boatmen it accounted for ten good trout.

The Parmacheene Belle, which was apparently named after a lake, was invented by Henry P. Wells with the help of a friend.

It has a lemon-yellow seal's fur or mohair body ribbed with silver tinsel. Its tail consists of strands of white and scarlet goose feathers (red below and white on top) and its hackle is a mixture of white and scarlet hen hackle fibres.

The wing is white with a scarlet stripe, and is also made from goose feathers.

Apparently the fly is a very killing pattern in America and Canada for river and lake fishing, but I have been told that it will also do well as a sea-trout fly for night fishing in this country, though I have not so far put it to the test.

It can be tied in sizes ranging from 10s to 6s (old numbers) for trout and sea trout.

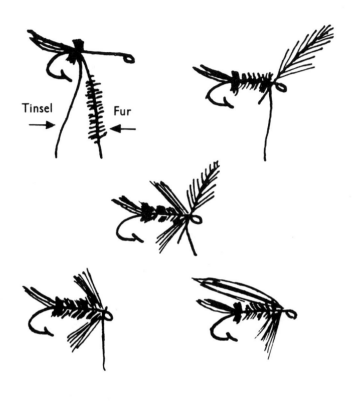

Tinsel   Fur

No. 21

Angus Stuart's Fancy

ANGUS STUART'S FANCY is another deadly salmon pattern from the same stable as the renowned Stuart Killer. I gather that it is also an excellent fly for sea trout in appropriate sizes. Indeed, Angus Stuart's Fancy was originally dressed, I am informed by J. R. Stuart, son of the originator, Mr. Angus Stuart, for sea-trout fishing but has been proving successful for salmon all over the country.

Mr. J. R. Stuart, who has a tackle business in Grantown-on-Spey, tells me that one of his customers has described the fly as the best he has ever come across for the Don, in Aberdeenshire.

Mr. Stuart kindly sent me the original pattern of Angus Stuart's Fancy and it is this which has been photographed to accompany this article.

This pattern has been dressed on a size 6 (1-inch) double hook but the fly can be busked on low-water hooks as small as size 10 (11/16ths inch) for both salmon and sea-trout fishing.

Tie in and wind on a tag of round or oval silver tinsel. Then fix in the tail, which consists of a short piece of golden pheasant topping.

The rear two-thirds of the body is of flat silver tinsel, ribbed or unribbed (the original pattern had no rib), and the remaining third is of red wool or seal's fur in a small bunch.

Now tie in the hackle, which is black hen or henny-cock.

The underwing of the fly consists of strips of white swan or goose and the overwing of bronze speckled mallard plumage, with a topping over. Jungle-cock cheeks add to the fly's attractiveness but these should not be too large.

I am indebted to Mr. J. R. Stuart for the information he has given me about this pattern.

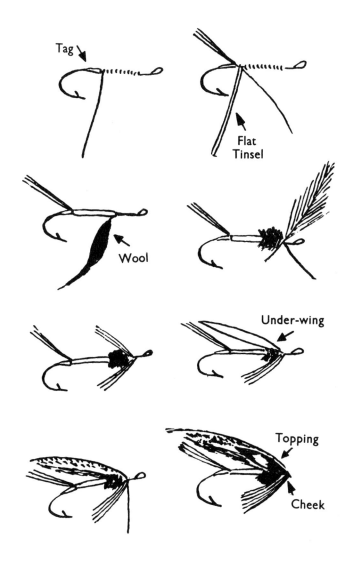

No. 22

Doctor

SEVERAL anglers have written to me in recent months asking for the dressing of this fly. I have not used it myself but it is popular in some parts of the country and here are the details of making it.

I understand that this pattern derived from what is known as the Devonshire Doctor, which is normally ribbed with flat gold tinsel and does not have the yellow rabbit-fur rear quarter.

It is not a very difficult fly to dress, though care should be taken to ensure that it is fairly fully dressed (almost bulky) for the perfectly simple reason that it is meant to imitate a beetle. The Doctor can be used wet or dry and is usually dressed on old number hooks ranging from 15s to 12s, but may be dressed on hooks as large as 8 (old number) for big-lake fishing.

Tie in a few fibres from a fairly stiff coch-y-bonddu cock hackle as a tail. Then wind on a small bunch of white rabbit fur which has been dyed bright yellow. Allot about one-third of the body to this, then clothe the remainder in black rabbit fur, put on reasonably heavily.

The hackle should also be thickly put on and consists of a large coch-y-bonddu cock feather which is not confined to the neck but can be carried down over part of the black rabbit fur.

I am informed that this is a very good imitation of a beetle and that it can be used with success from the beginning of the season to the end on rivers and lakes.

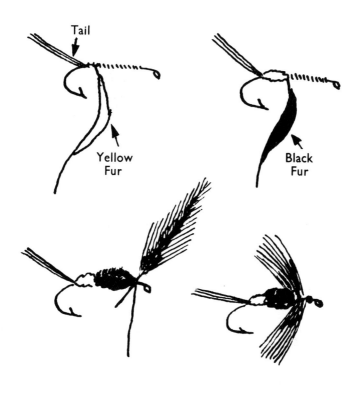

No. 23

Sweep

ORIGINALLY intended as a salmon fly this pattern has quickly assumed importance and popularity for sea-trout fishing. I am told that it has been accounting for quite a number of the big migratory trout in Ross-shire's Loch Maree.

From what I have heard, too, its usefulness is not confined to that water. I have had reports of salmon and sea trout being taken with it from waters as far apart as the River Tay in Perthshire, and the River Naver in Sutherland.

It is not a very prepossessing fly so far as looks go, but, like so many flies that do not catch the angler's eye, it seems to interest the fish.

The dressing is fairly simple and the materials used in its make-up are not particularly difficult to obtain. It has no tag. The tail is a small golden pheasant crest feather or topping, and the black floss silk body is ribbed with oval gold tinsel.

The hackle is black henny cock, not too stiff and put on only at the throat.

Almost any black feather will serve for the wing and although some fly dressers elect to use dyed feathers for this, a good hard-wearing wing can be obtained from crow quills or those of a black cock.

After the wings have been put on add "cheeks" of blue kingfisher, but as this feather is not very easy to obtain I would suggest the use of bright blue hackle tips, which serve equally well.

There are those who say that dyed feathers like these quickly fade through immersion in the water and exposure to light, but I have not found this to be the case. I think it is a question of how well the dye is set. And, in any event, I do not believe that a slight fading of the cheek feathers spoils their effect, but may, indeed, enchance their attractiveness, superimposed as they are against the black of the wing feather.

Dress the Sweep on hook sizes ranging from 6s to 8s in singles, and to as small as 10s in doubles when you are fishing for sea trout.

There is also a very good hair-winged version of this fly, using black squirrel or bucktail for the wing, with blue hair fibres as cheeks (or jungle-cock "eyes" as an alternative.)

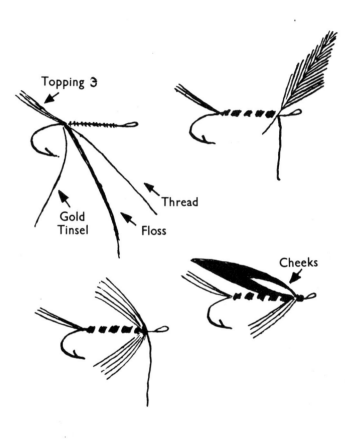

Topping

Thread

Gold Tinsel

Floss

Cheeks

No. 24

Langholm Silver

ESSENTIALLY a local pattern, more or less confined to fishing on the Border Esk for sea trout and herling, this is a very attractive-looking fly, held in much esteem by anglers who fish that river.

Winged, as it is, with the barred wing quill feathers of the curlew or whaup, as it is called in Scotland, it has a flat, silver-tinsel body, ribbed with oval silver tinsel or wire, or left unribbed.

The fly was originally known as the Whaup and Silver, but holiday-making visitors to the Border Esk discovered its great worth and gave it the new title. There is an associated pattern known as the Whaup and Yellow, which is often used in conjunction with the so-called Langholm Silver.

The latter is dressed with a tail of golden pheasant tippet fibres, or a small golden pheasant topping. One can also use a piece of red or yellow feather for the tail.

After putting on the tail fibres, tie in the oval silver tinsel, to be used for the ribbing, and the flat silver tinsel. Wind the flat silver tinsel on to the hook stem in tight overlapping turns and rib this with the oval tinsel or wire.

Then put on a black hen or henny-cock hackle (some anglers prefer a brown partridge hackle) and tie in corresponding pieces of the curlew wing quills for the wings.

Make sure that these wing strips are uniformly marked, for the contrast between the dark and light shades in the wing adds to the fly's attractiveness.

Dress the fly on a size 8 to 12 single or double hook (old numbers).

To tie the Whaup and Yellow, which is usually fished on the bob position of the two-fly, sea-trout cast, use golden pheasant tippets for the tail, a yellow wool or seal's fur body, ribbed with oval gold tinsel, a ginger hackle, and the same barred feather for the wing.

These two flies are especially useful for night fishing.

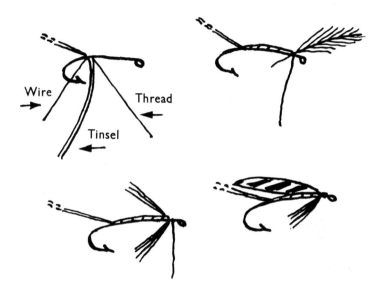

No. 25

Amber Nymph

THERE are two versions of this pattern, one slightly larger than the other. The bigger one has a brown floss silk or seal's fur thorax and the smaller one a hot orange seal's fur or floss silk thorax. Both are very popular among anglers who fish Blagdon and Chew Valley Lakes.

The larger one is dressed on a size 10 hook and the smaller one on a size 12 (both old numbers), and they are usually used as droppers, the bigger one from late April till the end of June and the smaller pattern from July onwards.

I can only speak by hearsay about their worth for I have not fished them but I am reliably informed that they each kill a lot of fish at the lakes mentioned during each season.

The bigger version is dressed as follows: Body—Yellow amber floss silk or seal's fur wound fairly thickly round the hook stem. Thorax—Brown seal's fur or floss silk, extending for about a third of the way along the body, starting from the throat. Wing-cases—A strip from a woodcock wing quill, tied in at the tail end of the body, laid flat along the back of the body and tied in again behind the thorax. Hackle (representing the legs)—A small bunch of fibres from a pale honey-coloured hen hackle, tied in under the head and the fibres stroked backwards towards the tail.

Both these patterns owe a great deal of their popularity to Dr. Bell of Wrington, who designed them for lake fishing and found them to be tremendously successful, as so many other anglers have done since they were introduced.

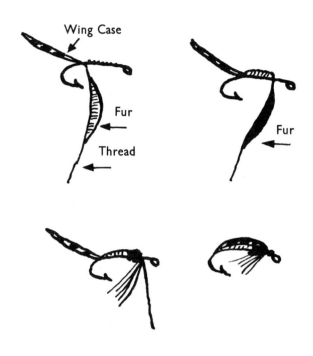

Wing Case

Fur

Thread

Fur

No. 26

Green
Highlander

HERE is a salmon fly that is very popular in the north of Scotland, but which, by repute, does not fare so well in southern waters. Why it should be less favoured in the south I do not profess to understand. It is a very attractive-looking fly and I can only surmise that it owes its success in the north to the fact that it is more often used in the rivers there.

A friend of mine was fishing a stretch of the River Helmsdale, in Sutherland, a couple of seasons ago and out of eight salmon he had during his week's stay five were caught on the Green Highlander.

To dress this pattern tie in a piece of oval or round silver tinsel as a tag, following this with several turns of pale yellow floss silk as a tip. Now tie in the tail, which consists of a small topping from the golden pheasant's crest, surmounted with a few fibres of barred teal plumage.

The butt, which separates the tail from the body, can either consist of a piece of black ostrich herl or black wool.

The first quarter of the fly's body is made of golden yellow floss silk and the remainder of bright green silk floss or seal's fur according to preference. Most anglers prefer the seal's fur, and there is a special dye, obtainable from dealers in fly-tying materials, with which one can obtain the correct shade of green.

The body is ribbed with oval silver tinsel, which is put over a henny-cock hackle dyed a slightly paler shade of green than the body. This hackle extends from the yellow silk part of the body.

A throat hackle of lemon yellow is added before the wings are put in. The wings are mixed and consist of golden pheasant tippets in strands, followed by "married" strands of yellow, orange, and green swan, bustard (or oak-speckled turkey), marled peacock (not strictly necessary) and golden pheasant tail.

Narrow strips of teal, with or without barred summer duck, are added to the sides and a piece of brown-speckled mallard folded over the back of the winging feathers to slightly veil them.

A topping from the golden pheasant crest is added. This should extend the length of the wing to join up with the uptilted tail.

Jungle-cock "eye" feathers are tied in on each side of the fly, but the original fly did not have these and they can be left out, though I think they add to the fly's attractiveness. Cheeks of Indian crow can be added, if you wish.

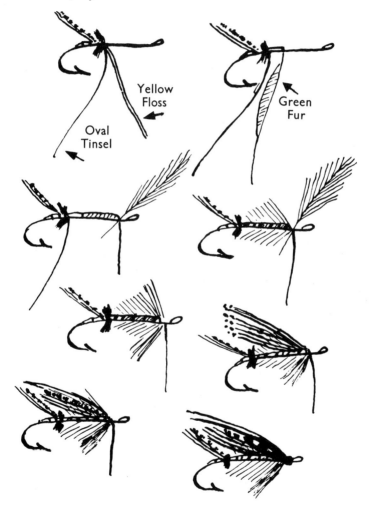

No. 27

Oak Fly

IT IS one of the pleasures of writing about fly patterns that one gets correspondence on the subject from anglers in various parts of the country.

Very often their letters contain little snippets of information and comment which are useful to me in preparing my articles. At other times I am able to help in identifying artificial flies or by giving the dressings for certain patterns.

Such was the case a short time ago when I was asked to identify a pattern which I recognized at once as the Oak fly, also known as the Downlooker.

The fly, in this instance, was in a rather worn condition, bearing witness to the fact, as my inquirer pointed out, that it had killed many fish in an English brook.

There was only one slight variation in this particular pattern from the accepted dressing of the Oak Fly—it had its orange silk body ribbed with fine black thread instead of being ribbed with the stripped quill from the stem of a peacock tail herl strand.

I have since discovered, however, that this way of dressing the Oak Fly's body is recommended by J. Edson Leonard, an American writer of a book about flies.

My correspondent told me that the fly he sent me had been particularly deadly on a tiny stream with well-wooded banks. I was not surprised at this, for the fly that the Oak Fly represents is land-born and one very often finds the natural flies in the vicinity of trees.

I have found many of them on the banks of Loch Awe where the trees grow down to the waterside. Moreover, I have taken fish from Loch Awe with a floating version of the Oak Fly during rises of trout in near-calm conditions.

The natural Oak Flies are usually to be found from April onwards through the summer and it is then that the fly will be found to fish well.

To dress the Oak Fly one ties in two or three strands of natural red cock or hen hackle as a tail. The body is made from orange floss silk or raffia dyed the same colour and ribbed with the peacock quill, which should not be taken from the "eye" feather.

The wing consists of two corresponding pieces of woodcock wing feather, though in some cases two dark grizzled cock hackles are used for the same purpose. If you use the woodcock feathers tie them in close and low down over the back of the fly's body.

The hackle is coch-y-bonddu cock or hen, though it can also be black, or dark red-brown.

Dress the fly on size 14 to 12 hooks (old numbers).

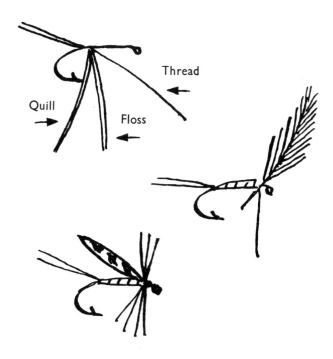

No. 28

Muddler
Minnow

SOME months ago, Les Bishop, an angler from Wisconsin, who was then residing in Edinburgh, was kind enough to send me details of this lure-like fly with which, he told me, he had had some capital sport on the River Tweed.

Mr. Bishop informed me that the Muddler Minnow has probably taken more large trout than any other single pattern in use in America. It was a favourite pattern, he said, of such well-known anglers as Joe Brooks and Al MacLane, who fished it in sizes all the way up to 3/0!

Mr. Bishop was good enough to provide me with a specimen pattern of the Muddler Minnow, which I am using by way of illustration for this article.

The dressing is not particularly difficult. The tail of the fly, which according to Mr. Bishop, is best tied on 10 to 6 (old number) hooks, consists of a folded strip of oak-turkey, wing-quill feather.

The body is flat gold tinsel, which may be ribbed with fine gold wire or left unribbed.

I prefer the ribbed body because there is always the risk of the flat tinsel being torn off by the teeth of fish if it is unprotected. It is also a good plan to put a slight coating of clear celluloid varnish over the tinsel.

The wing consists of two matched pieces of oak-turkey, wing-quill feather on each side of a small bunch of grey squirrel hair.

The original pattern, I am told, had coyote hair, but I do not suppose this would be easy to obtain on this side of the Atlantic. I have also heard that white impala hair, which is more readily obtainable, can be used but the white-tipped grey squirrel serves equally well.

It should be noted that the feather and hair wing should be dressed some way back from the eye of the hook to leave room for a neck ruff.

This is formed with a small bunch of deer-hair fibres held parallel over the back of the hook and flared round the neck of the hook with a couple of turns of tying thread.

After the finishing whip knot has been tied, the ruff or collar is shaped with a pair of scissors to correspond to that of the fly used in the illustration.

The Muddler Minnow kills sea trout as well as brown trout.

Since I wrote about this pattern of the Muddler Minnow, I received details of another dressing from Major R. Lovatt. These are: Tag—gold (flat) tinsel; tail—a strip of speckled brown turkey quill feather; body—flat gold tinsel; wing—sparse black bear hair with a strip of speckled brown turkey feather at either side; hackle—bunch of brown deer hair tied about 2/3rds hook length, butts cut off to form a bulky head. Major Lovatt says this pattern should be dressed on a long shanked hook and fished on its own.

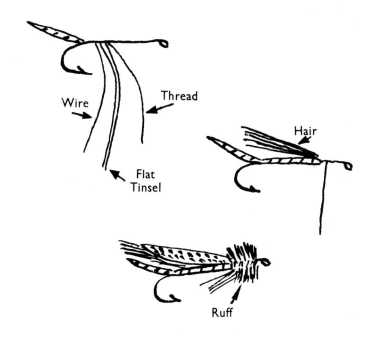

Ruff

No. 29

John Storey

NOBODY seems to know what trout take the John Storey for, but it is certainly a very popular and deadly pattern when fished in the streams of Yorkshire.

It has been the subject of correspondence in *Trout and Salmon* from time to time. And on looking over what various writers have said about it I am torn between attributing its origin to a certain John Storey, who was a keeper until his death, for the Ryedale Anglers' Club, and to another gamekeeper—employed by the Earl of Feversham.

But, whoever devised the fly, it is accepted that the original pattern was dressed with a plain bronze peacock-herl body, without ribbing; a stiff, dark-red cock's hackle; and a wing (tied in front of the hackle and pointing forward over the eye of the hook) from the tip of the speckled feather from a mallard's breast.

However, there have been variations on the theme where the wing is concerned.

I recall that Mr. Eric Horsfall Turner, of Scarborough, claimed that the wing could be made from either pale partridge or teal and that the hackle could be of any shade of medium to dark-red cock.

I agree with Mr. Turner that it scarcely matters what the trout take the John Storey for and that it is as good a general type of floating fly as anyone has yet devised for the northern rivers where it is most often used.

Another reader of *Trout and Salmon*, Colin Dales, of York, who claimed that the John Storey was devised by one of the Earl of Feversham's gamekeepers, said that the fly was just as good and sometimes better if it was dressed with a black hackle—and that he often used the mallard wing dressed in sedge-style (over the back of the fly's body) and got just as good results.

I might add that two hackles are often used to give the John Storey greater buoyancy, but this should not be necessary if a good hard cock hackle is used.

The fly is usually dressed on hooks ranging from size 10 to 14 (old numbers).

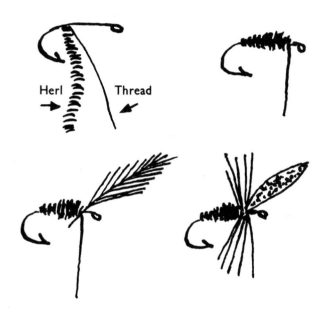

No. 30

Black
Lure

BLACK-BODIED flies or lures, ribbed with tinsel, have an uncanny habit of doing well when used in lake or reservoir fishing. There are some notable examples, among them being Black Pennell, Black Zulu, and Williams Favourite.

The Black Lure corresponds to these only in the respect that it has a black, silver-ribbed body. It differs in that it has no leg hackles and is made in the form of a tandem, dressed on a two-hook tackle, with two black cock hackles tied back to back or split in "V" style.

The popularity of this lure has grown rapidly among still-water fishers. This is not so much because it has any particular resemblance to any known insect or immature fish but rather because that when properly worked, with long drags and quick, darting movements, it seems to arouse the predatory instincts in the fish.

It has been suggested that it might be mistaken by the fish for a tadpole as it swims through the water, or even as some large, aquatic beetle.

I prefer the former idea—and if you dress the Black Lure with its wings splayed out from the body in "V" shape and draw it through the water you will certainly see the tadpole resemblance as the wings open and close.

There are various other lures, of course, in different colours, which are not direct copies of anything in the water but which are strangely attractive to the fish. I fancy that the Black Lure falls into this class and owes most of its appeal to the way it is operated.

The original pattern had no tail but some fly dressers decorate the end fly with a few fibres of red feather (as used in the tail of the Silver Butcher).

The two size 14 to 12 (old number) hooks are joined with nylon or wire preparatory to putting on the body materials.

Start off by dressing the tail hook first, covering the stem slimly with black floss silk, then ribbing it with oval silver tinsel in evenly-spaced turns. Do the same with the second hook, leaving sufficient room at the head for tying in the winging hackles.

After securing the wings with a whip knot, apply black celluloid varnish.

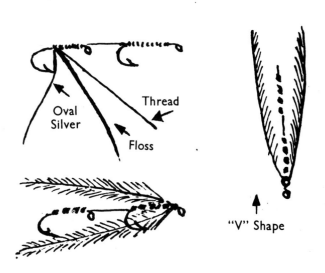

Oval Silver

Thread

Floss

"V" Shape

No. 31

Bill's Badger

HAIR-WINGED flies for salmon and sea-trout fishing are now legion, many of them the products of much trial and error by their innovators.

Some of them, like the Hairy Mary and the Stoat's Tail, to mention only two, have established very fine reputations for themselves in different localities.

Bill's Badger, however, is perhaps not so well known as it deserves to be, for it has done well not only for salmon but for sea trout, in its smaller sizes.

It is particularly good at dusk on a river in high summer, though its usefulness is by no means confined to that time.

Dressed, for instance, on small low-water, double hooks (sizes 12 to 10) it is a good pattern for greased-line fishing—and could, no doubt, be devised in tube-fly form to fish with equal success.

The body consists of black, floss silk, very thinly put on, with a ribbing of narrow-gauge, flat, silver tinsel, evenly spaced.

Next stage in the dressing is to reverse the hook in the vice and tie in a small tuft of dark blue cock or hen hackle fibres. Or you can put the hackle on by winding it round the throat of the hook and snipping off the uppermost part of the hackle.

Now tie in the wing, which consists of well-marked badger (black and white-tipped) or squirrel of almost similar type. This wing should be long enough to extend the length of the body but should not be too thick.

If you are dressing a tube-fly version, tie in a few fibres of hair, dyed dark blue, before you put on the badger hair. The tube can be painted black and then ribbed with the narrow tinsel. As in all tube-fly dressing the hair should be put on sparingly.

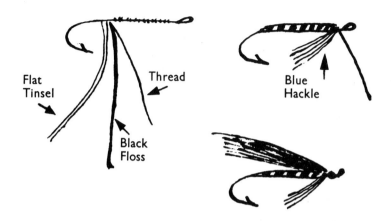

Flat
Tinsel

Thread

Black
Floss

Blue
Hackle

No. 32

Woodcock and Mixed

LIKE all the other patterns in the Woodcock series this fly takes part of its name from the feather with which it is winged.

To some extent it has gradually usurped that one-time favourite of the loch fisher, the Woodcock and Yellow, from which it only differs in that it has the addition of red wool or seal's fur in its body.

It is an extremely popular fly in Scotland, especially at Loch Leven, where, as a tail fly or a central dropper on the wet-fly cast, it kills many fish per season.

Moreover, it is one of those stand-by flies that anglers can use with some measure of built-in faith all through the season. It will kill at the back-end just as well as it does in early spring but is perhaps at its deadliest when the Sedges are about in the late spring and summer.

The tail consists of a few fibres of golden pheasant tippet fibres and the body is made in two equal parts of bright yellow wool or fur and red wool or fur (the yellow at the tail end). Both are ribbed with fine oval silver or gold tinsel.

A bright ginger or red-brown hen hackle, taken from the hen's neck, is used for the legs. No more than two or three turns are necessary. The winging feathers are corresponding pieces from the woodcock's flight feathers, tied in with the shiny side out so that the barred markings are clearly visible.

Woodcock and Mixed can be used for brown, rainbow and sea trout, in sizes ranging from 16 doubles to 8 singles. Loch Leven anglers normally use the small doubles during the daytime and size 14 (Outpoint 12) during the late evenings in the summer months.

In some cases narrow strips of barred teal feather are added to the sides of the woodcock wing, a device which changes the fly into the Teal, Woodcock and Mixed, another popular pattern for the lochs of Scotland.

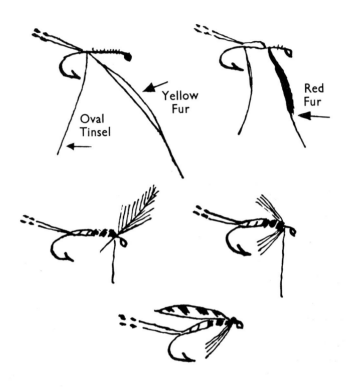

Yellow Fur

Oval Tinsel

Red Fur

No. 33

Green Monkey

AFTER the publication of my earlier article on the Grey Monkey I received numerous letters of thanks from readers of *Trout and Salmon*, who had heard about it but had not previously known the dressing of that very popular fly.

And in the light of the interest evoked then I feel I have no option but to supply the recipe for this variation of the Grey Monkey, for the Green Monkey is an equally deadly pattern for brown and sea trout.

I should say, at the outset, that the Green Monkey is in no sense a new pattern. It is believed to have originated on the Spey, but its use is nowadays probably greatest in the rivers of southern Scotland.

I have never found it much of a success in sizes larger than 8s (old number) and prefer to fish it as a small double (size 14 to 12).

To dress the Green Monkey, tie in a short golden pheasant topping as a tail. The body consists of no more than a couple of turns of wool or seal's fur dyed a Green Highlander shade, the remaining two-thirds of the body being grey wool, seal's or monkey's fur, all ribbed with fine oval gold tinsel.

The hackle put on at the throat only is also of the Green Highlander shade (a suitable dye of the name can be obtained from fly-tying material suppliers).

The wing is palest starling with jungle-cock cheeks on each side. In the larger patterns you can use the palest parts of a mallard drake's blae wings, shiny side out.

I have used both patterns, the Grey Monkey on the tail and the Green Monkey as a dropper, on the same cast and have had success with both.

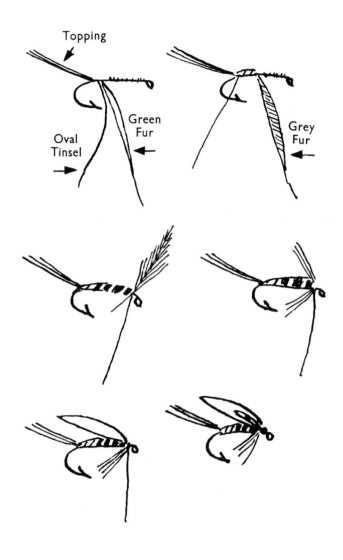

Topping

Green Fur

Oval Tinsel

Grey Fur

No. 34

Iron Blue Dun

FOR AN insect that is common to most waters in this country this diminutive fly has been subjected to much-varied treatment from amateur and professional fly dressers.

So I will confine myself to three dressings of the pattern—one for a wet fly and the other two for dry-fly angling. These two dry flies are representations of the male and female of the species.

These three are generally recognized as worthwhile patterns—and are, in fact, the types that might be bought from most of the leading tackle suppliers.

I shall begin with the popular wet-fly version. The tail consists of several fibres of an iron-blue, dyed hackle of a similar shade to the feather used for the leg hackle.

Use red tying silk for putting on the mole-fur body dubbing, leaving a tip (about one-third of the body) of the red tying silk or red floss silk at the tail end.

The winging feather varies from dark starling to cock blackbird and pale starling dyed in blue-black ink, the last mentioned making a wing that is very similar in colour to that of the natural insect.

While this pattern is usually fished sunk it can be converted into a floating or dry fly by using a cock hackle of the appropriate shade and upright single or double wings.

A popular dressing for the Iron Blue Dun (female) for dry-fly fishing is: Tail—a few fibres of pale blue-dun, cock hackle. Body—peacock quill dyed claret. Wings—cock blackbird (upright). Hackle—dark-blue, dun cock.

For the male of the species a good dressing for dry-fly fishing is: Tail—three cock hackle fibres dyed dark brown olive. Body—peacock quill dyed olive. Wing—cock blackbird. Hackle—cock hackle dyed dark brown olive.

As the natural form of the Iron Blue Dun is such a small item the artificials should be dressed in sizes no bigger than 14 and are probably most deadly on 15 or 16 hooks (old numbers).

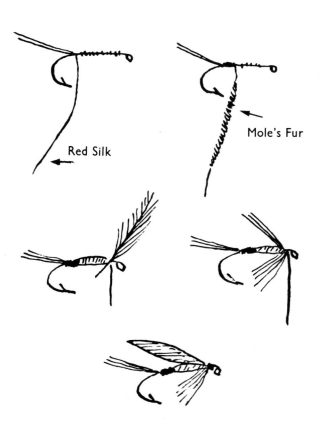

Red Silk

Mole's Fur

No. 35

Lemon Grey

ORIGINALLY an Irish pattern, the popularity of this salmon fly is by no means confined to Ireland but it is probably more favoured there than elsewhere.

It is one of those mixed-wing flies which seem to be improved by the omission of a number of the winging materials initially deemed essential.

For example, one can safely leave out such feathers as florican, and substitute oak-speckled turkey for the bustard. Barred teal can be used on its own instead of in conjunction with barred summer duck without noticeably impairing the fly's efficiency.

Begin the dressing of the Lemon Grey by tying in several turns of fine round or flat, silver tinsel, following this with a tip of golden-yellow, floss silk. The tail consists of a short golden-pheasant topping, with a smaller sliver of Indian crow (red feather substitute) on top.

Now wind on a black ostrich herl butt and tie in the oval, silver tinsel which will be used to rib the grey wool or seal's fur body.

Before applying the throat hackle tie in a grizzled (white and black) cock or henny-cock hackle doubled and wind this down towards the tail. Fix the tip of this body hackle down with the ribbing tinsel and carry on the ribbing in evenly-spaced turns through the body hackle towards the head of the fly.

Do not make the wool or fur body too bulky or you will throw the wing out of its true position, which should be as close to the back of the body as possible.

Now tie in a lemon cock hackle at the throat, cutting off the upper-most fibres.

The first step in putting on the winging material is to tie in golden-pheasant tippets in strands. Then veil these with "married" strips of

282

green, yellow and orange swan or goose, oak-speckled turkey and a strip (on each side) of barred teal of distinctive markings.

Dress the wing overall with strips of bronze mallard plumage and black varnish the head. Some of the earlier fly dressers added a head of black ostrich herl or peacock herl but these refinements are not really necessary.

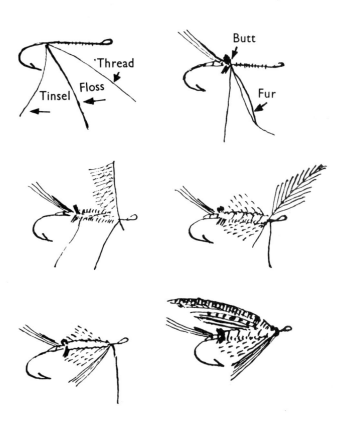

No. 36

Silver
Shrimp

MY INTRODUCTION to this fly came during a visit some years ago to the River Brora, in eastern Sutherland.

The local fishing tacklist, Robert Wilson, showed me the pattern and said that it was a very good tail fly on a sea-trout cast.

Fundamentally, of course, the Silver Shrimp is not very much different from the Silver March Brown and the Silver Invicta.

The chief difference is in the hackle. The Silver March Brown has a brown partridge hackle, the Silver Invicta has one of barred blue jay, and the Silver Shrimp has two hackles, one of white cock under one of barred blue jay.

On Mr. Wilson's advice I used the Silver Shrimp as a tail fly and because of my success with it, I now prefer it in this position for sea-trout fishing.

I dress it slimly on a size 8 (old number) hook and find that it does its best work in the evenings just when darkness is coming down.

The dressing is as follows: Tie in a short golden pheasant crest feather or topping as a tail. Then fasten in a short length of oval silver tinsel or wire and a piece of flat silver tinsel. The oval tinsel or wire is used for ribbing the flat silver body.

Now tie in and wind on a white cock hackle and trim off the uppermost fibres. Wet the hackle fibres slightly and smooth them back towards the barb end of the hook. Fasten down the hackle with half-hitches of the tying thread, then strip off a small bunch of the blue-barred jay feather and tie this in front of the white hackle.

My method of putting on this second hackle is to reverse the hook in the vice and tie the jay plumage fibres slightly off centre and towards me, so that when I turn the tying thread round the fibres these spread round the hook and distribute themselves neatly over the white hackle.

Now take corresponding pieces from each side of a hen pheasant's centre-tail feather and tie them in as wings. Keep the wings slim and make a special point of keeping them well down over the back of the fly's body.

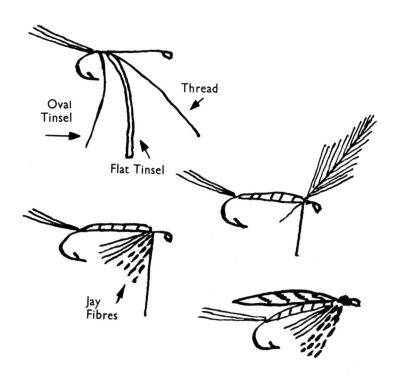

No. 37

Black
Brahan

INTRIGUED by so many favourable references to this salmon fly in reports in *Trout and Salmon* about waters in the far north of Scotland, I finally traced its origin.

Mr. William Brown, a well-known angler and writer of Strathpeffer, kindly sent me a copy of it which had been dressed by his friend, John McKenzie, a gillie on the River Conon, who invented the pattern.

The Black Brahan is a hair-winged salmon fly. The wing is black squirrel and the body consists of red Lurex tinsel, ribbed with oval silver tinsel.

The tail is a short golden pheasant crest feather or topping, and there is a tag made of three turns of the ribbing tinsel.

The hackle can be either black henny-cock (tied-in beard style) or hot orange hen.

Mr. Brown tells me that he uses the Black Brahan as a summer fly on a floating line and has extremely good results with it. Often, in low water, when fish were hard to move, this fly has attracted them. He has taken fish with it from the Blackwater, the Ewe and the Conon.

The fly is tied on size 6, 8 or 10 hooks, preferably 8 or 10 doubles (low water irons).

Mr. Brown informs me, too, that he fishes the Black Brahan in a way that is directly opposed to that most fly fishers advocate—he works the fly very quickly through the pools.

Since he sent me the original pattern, friends of mine have taken fish with dressings of it from rivers in the south of Scotland.

In a subsequent letter to me, Mr. Brown told me that he has also had fish with a Black Brahan dressed with a pink Lurex body.

This is also a good sea-trout fly, well worth a trial when fish are hard to get.

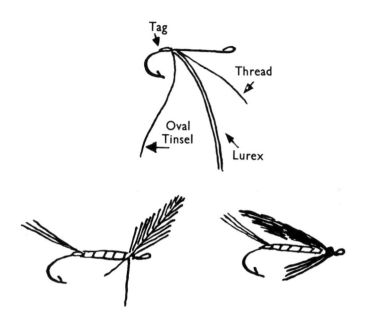

No. 38

Twilight Grey

DURING correspondence with the late Captain J. Hughes Parry, that well-remembered angler of the Welsh Dee, I was put in touch with Gordon Hay, who has done so much to popularize the use of fluorescent materials in fly tying.

Mr. Hay graciously sent me copies of three flies of his own tying—and among them was the Twilight Grey.

He did not claim to have originated the pattern. It seems that the Grey Fly, as it was previously called, was devised by George Marbury and was a very old Welsh Dee pattern.

Mr. Hay has written of the extraordinary success that Captain Hughes Parry enjoyed with the pattern on lakes and rivers.

I was immediately impressed and tried out the fly on my favourite reservoirs in Scotland and had many trout with it.

Mr. Hay states that the Twilight Grey can be used throughout the season on lakes and rivers and, as its name implies, it was originally tied for evening use.

The body of the fly consists of a grey wool mixture (grey and fluorescent white—one-third of the latter to the former is about the right proportion). The tying silk is grey or olive, and the hackle is Grizzle (Scots Grey) cock.

Mr. Hay advises teasing out the body wools in advance in the proportions stated. He says that there is no grey among the American Gantron wools but that Messrs. Veniard's, of Thornton Heath, produce a grey fluorescent wool, which, when mixed in place of the white fluorescent wool, is equally successful.

He adds, however, that when used "raw" this wool seems to be too bright and that masking, by mixing with ordinary wool, has done better.

288

The Twilight Grey has a very slim body, thickest at the thorax. For sea-trout fishing the hackle should be slightly longer in its fibres.

It has taken fish tied on a size 5 long-shank hook and on a hook as small as 00. Two or three turns of hackle are sufficient if the fly is to be fished sunk, but more if it is to be fished as a floater.

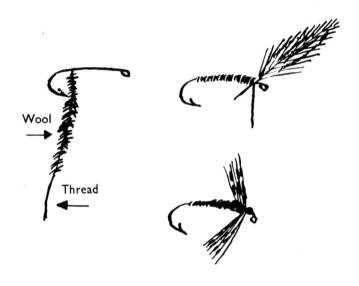

Wool

Thread

No. 39

White Moth

I HAVE already referred in an earlier volume of *Popular Flies* to the Brown Moth or Hoolet, which is a great favourite for night fishing on lakes and reservoirs.

The White Moth is another of the same type—a fly that does its best work in the dark or at dusk on midsummer nights, a wake fly in the truest sense of the word.

It is fished dry, in the same manner as the Hoolet, and is made to trip across the surface.

You will frequently see white moths on or above the surface long before the large caddis flies (which the Hoolet represents) make their appearance towards the end of May or the beginning of June.

These moths come in various sizes. The smaller ones are represented by artificials obtainable from many tackle shops, but the bigger pattern I am chiefly referring to is not so readily available. But they are easy to make.

For the very small ones, dressed on hook sizes ranging from 14 to 12 (old numbers) the body can be of white floss silk, ribbed with oval silver tinsel or left unribbed but, in the larger sizes (6, 8 or 10 old numbers, light wire hooks), I prefer to use white wool or white ostrich herl, unribbed, or with a white cock hackle tied down the body in palmer fashion.

For the smaller flies, the wings can be formed from the white satin feathers obtained from the under-wing of the wild duck, the same feather as is used for small dressings of the Coachman.

But, for the bigger patterns, white-owl feather is probably best. It should be made into a small wad and tied to lie down flat over the back of the fly's body.

I have also seen wingless dressings of the White Moth—made entirely of wool and cock hackles; and there is a pattern in my part of the country which is known as the White Zulu. It has a white wool, silver-ribbed body, with a white cock hackle dressed in the usual palmer style and boasts a red wool tail!

It might be thought that this is stretching things too far, but there is no accounting for the tastes of trout—and anything that has a passing resemblance to a White Moth will seemingly take fish when conditions are right.

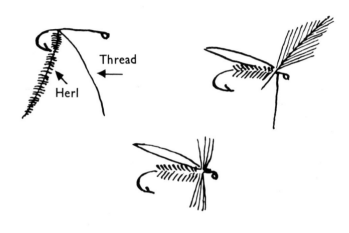

No. 40

Bradshaw's Yellow

THIS is a very good sea-trout fly much used in night fishing. It was invented by Henry Bradshaw of Leeds, who was a Yorkshire angler of some repute.

It is not nearly so popular as the Mallard and Yellow, which it so closely resembles, but those who have used it for sea-trout fishing claim that it is equally reliable.

The body consists of yellow pig's wool (seal's fur, being more manageable, is a better material), ribbed with broad silver tinsel. The hackle is red-black or coch-y-bonddu; and the wing is made from matched strips of bronze speckled mallard plumage. The original pattern does not appear to have had a tail but if you find one a necessity you can use a small piece of dyed red feather or silk.

While this fly was first intended for migratory trout, I have used it with marked success for brown trout when fishing lakes and reservoirs at dusk and during the hours of darkness on summer nights when, presumably, the fish were taking it as an imitation of a sedge fly.

Dress the fly by tying in the tail, then the broad silver tinsel. Now dub the tying silk with a pinch of yellow seal's fur, which should be wound on with the tie thread to the hook shank to make a tapered body, thickest at the throat.

Wind the broad tinsel over the seal's fur fairly tightly in three evenly-spaced turns.

Put on a dark coch-y-bonddu henny-cock hackle and add the speckled mallard wing.

It is not strictly necessary to use matched pieces of the mallard feather. You can, if you prefer, fold broad-webbed pieces of the mallard plumage into a small wad to make an equally satisfactory wing.

You can tie the fly in hook sizes ranging from 10s to 8s (old numbers).

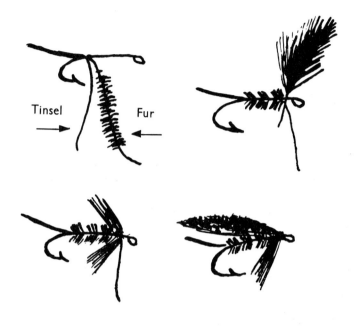

No. 41

Conon
Lure

MANY sea trout and finnock are caught in the estuary waters of the rivers Conon and Beauly in the north of Scotland every season by anglers using this feathered lure.

It was first used on the Conon estuary before the First World War and was known at that time as the Heron Hackle Lure, presumably because of the fact that it was winged with the hackle of that bird.

Later, as its fame spread, it came to be called the Conon Lure, though it is sometimes referred to as the Grey Lure.

It owes its considerable popularity on the Conon and Beauly estuaries to its resemblance to herring fry or sprats on which the sea trout and finnock feed.

While it will account for large numbers of these fish at any time when there are fish in the estuaries, it is particularly deadly, according to the local experts, from the end of July to the finish of the season at the end of September.

The Conon Lure dressing is simple enough. It is tied in the shape of a three-hook terror in singles or doubles, or with two singles and a double at the end.

It can be tied with, or without, a red silk or feather tail. All the hooks are given a flat silver tinsel body, ribbed with oval silver tinsel in each case to strengthen them against the ravages of the fish's teeth. There is no throat hackle.

The wing consists of two or three suitably long and well-marked badger (black with white tips) cock hackles. If three are used, one is tied in as a central hackle with one on each side of it.

Alex Shanks, fishing-tackle dealer of Dingwall, kindly sent me one of these lures to enable me to make a copy of it for the photograph.

I am indebted, also, to William Brown of Strathpeffer, a very experienced angler, for some details about the lure. It is vital, he says, to have the black streak extend down the whole of the hackle wing.

The hooks used in this lure can be 10s to 8s (old numbers), singles or doubles. The lure dressed with the double hooks is most in favour.

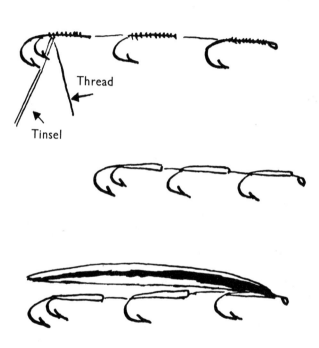

No. 42

Treacle Parkin

HERE is a trout fly that approximates very closely to a coch-y-bonddu with a yellow tail.

For many years now I have used a coch-y-bonddu variation which has an orange wool or gold floss silk tail and I can speak highly of its killing qualities.

It seems that the Treacle Parkin enjoys a similar reputation on the chalk streams of Yorkshire where, I am told, it kills trout throughout the season.

Angling writers like Charles Derrick and the late T. K. Wilson have spoken very highly of this fly, which would appear to have had its origin in the north of England.

Because of the bright yellow wool in its make-up it is sometimes referred to as the Yellow Tag, in the same way as the Red Tag takes its name from its red tail.

It is not a particularly difficult fly to dress. The body, which should be dressed fat, is made from one or two strands of bronze peacock herl wound round the hook stem from the tail towards the head. The hackle is dark red or reddish-brown cock and is tied in and wound on at the throat. The tag or tail is bright yellow wool.

In his little book *Trout Flies*, John Veniard refers to a dressing of this fly with a tag of orange wool, floss or fibres of an orange feather, a fly which he also describes as the Orange Tag.

The latter is perhaps nearer in likeness to the coch-y-bonddu variation which I have been using for lake and reservoir fly fishing for many years. The only difference is that this variation has a Furnace (red-black) hackle.

All these dressings can be made on size 16 to 14 (old number) hooks, and the fly can be fished either dry or wet.

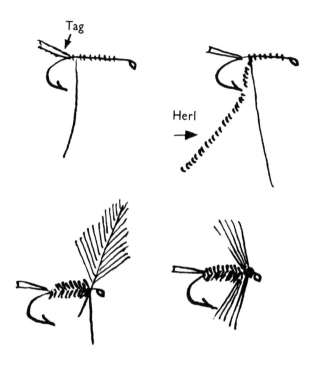

No. 43

Feather Duster

A FRIEND of mine, proprietor of a stretch of an Ayrshire river, tells me that he has had some remarkably good sport while fishing this fly for sea trout on broken water. He was using it as a floater.

I also understand that it is very popular in some of the Welsh rivers, where it is apparently used for both trout and sea trout.

I suppose moreover, though I have never had the opportunity to try it out, that it might also serve as a fair imitation of the heather moth that is so familiar on Highland lochs and rivers.

It is probably one of the simplest flies to dress, the materials being reasonably easy to obtain, except that the natural blue-dun, cock hackle, wound round its neck, is in short supply and a dyed hackle has to be employed.

The body is made from either grey wool or seal's fur, with the merest pinch of blue rabbit fur, obtained from near the skin, inter-mixed before being dubbed on.

The hackle, which can be either cock or hen, is dressed full style; that is, in palmer fashion from head to tail. In some cases, too, a very fine silver wire is used to rib the body—not so much of a decoration as a safeguard against the hackle being pulled off by the trout's teeth.

I suppose this fly could be used for wet-fly fishing, but it is best known as a dry fly to be fished in fairly small sizes.

The normal practice is to dress it on a size 14 (old number) hook, but I have seen it tied on hooks as big as 10s for fast and broken water.

When dressing a fly with a grey body it is a good plan to use a grey or white thread. The fur or wool is dubbed on to this by twisting between the thumb and forefinger of the left hand. Try to achieve a good taper with the dubbing so that the veiling hackle will sit nicely on the fly's body.

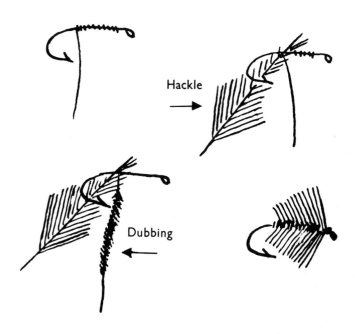

Hackle

Dubbing

No. 44

Teal and Black

AS AN early-season, wet fly for brown-trout fishing, this pattern enjoys the same kind of reputation as the very popular Blae and Black. It is a good alternative to put on the sunk cast in lake and reservoir fishing. Indeed, in some lochs in Scotland, notably at Loch Awe, it is one of the best flies an angler can have on his cast.

It can either be fished on the tail of the cast or as a dropper. I prefer it as a dropper fly placed next to the point fly.

I remember reading in *Trout and Salmon* that an angler had eschewed all other wet flies in favour of this one because he had caught so many fish with it.

While I have said that it is a good early-season fly I have to confess that I have had trout and sea trout with the Teal and Black all through a season. I have found it particularly deadly where sea trout are concerned and invariably include it on my cast when I go after these migratory fish.

When fishing for brown trout in lakes it should be used in fairly small sizes. My own dressings of the pattern are on size 14 (old number) round bend hooks. But when fishing for sea trout I use a size 8 Limerick, which is the type shown in the photograph. And, in the case of the sea-trout fly, I apply the black henny-cock hackle as a beard rather than wind the hackle round the hook.

Apart from the tying in of the barred, teal wing—always a problem with some fly dressers, because they find the fibres splitting up—it is a fairly easy fly to tie. And if you are making small flies with teal wings it is best to snip corresponding pieces from each side of the teal feather and tie these in firmly. When dressing the larger sizes of fly you can either use the same method, doubling the corresponding pieces, or you can fold the whole feather over and over to make a thicker and more durable wing.

300

In dressing the Teal and Black, tie in a few fibres of golden pheasant tippet as a tail. Then fix in the narrow flat silver or oval silver tinsel which is to be used for ribbing the black seal's fur or wool body. Put on the hackle in the usual manner or as a beard and tie in the wings.

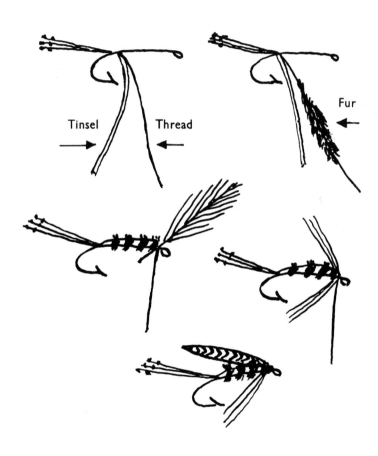

No. 45

Pink Lady

THERE are various patterns of this name, most of them emanating from America. But they are all different from the one being described, which is a hair-winged pattern owing its origin to the late Tom Finlayson of Houston, Renfrewshire.

Tom tied this fly for use on West of Scotland rivers, where it was very attractive not only to salmon but to sea trout when dressed in appropriate sizes.

Duncan S. Drysdale of Greenock kindly supplied me with a pattern of the fly as it was originally dressed by Mr. Finlayson. It is the one in the photograph, and it will be noticed that the wing is tied well down on top of the back of the hook.

Mr. Drysdale took many grilse with it, but emphasized that the hair wing should not be put on too thickly. He suggested eight or nine fibres of badger hair, with the equivalent number of fluorescent pink hairs on top.

These two types of winging hair should extend approximately half-an-inch beyond the bend of the hook to give the fly a streamer effect.

To dress the Pink Lady, tie in and wind on two or three turns of fine, silver tinsel as a tag. Then put on the tail, which is a small golden pheasant crest feather or topping.

The body is a two-part one. The rear half is of green (olive) Lurex tinsel and the front half of silver Lurex tinsel—flat in each case. Both are ribbed with size 16 round silver tinsel.

After the body has been completed secure it with a couple of half-hitches and reverse the fly in the vice to put on the beard hackle, which consists of fibres of the barred blue feather from the outside of a jay's wing.

These should not be cut from the feather but torn from it in a little bunch and put on to the side nearest to the fly dresser so that they wrap themselves centrally below the fly when the tying thread is tightened.

Now apply the wing in the proportions described and you will have a salmon fly that not only looks attractive to the angler but kills fish as well.

The Pink Lady can be dressed on size 8 (old number) Limericks for sea trout, but remember that the proportions of hair for the wings should be reduced correspondingly.

Incidentally, Mr. Drysdale, who passed on some years ago, used the salmon pattern in sizes 5 and 6.

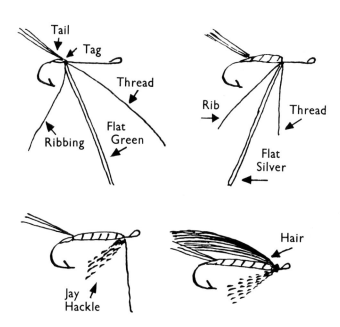

No. 46

Red
Devil

EVER since the introduction of fluorescent materials for fly dressing there has been a spate of experimental patterns for all types of fly fishing.

Some have proved successful; others have not. And it would appear that where success has been achieved it has chiefly resulted from the incorporation of the fluorescent materials with the recognized silks, wools and furs.

Some old patterns, in fact, have been greatly improved by the careful and modest involvement of fluorescent materials in their make-up.

One of these is the Red Devil, which was previously nothing more than a Black Spider with a red body, a fly that has been known to Scots anglers for many years.

The pattern is normally dressed on a size 14 (old number) hook. I fish it on the tail of the cast and have found it to do well at the start of the trout-fishing season, when I suppose it is taken for a midge pupa.

It is quite a sombre-looking fly, despite the inclusion of the fluorescent ribbing, though I guess the trout will see it differently through their eyes.

One of its advantages from the fly tyer's point of view is that it is fairly easy to dress. Even those who are just embarking on fly dressing should find it within their capabilities.

There is no tail. The body consists of red floss silk, ribbed with the fluorescent Fire Orange silk fibre. When I am ribbing the fly, I run this silk through a piece of clear wax so that it does not spread out when ribbing is being carried out.

Carefully space the turns of ribbing and add a black hen hackle. Then finish off the head with a whip knot and apply shellac or Cellire varnish.

The Red Devil was invented by Mr. Tom C. Saville, of Notting-ham.

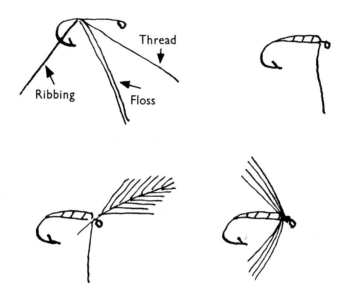

No. 47

Silver
Doctor

WHEN I referred earlier in this series of fly dressings to the composition of the Silver Wilkinson, I mentioned that it and the Silver Doctor were very much the same fly—except that the hackle of the Wilkinson is magenta while that of the Silver Doctor is bright blue. Both have an additional hackle of widgeon or lightly-barred teal.

A further difference is that the scarlet head of the Silver Doctor is often omitted from the Silver Wilkinson.

The dressing I am giving of the Silver Doctor is only approximate to the one propounded by the late T. E. Pryce Tannatt in his wonderful book *How to Dress Salmon Flies*.

I trust I will be forgiven for omitting some of the more exotic feathers that Pryce Tannatt mentioned. The point is that many of the patterns you buy in the shops today do not include *all* the materials used for the original pattern—and the fish do not seem to mind.

For instance, in winging the Silver Doctor I think the fly dresser can safely leave out florican bustard and barred summer duck—and one can usefully substitute a blue hackle point for the blue chatterer feather recommended as a top for the golden pheasant topping used in the tail.

To dress the Silver Doctor, tie in a tag of fine silver round tinsel, followed by a tip of golden yellow floss silk. Now add the tail topping and put the blue hackle point over the top of it.

The butt consists of a piece of ostrich herl dyed scarlet, but wool of the same colour is much better, more lasting and keeps its colour.

The body consists of flat silver tinsel, ribbed with oval silver tinsel.

Now tie in the first of the two hackles—a bright blue one first, then a few turns of the widgeon or lightly-barred teal.

The wings are made from golden pheasant tippets in strands, with strips of the mottled tail feather from the same bird placed over them. Then add "married" strands of scarlet, blue and yellow swan, and oak turkey (substitute for bustard), adding long strips of barred teal to the sides.

The minimum of materials should be used in the winging process, otherwise one gets a heavy-looking fly.

Narrow strips of brown, speckled mallard are placed over the top of the composite wing as a kind of top veil, and a golden pheasant topping is fitted over the top of the length of the wings. The fly's head can then be formed with red or scarlet Cellire varnish.

In these days when hair-winged flies are so popular, it is worth mentioning that a suitable wing can be made by sparse use of brown squirrel, with red, yellow and blue bucktail on each side.

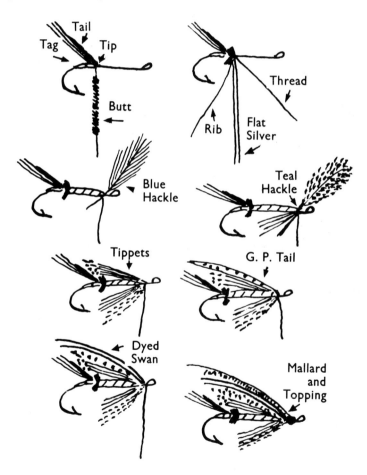

No. 48

Jock

WHEN I first saw this fly it was in a Glasgow's tackle-maker's showcase and I was struck by its tolerable resemblance to a Jock Scott salmon fly in miniature. The tackle-maker told me that it probably derived from that more famous pattern.

It is indeed, only in the body and hackle that it bears any relationship to the Jock Scott.

The Jock has a small golden pheasant topping for a tail. The front half of the body is of black floss silk and the rear half of yellow floss, the two being ribbed with oval gold tinsel.

Its hackle is spotted guinea-fowl plumage from the neck of that bird and the wing consists of paired pieces of the white-tipped, blue-black feather from the side of mallard drake wings—the wing feather used in dressing the Heckham Peckham series of flies.

I have since found the Jock to be a very useful fancy fly on waters such as Loch Awe and Loch Leven. It is particularly good in the evenings for brown trout but friends who have used it for sea-trout fishing have also taken fish with it.

Dress the Jock on hook sizes ranging from 10s to 12s (or even 14s)—old numbers. If you are dressing the small sizes, however, you would be wise to cut off a small bunch of fibres from the guinea-fowl plumage and tie these in, according to the size of the hook, to form the hackle. The ordinary guinea-fowl hackles are too large by themselves to try to put on so small a fly as on one dressed on a size 14 hook.

I use this fly mainly on the tail of the wet-fly cast where I have had most fish with it, but it has also proved a useful top dropper.

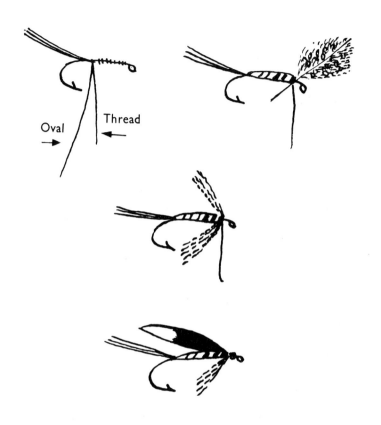

Oval

Thread

No. 49

Cock
Robin

MY ATTENTION was first drawn to this comically-named trout fly when I was fishing in Ireland some years ago. But although I fished it for the trout in the lakes there I did not make any spectacular catches with it.

Then, in a subsequent angling holiday in Wester Ross, I was fishing Loch Fionn when I discovered the pattern in my fly box and was agreeably surprised when, on trying it, experimentally, on the tail of my wet-fly cast, it took five out of seven in one outing and eight out of eleven good trout in a later visit to that loch.

I would not care to suggest that the Cock Robin is a popular fly. No doubt many anglers have never heard of it. But I think it is a good pattern to try when others fail.

The materials used in the dressing are not particularly difficult to obtain. For the tail, use several fibres of bronze speckled mallard plumage. The rear half of the body consists of golden olive seal's fur or wool and the shoulder half of scarlet seal's fur or wool, both rather sparingly put on. The entire body is then ribbed with oval gold tinsel.

Now wind on a natural red-brown cock or hen hackle—no more than a couple of turns. Smooth the hackle fibres back towards the tail.

Wing the fly with bronze speckled mallard feather and dress it in sizes ranging from 14s to 10s (old numbers) according to require- ments.

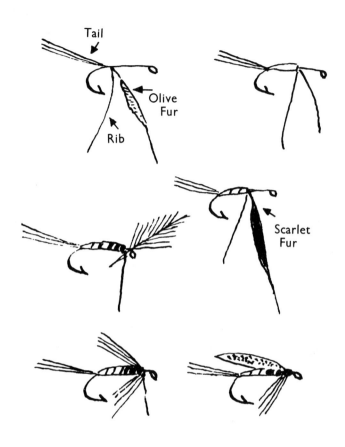

No. 50

Jungle and Silver

THIS is one of those fancy flies which anglers tend to trot out of their fly boxes on dour days when the fish are particularly difficult to entice.

With its silver body and jungle cock "cheek" wings it is something of a cross between a Butcher and a Col. Downman.

While useful as a brown-trout fly—it is presumably taken by the fish for a tiny minnow or other minute type of fish rather than a nymph or beetle—it is also favoured for sea-trout fishing.

When used for migratory trout it is often dressed with a turquoise or pale blue hackle instead of the ordinary black one.

To dress the fly tie in a short piece of red feather or silk as a tail (you can also use several strands of golden pheasant tippet feather, as in the illustrations), then a piece of oval silver tinsel or wire with which to rib the flat silver tinsel body. The ribbing tinsel helps to reduce the chance of the flat tinsel being ripped off by the fish's teeth.

Now tie in a black (or blue) hackle and make two turns of this round the neck of the hook.

Add the wings—two well-marked pieces of the jungle-cock "cheek" feather which should extend the length of the fly's body. Varnish the head with shellac or black cellulose paint.

Dress this fly in hook sizes ranging from 14s to 6s (old numbers) in singles or doubles. I particularly like the pattern dressed on a small double, even as small as size 16.

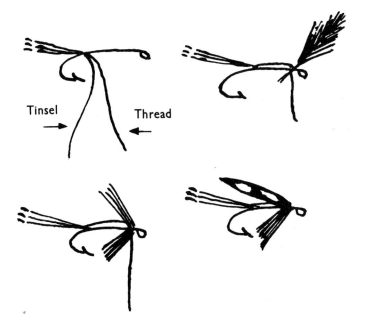

Tinsel   Thread

BOOK FOUR

No. 1

Camasunary Killer

UP IN the north of Scotland, salmon and sea trout are being caught regularly on this pattern, which was originally known as the Blue Fly and was designed by Stephen Johnson, author of that delightful book, *Fishing from Afar*.

In the original Johnson fly, the dressing was: Tag—Flat silver tinsel; body—Royal blue seal's fur or wool, ribbed with oval or flat silver tinsel, with at least three turns of a long-fibred, black cock hackle. The pattern had no tail.

Later, the fly acquired a tail of royal blue wool and the body was made up of two halves—royal blue wool for the tail half and red "Firebrand" DFM (Daylight Fluorescent Material) for the front half. The ribbing tinsel remained oval silver, and the long-fibred black cock hackle was also retained.

This, under the name of the Camasunary Killer, is the fly that is doing such great execution in northern waters, both in its orthodox dressing or tied as a hair-wing fly with black squirrel-tail wing and hackle.

In a contribution to that most informative book, *A Further Guide to Fly Dressing* by John Veniard, Peter Deane claimed that this fly was the most successful wet fly (for sea-trout) that he had ever come across. This view is shared by anglers in Scotland who have used it.

The dressing is easy enough. Tie in the royal blue wool tail, then the oval silver tinsel for ribbing the body. Now dub on the royal blue wool for the rear half of the body and then the Firebrand red for the other half. Rib both with evenly-spaced turns of the ribbing tinsel.

Now wind on the hackle, making extra turns as required for the larger dressings.

It is normal to dress this fly, which is mainly for sea trout, on a size 10 or 8 hook (old numbers), single or double. A size 8 low-water double makes a perfect hook for the purpose. If used for salmon, it can also be dressed on larger hooks, but salmon take the smaller patterns just as well.

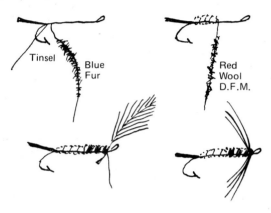

No. 2

Bibio

DURING A RECENT angling holiday in Ireland I was impressed by the popularity of this quaintly-named fly, and intrigued to find that it has a number of variations. Veteran Westport angler Mr. William Hewetson told me he invented the Bibio and had used it with great success on Lough Mask, on which water he had three times been champion. The pattern I am using by way of illustration is one he presented to me. It is tied on a size 8 (old number) hook and is normally used as a top dropper or bob fly.

In some respects the Bibio resembles that great old campaigner, the Black Zulu (dressed palmer style), but it has no red tail. Instead, its body is made up of black and claret wool or seal's fur, with the claret in the centre and the black at head and tail. There is also a fine oval silver tinsel ribbing.

The black cock hackle is dressed full—that is, from the head to tail or *vice versa*, depending on how you put the hackle on. I prefer to tie the hackle in at the head and wind it down the body, securing the end with a turn or two of the ribbing tinsel.

During my stay in Ireland I was to come across another version of the Bibio—with a red and black body—but otherwise dressed similarly to the one given to me by Mr. Hewetson. This other version of the fly had four distinct bands of red and black wool or seal's fur for its body. The order was black at the tail, then red, then black and red at the throat.

After publication of this fly in *Trout and Salmon* Mr. A. G. Prideaux, of London, gave details of another variation in which the body was black with an orange band.

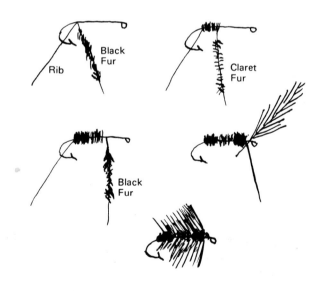

No. 3

Donna
May

THE DRESSING for this hair-winged salmon fly was given to me by an Elgin angler and tackle-dealer, who told me that it is used with some success on the River Beauly. He was unable to tell me the name of the inventor or how the pattern got its name.

Begin the dressing by tying-in the tail which consists of a piece of red ibis (or substitute) with several strands of pintail or barred teal plumage on top. Then wind-on a butt made of a strand of bronze peacock herl.

The body of the fly is composed of orange seal's fur or wool (one third, at rear) and the remaining two-thirds are of green seal's fur or wool. Both are ribbed with flat gold tinsel.

Put on a hot orange hackle, preferably in beard fashion. To do this correctly you have to reverse the hook in the vice and tie-in a small bunch of the hot orange hackle fibres, preferably from a cock hackle, on the side of the hook nearest to you. Then when you apply thread pressure the hackle fibres will splay out suitably for your purpose. Now add the hair wing comprising a mixture of light blue bucktail and undyed black, white-tipped badger hair.

This fly is usually dressed on singles and doubles ranging from about size 8 upwards.

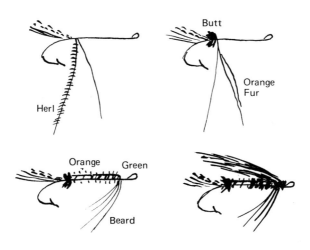

Herl

Butt

Orange
Fur

Orange   Green

Beard

No. 4

Governor

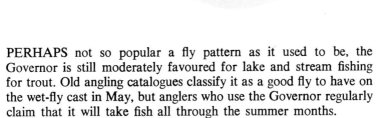

PERHAPS not so popular a fly pattern as it used to be, the Governor is still moderately favoured for lake and stream fishing for trout. Old angling catalogues classify it as a good fly to have on the wet-fly cast in May, but anglers who use the Governor regularly claim that it will take fish all through the summer months.

Apart from its bright yellow floss tag, which constitutes the rear third of the bronze peacock-herl body, the Governor is a sombre-looking pattern. It is not too difficult to dress.

The tail consists of a few fibres of red cock hackle or golden pheasant scarlet breast plumage. Next comes the yellow floss part of the body, followed by the peacock herl, which is wound on and tied down at the neck.

Now tie in a red-brown cock or hen hackle and give it two or three turns. Take two matching pieces of woodcock wing feather and tie them in (inside out) for the fly's wings. Some fly dressers have been known to use hen pheasant wing feathers for the wings of this fly, but if you use these keep the shiny sides innermost.

Dress the Governor in old-number hook sizes ranging from 14 to 12. It can be fished anywhere on the three-fly cast, but is possibly best used as a top dropper or bob fly.

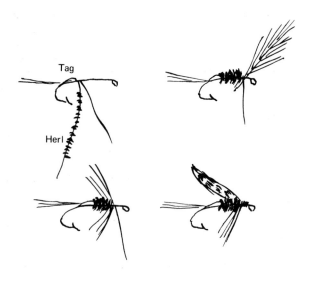

No. 5

Corrie Fly

THIS fly has been on the go since long before the Second World War and is chiefly known as a sea-trout pattern. It is particularly attractive to herling or whitling and is most often used on the tail of the cast.

It is a gaudy-looking fly, a sort of cross between a salmon and a trout fly. Indeed, I have heard of it being dressed as a low-water fly for salmon and of having taken fish at the end of a greased line.

No doubt it could also take brown trout from lakes and reservoirs if it were dressed in smaller sizes than the 10s to 8s (old numbers) on which it is normally tied.

Tie in a sliver of red ibis (or red-dyed substitute) for the tail. Then tie in fine silver oval tinsel which will be used in ribbing the body.

The body itself is made of flat silver tinsel, with the ribbing over in evenly-spaced turns.

The hackle is usually of bright claret cock or hen, but some fly dressers replace the claret with a shining magenta, though I don't see that it makes much difference.

Wings for the fly are made from corresponding strips of grey mallard wing feather, with small pieces of jungle cock tied in on each side of the wings as "eyes".

It is a matter of choice whether you use the mallard feathers inside or out, but if they are tied with the shiny side out they have a slightly more flashy appearance and do not have the same tendency to separate.

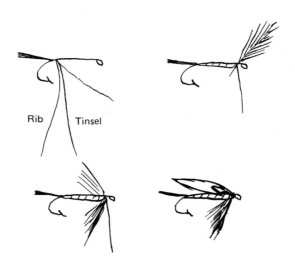

Rib   Tinsel

No. 6

Goshawk

IN THESE days when hair-winged flies are becoming increasingly popular for salmon and sea-trout fishing, the Goshawk is a good pattern to have in the fly box.

This attractive-looking fly has already proved its worth in Scottish and Irish rivers. It was first brought to my notice by an Aberdeenshire angler and fly tyer, William Forrest.

He told me that he had taken nine salmon with it in a week's fishing. It has been further tested on the Nith and the Annan with satisfactory results.

While the tails and tags used for this fly are subject to variations in the hands of different fly dressers the following dressing is recommended. The black seal's fur used for the body should not be too heavy. It should be applied thinly enough to show the gold ribbing.

Tie in and wind on the oval gold tinsel tag. Then apply the tail, which consists of a short golden pheasant crest feather, topped with a few fibres of barred teal plumage. A small piece of dyed red feather may be added if you think this refinement improves the fly.

The body is black seal's fur. Mohair is often used, but the seal's fur is better. Use oval gold tinsel ribbing of the appropriate grade according to the size of the fly being dressed.

The hackle is white cock dyed claret—and the wing consists of a slender bunch of white bucktail or impala dyed yellow.

This pattern can be dressed in standard singles (8–6) and low-water doubles in similar sizes. It is a particularly good fly for autumn fishing.

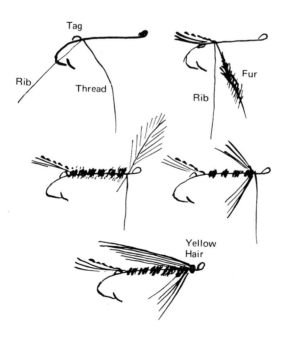

325

No. 7

Infallible

THIS IS A DEVON pattern, which first came to my notice many years ago, in a very old edition of Hardy's catalogue. The fly's name intrigued me, since it suggests a fail-me-never and every angler worth his salt is always on the look-out for a pattern that will never let him down!

The Infallible, which is suggestive of the Iron Blue Dun, may not always live up to its descriptive title, but it does catch a lot of fish wherever hatches of iron blues occur. It can be used as a dry fly, floater or a sunk fly, the latter corresponding to a nymph.

For the dry fly make the body of mole fur or crimson tying silk, which may be shown at the tail end of the body if the mole fur is used. The hackle and whisks, or setae, are of dark blue dun cock.

When dressing the wet fly or nymph-suggesting pattern you use dark blue dun hen fibres for the tail or setae. Then wind on a body of waxed claret tying silk, keeping it very thin.

You can also use the mole fur sparingly for the wet pattern, but in this case rib it with fine claret tying thread.

A good feather to use for the wet fly is the small metallic-coloured one from the shoulder of a crow's wing. Put it on scantily, for it has to be remembered that the nymph of the iron blue is very small and slender.

Because of the natural insect's smallness, use 15 and 16 (old number) hooks.

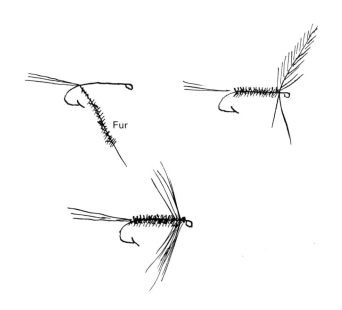

Fur

No. 8

Waterhen and Black

BY NO means a well-known pattern, though it would appear to be a fairly old fly, this one is popular enough among those West of Scotland anglers who know its worth for sea-trout fishing.

I first heard of its use on an Ayrshire river, where a local doctor fished it with considerable success, dressed on hook sizes seldom bigger than size 10 (old number).

So far as I am aware, you will not find it in any of the tackle shops and I have not been able to trace its origin, though I have since heard of its use on the rivers of Skye.

The dressing is quite simple. The tail consists of a few barred teal or pale mallard fibres. There are two parts to the body; the rear half is flat silver tinsel, ribbed with oval silver tinsel, and the foremost half is black floss silk, also ribbed with the oval tinsel. The hackle is black hen or henny cock.

This fly is dressed slimly and is normally fished on the tail of the cast.

Tie in the teal or mallard fibres (three at the most), then tie in the ribbing tinsel (silver oval), and the flat silver tinsel for the rear half of the body. Wind on the flat tinsel and rib it with the oval silver tinsel. Now tie in a piece of black floss silk and continue the ribbing over this after the floss has been thinly wound on.

Put on the black hackle in the ordinary way (two turns) or in the beard fashion, and tie in corresponding pieces of waterhen wing feather quills, fixing these in so that they lie down well on the back of the fly's body.

I dare say this pattern might also be used in smaller sizes for brown-trout fishing but I have never heard of it being put to this use.

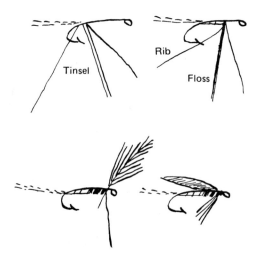

No. 9

Silver Ghost

THERE ARE PROBABLY other names for this pattern, which is a sea-trout fly used with a great amount of success in northeast Scotland rivers. In a sense it is a derivative of the Silver Shrimp or Silver Invicta. But it differs from both in having a hairwing.

I know for a fact that this fly has killed salmon and sea-trout on the Deveron, at Turriff and on the River Spey. It has also accounted for grilse and sea-trout in south of Scotland rivers and on the Teifi in Wales.

The tail consists of a small golden pheasant topping. The body is flat silver tinsel, unribbed, and the wing is pale fawn white-tipped deer or other hair sparingly applied. I have seen a fly of this type which had no more than six single strands of hair for its wing kill many sea-trout when the fly looked like nothing more than a silver-bodied hook in the water.

The hackle consists of several strands of white cock hackle, with three or four fibres of barred blue jay overmounting it. The jay fibres are tied in, as is the white hackle, by the beard method, not wound on.

This fly is particularly deadly at night, just after sunset. It is usually dressed on a small double hook—seldom bigger than 12 (old number)—and has been known to be most effective dressed on a 14 double, when it can be fished in the company of a similarly-winged fly with a flat gold body.

It is normal practice to fish these small flies on a floating line, making sure, of course, that the cast is kept free of grease so that the flies swim just under the surface.

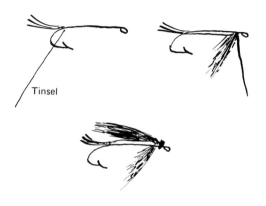

Tinsel

No. 10

Jerram's
Fancy

DURING a short visit to the Turriff Angling Association waters of the River Deveron, in Aberdeenshire, I was fortunate enough to hook and land several salmon. And one of the successful flies was a black, hair-winged pattern which bore some resemblance to a Stoat's Tail and was dressed on a size 8 double hook.

This particular fly was passed on to me by a friendly Deveron angler who informed me that it was called Jerram's Fancy and was invented and named by the late Tom Jerram, a former prominent member of the Turriff Angling Association.

Normally, in Deveron practice, this fly is fished on its own, but

I was using it as a bob fly on a two-fly cast, with a Curry's Red Shrimp on the tail.

Jerram's Fancy took two of the five salmon I caught in my three outings to the river. Two of the fish were taken from the pool known as the Kirns. The other three were caught in the Flats below the bridge, nearer Turriff.

Jerram's Fancy is not a particularly difficult fly to dress. It has a short piece of pale blue feather for its tail. Incidentally, I think it might be improved upon by using a short piece of horizon blue Depth Ray Fire fluorescent silk instead of the feather for the tail.

The rear third of the body is red floss silk and the remaining two thirds black floss silk. Both are ribbed with oval silver tinsel.

The short hackle is pale blue hen and the wing consists of a small bunch of black squirrel tail fibres or bucktail dyed black. Care should be taken not to make the wing too bulky and not to carry the fibres much beyond the end of the hook.

This pattern can be dressed in size 8 to 10 low water hooks.

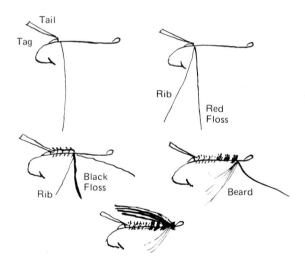

No. 11

Kate

THIS IS ONE of those trout flies—principally used in lake fishing —which is not so generally well-known as it might be. Its only claim to popularity is that it is much esteemed by the anglers who do use it.

Once, at Loch Leven, I was showing the contents of my fly-box to a fellow-angler and he took a fancy to this pattern, the only one of it that I had, and I presented it to him. Oddly enough, he returned to the jetty at the end of the day with the heaviest catch —and most of his fish were taken on the Kate.

As most of the trout I caught that day were got on the Woodcock and Mixed, with red and yellow body, I concluded that the marked resemblance between the two flies might have had something to do with my friend's success.

The Kate should be dressed on small hooks, never bigger than 12s. I have tried it as a sea-trout fly in bigger sizes, up to 6s (old numbers), but have not achieved much with it.

The dressing procedure is: Tie in a small golden pheasant topping as a tail. Then tie-in a piece of fine oval gold tinsel, to be used for ribbing the body which consists of pale yellow seal's fur or wool (at the rear) and bright scarlet seal's fur or wool nearest the wing. The hackle is black henny-cock, and the wing comprises two strips of the fawny brown feather from a jay's wing.

I normally tie the fly on size 14 singles and size 16 doubles, and I fish it as an intermediate or tail pattern on the wet fly cast.

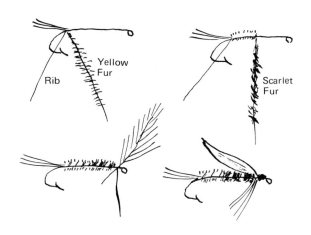

Yellow
Fur

Rib

Scarlet
Fur

No. 12

Bluebottle
Spider

ALSO KNOWN as Murray's Spider, this extremely popular lake
or river fly was invented by Mr. David Murray, of Hurlford, in
Ayrshire, though I first got it from Cafaro Brothers, the Glasgow
fishing-tackle shop, in the early '50s, and I am basing my present
instructions on the dressing of it on the fly purchased then.

Since it was invented, however—good fly though it is in its
original form—the Bluebottle Spider has been subjected to a

number of variations. Some modern dressings give it a tail consisting of several black hackle fibres, but the original fly had no tail, just a green fluorescent tinsel body and a black hackle.

Other versions of the fly have a blue fluorescent tinsel body—and I have seen variations in which the green or blue Lurex tinsel was wound on in ribbing style over a black thread body.

A striking feature of this fly is that it can be fished with confidence from the beginning to the end of the trout season, and is successful at any position on the cast.

It is a very easy fly to dress. Tie in a piece of green or blue Lurex tinsel and closely wind this towards the neck of the hook. Then wind on several turns of a black hen hackle.

This is the dressing for the wet or sunk fly. If you are dressing the floating fly, use a cock hackle. The dry fly is particularly deadly in the hot days of midsummer and again in the autumn. Hook sizes are 12 to 16.

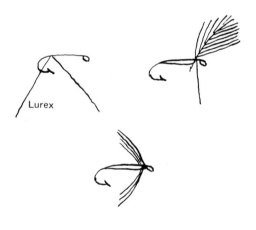

No. 13

Mystery

THERE ARE TWO FLIES with the name Mystery, and they are both referred to by J. Edson Leonard, the American, in his *Dictionary of Flies.* I cannot speak for Mystery No. 1, which has a pink floss, silver-ribbed body, but I can certainly testify to the efficacy of Mystery No. 2, which has a flat silver body.

I have used this fly and taken salmon with it from the Deveron, in Aberdeenshire, and I have also had fish with it from the Annan, so it has some claim to success both in the north and south of Scotland.

Mystery No. 2, which had its baptism in Nova Scotia, seems to have been introduced to Britain during the war or shortly afterwards. But it is relatively unknown to a great many salmon fishers.

The tail consists of a small golden pheasant topping, tied in after putting on a small silver tag. The tip is bright yellow floss followed by a butt of black ostrich herl or chenille, or even of black wool thinly wound on.

The body itself is flat silver tinsel, unribbed, and the hackle, tied in beard-fashion, is brown henny cock. Fox squirrel is used for the wing, and this has jungle cock cheeks on each side.

The fly, which can also be used in smaller sizes for sea-trout fishing, is tied on low-water singles and doubles up to 1 in. irons.

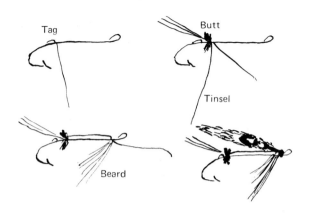

Tag

Butt

Tinsel

Beard

No. 14

Badger
Variant

THE BIG TROUT in the River Don, in Aberdeenshire, are very partial to quill-bodied dry flies, and this one has regularly proved its worth in the pools and runs near Inverurie.

The Badger Variant should be dressed with the minimum of material—a fairly short undyed peacock quill (taken from the eye feather) for the body and a long-fibred, bright and stiff badger cock hackle. The original fly had a starling wing, split, but this can be omitted, though some anglers prefer their dry flies to be winged.

336

No setae or tail whisks are necessary, though, again, some fly-dressers prefer these as they help to cock the fly up well in the water—and there is nothing nicer than a fly that rides gracefully, with wings perked up, on a rippled pool or stream.

Omitting the whisks, however, tie-in the undyed quill with a dark (brown or black) tying silk. The purpose in using this dark silk is to ensure that the fly's body has that attractive segmented look when the quill is wound on, fractionally exposing the tying silk at each winding.

If you prefer the starling wing, make it of two slender, upright slips, and wind on no more than a couple of turns of the badger cock hackle, making sure that the fibres are long and bristly, of almost glassy texture.

This pattern is dressed on a 16 to 14 (old numbers) up-eyed or down-eyed light-wire hook.

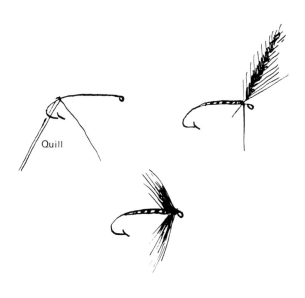

No. 15

Conway Blue

MAKING a present of flies to a Welsh friend I included this pattern, the dressing for which I had found in John Veniard's most informative book, *A Further Guide to Fly Dressing*.

Mr. Veniard mentions the dressing among a selection of Welsh salmon and sea-trout flies which were given to him by Mr. R. H. Hughes, the Llanwrst fly tyer.

My friend fished the Conway Blue on the Towy and took two salmon with it on its initial trial.

This is an attractive-looking pattern which presumably had its baptism on the River Conway, though I cannot swear to this.

The fly I dressed for my Welsh acquaintance was tied on a size 5 (low water) 1⅛th-inch salmon double hook, identical to the one shown in the photograph. He told me that he took his fish by stripping the fly fairly fast through the water.

The dressing of this fly looks a bit more difficult than it really is. The main thing to watch for is that the pattern is not over-dressed. Use the minimum of materials so that the fly has a slim, almost rakish appearance.

Tie in a small round silver tag, followed by a tip (two turns of golden yellow floss). Now tie in a golden pheasant crest feather (small topping) and put on a butt of black ostrich herl or wool.

The body consists of royal blue seal's fur (though wool was used in the present case), ribbed with oval silver tinsel.

There are two throat hackles, dyed royal blue first, with blue-barred jay (the merest suggestion) in front of it.

The wings are made by setting in two golden pheasant tippet feathers back to back, and roofing them with bronze mallard flank

338

feather. A golden pheasant topping is then set in over the top of the wing, sloping so that it comes down to converge almost with the tail. No attempt should be made to hide the tippet feathers.

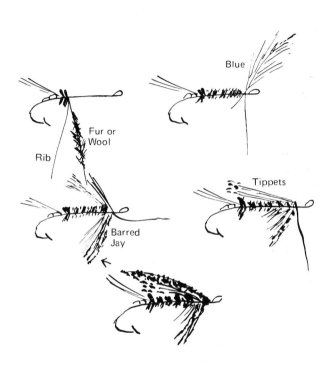

No. 16

Mairi

WHEN Mr. Niall Campbell wrote about the pattern known as Mairi and another called Ronald in the August, 1963, issue of *Trout and Salmon*, he can hardly have dreamed of the interest they would arouse. Indeed, he has been asked for the dressings so many times since then that he has suggested I might like to pass them on in this series.

I must confess, though, that I have felt bound to put the two flies to the test before including them. I have used them for loch fishing since and I can vouch for their trout-enticing qualities. I have not used them for sea-trout fishing, but Mr. Campbell, by his own account, took a $7\frac{1}{4}$ lb. sea-trout with the Mairi.

Mr. Campbell replaces the Grouse and Claret with the Mairi in early June, unless trout are observed taking sedge pupae and adults. I tried the Mairi on Renfrewshire lochs where there is a good sedge hatch in June and got many fish with it, especially during evening rises. The trout took boldly, with that fierce slashing attack that is so characteristic of fish taking sedges. And long after June I was still taking fish with this pattern.

The Mairi is not difficult to dress. It has no tail. The rear half of the body is pale green wool ribbed with yellow thread, and the second half is pale yellow floss, also ribbed with yellow thread. The winging feather is hen pheasant, though you might care to use the speckled feather from a partridge tail. Round off with a cinnamon hen hackle tied in front of the wings.

The pattern sent by Mr. Campbell was dressed on a size 12 (old number) hook, but I have been using size 14 and 13 (old numbers) for the well-educated trout in the waters where I customarily fish.

The dressing for the Ronald is given in a later article.

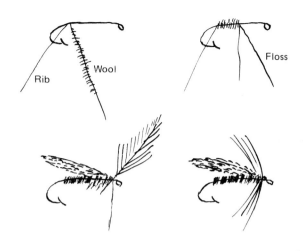

Rib

Wool

Floss

No. 17

Ronald

THIS IS THE SECOND fly from Mr. Niall Campbell, of Pitlochry, and follows the dressing of the Mairi. It is his version of the heather fly *(Bibio pominae)* which differs in many particulars from my own dressing of the fly, known in my part of the country as the Red Legs.

Both are imitations of the big, gaudy fly that is often found on the surface of lochs and lakes about the middle of August, a time when, if you are fishing when these flies fall on the water, you will probably experience a rise such as you have seen only to a fall of ants on a mild and windless day.

Mr. Campbell devised the Ronald as a representation of one of these large flies, and though I was loath to depart from my own favourite Red Legs, I was fortunate enough to be fishing Loch Ard during a fall of the heather fly in August and was able to put Mr. Campbell's fly to the test. It took six of the eight trout I caught.

The dressing is somewhat akin to the Black Joe, which I describe elsewhere, except that it has a blae wing and a silver tip to the body. The Ronald also has a few black fibres as a tail.

Tie in the tail fibres (no more than three), then wind on the flat silver tinsel (two turns), and the red floss silk (for the rear half of the body). The second half of the body is black floss (with no ribbing), and the hackle is black hen. The winging feather is mallard blae (grey) tied with the shiny side inwards so that the wings have a split appearance.

Mr. Campbell's fly was dressed on a size 12 hook which was just about right, for the fly the Ronald imitates is a fairly large one and might even be tied on a size 10 or 11 (old numbers) hook.

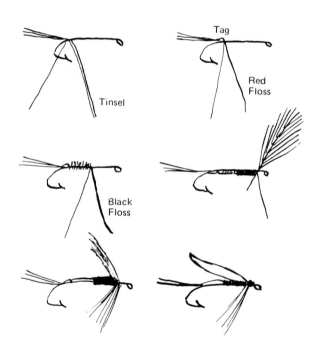

No. 18

Freeman's Fancy

HERE IS A FLY, or a lure, to be more exact, that can be depended upon to take its quota of trout and sea-trout each season. For a long time it was known to and used by a small number of anglers, but with the tremendous increase in lake fishing in recent years, it has tended to grow in popularity.

Its inventor no doubt tied it as a representation of a small fish. It most certainly looks like one when drawn through the water, and it is a first-class fly for lake fishing. I have also taken a lot of sea-trout with it from the Border rivers of Scotland.

The original dressing insisted upon a small bunch of orange toucan breast feathers for the tail, but dyed orange hackle tip or a small golden pheasant topping feather does just as well. The body is flat gold tinsel or Lurex, ribbed with oval gold tinsel, or unribbed.

After putting on the tail and the tinsel body, tie in a bright magenta hackle. This hackle is best if it comes from a cock bird, and it should not be dyed too deeply or it will lose its most attractive shine. For the wing use paired strips of bronze speckled mallard and add two small jungle cock cheeks, one on each side of the wing.

Dress this fly on hook sizes ranging from size 14 to 8 (old numbers) and strive for a slim effect.

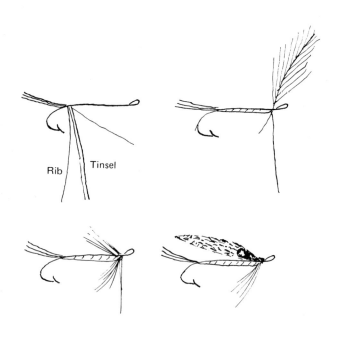

Rib   Tinsel

No. 19

Lady
Caroline

GIVEN its full dressing as a Spey fly, the Lady Caroline calls for
a different approach from that of most salmon flies in the winging,
the ribbing of the body and the application of the body hackle.

344

This hackle, which is grey heron, is tied in at its base, and wound up the body in even turns so that the largest fibres are nearest to the tail of the fly. They have a fluttering action in the water.

It is usual to wind on this hackle in reverse to the ribbing tinsel which protects it from the fish's teeth. The wings, consisting of corresponding right and left strips of bronze mallard plumage, are tied down low with a kind of dropping effect over the body.

Flies dressed in this fashion, with criss-crossing of the ribbing tinsel, have long been associated with the River Spey. But many anglers prefer the less-involved dressing on the lines of a low-water pattern.

This is the one discussed here and the dressing is more simple, yet does not seem to detract from the pattern's usefulness.

Tie in a few fibres of red, golden pheasant breast feather. Now fix in a piece of flat gold tinsel, one of oval silver and one of oval gold tinsel. Then wind on a mixture of one strand of olive green wool to two strands of light brown wool.

Rib the body with the flat gold tinsel in evenly-spaced turns and then wind the oval silver tinsel alongside (up against the flat tinsel) in similar even turns.

Follow that by winding the oval gold tinsel over the body to criss-cross the previous windings of tinsel.

Tie in a grey hackle (two turns) and follow that with a hackle from the red, golden pheasant breast feather.

Now put on the mallard wing, ensuring that it lies well down over the fly's body.

This fly can be dressed on 6 to 8 low-water hooks or on similar or bigger standard salmon irons.

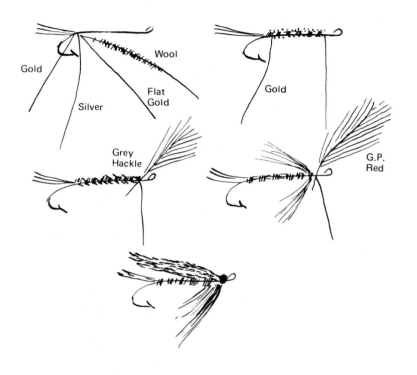

Gold

Wool

Silver

Flat
Gold

Gold

Grey
Hackle

G.P.
Red

No. 20

Black Joe

I LEARNED the dressing for this spider-type fly from an angler fishing Loch Ard, in Perthshire, who told me that it got its name from its originator, a Falkirk man called Joe Black. In some respects it corresponds to an old pattern known as the Black and Red, and it bears some resemblance to a Black Zulu.

I saw this fly take eight fish from Loch Ard and I was told by its user that it kills as well if not better than the Black Zulu when the water is scoury in high winds and heavy waves.

I have since used it on various positions on the wet-fly cast, and it has taken fish on all of them. I normally fish it, however, as a tail fly, and think it performs best when tied in small sizes, from 14 to 16 (old number) singles or doubles.

Unlike the recommended dressing of the Zulu, this pattern has the hackle tied at the neck only, and the hackle should be put on sparingly and should be long in the fibre.

The Black Joe has no tail. Half the body is red floss silk (a very bright red), though Fire Orange Depth Ray Fluorescent silk or wool might also be used. The remaining half of the body is black silk or black ostrich herl. The hackle is black hen.

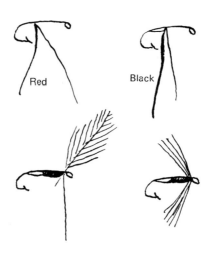

Red   Black

No. 21

Challoner

MENTION is made of this pattern in W. Earl Hodgson's very fine book *Trout Fishing*, published in 1920, and it no doubt enjoyed some measure of popularity about that time.

But it has not been heard of under the name of Challoner for a very long time. It is possibly better known today as Pheasant and Yellow, which is regarded by some lake or loch fishers as one of the best flies that can be used in late spring or early summer.

The Challoner differs from the accepted dressings of the Pheasant and Yellow in that its wings are made from the hard (and darker) side of the hen pheasant's wing feather.

The Challoner has a red ibis (or dyed substitute) tail and the body is made of yellow seal's fur, mohair or wool, ribbed with oval gold tinsel. It has a red-brown or dark ginger hen hackle.

Tie in the red tail feather and the ribbing tinsel. Dub the seal's fur, mohair or wool on to the hook stem with the tie-silk and rib it evenly with the tinsel. Now tie in the brown hen hackle and wind on no more than a couple of turns.

Snip corresponding pieces of the marled feather from the hard side of the hen pheasant wing quills and fix these in so that they lie well down on top of the fly's body. Strive for a thin and rakish-looking fly.

The Challoner can be dressed on size 14 to 12 (old number) hooks for trout fishing and is particularly good as a bob fly, especially on rough days of cloud and wind, when yellow-bodied flies invariably do well.

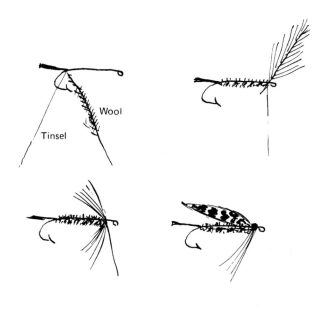

349

No. 22

The Burton

OVER the years I have received numerous requests for the dressing of this well-known Loch Lomond fly.

I understand that it originated in the River Nith, and that it was introduced to Loch Lomond by a Mr. Dargavel, who had used it on the Nith. Its success at Loch Lomond was immediate as a sea-trout fly. Very soon it was taking salmon as well.

In many respects it is akin to the Brown Turkey. It has a golden pheasant topping (small) for the tail, and the body is in three parts—yellow at the tail, then red, and finally black seal's fur, all ribbed with flat silver tinsel.

The hackle is Furnace or Coch-y-Bonddu, wound on round the neck of the hook or tied in as a beard, and the wing is brown turkey or dark cinnamon hen, with fibres of barred teal plumage tied in between the wing strips.

It was this fly, along with the Mallard and Yellow (on the bob), that enabled the late Alexander Frisken of Glasgow to make a record kill of salmon (five of them, weighing 60 lb.) at Loch Lomond on June 16th, 1919. This record, incidentally, was later broken (twice) by Ian Wood, former editor of *Trout and Salmon*.

But Mr. Frisken made his catch—13½, 12½, two of 12 and one of 10 lb.—in an hour-and-a-half. The cast he was using is still to be seen in the tackle shop of William Robertson and Co. of Glasgow.

These flies were size 6 and the Burton that Mr. Frisken was using then with such remarkable results was in no way different from the one that is marketed today in Glasgow tackle shops.

To dress the Burton, tie in the topping for the tail, then tie in the ribbing tinsel.

350

Dub the yellow, then red, and, finally, the black seal's fur (or wool) on to the tying thread and wind them in equal parts on to the hook stem as the body.

Tie in the Furnace (red-black) hackle, and fix in a bunch of barred teal fibres as an under-wing. The brown turkey or brown hen wing strips are then put in place to veil but not to hide completely the teal fibres.

This fly can also be used successfully for sea-trout and salmon fishing in rivers—and there are some anglers who use cinnamon hair instead of brown turkey or brown hen feather for the wings.

If using this pattern for sea-trout fishing, a size 8 (old number) is generally good, but a 6 is about normal for salmon.

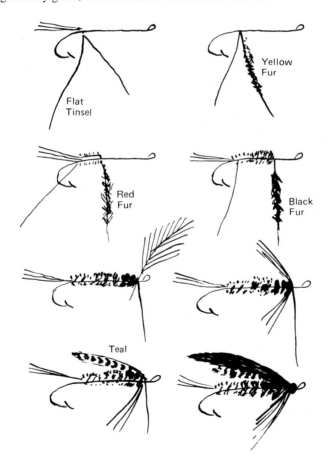

Flat Tinsel

Yellow Fur

Red Fur

Black Fur

Teal

No. 23

Slater

ONE OF the older lake flies, this one enjoyed a considerable vogue following the publication of its dressing in an appendix to the late W. Earl Hodgson's *Trout Fishing* in the early 'twenties.

It cannot truly be regarded as a popular pattern but it is still used by some anglers who dress their own flies. I have used it with moderately successful results for Scottish loch and reservoir fishing in June. I assume that it is taken for some kind of sedge fly rather than an imitation of the so-called slater, found under stones on the bottoms of lakes and streams.

Tie in the tail, which comprises a few fibres of the red breast feather of the golden pheasant. A red-brown cock hackle will do at a pinch.

The body is made of yellowish-green seal's fur or wool, ribbed with fine, flat silver tinsel. Wind on a red-brown hen hackle at the throat and finish off with wings consisting of corresponding pieces of brown or cinnamon hen feather.

Dress this fly on size 14 to 12 hooks (old numbers) and fish it mainly as a bob fly or top dropper. I have found it particularly good in the evenings when sedges were on the water's surface.

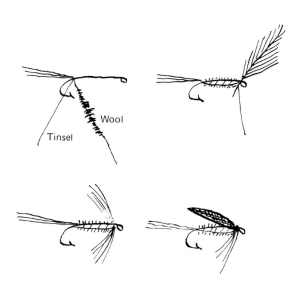

Wool

Tinsel

No. 24

Maxwell's Red

MAXWELL'S RED and the complementary Maxwell's Blue are two very old West Country patterns. I first saw reference to them in H. C. Cutliffe's book, *The Art of Trout Fishing in Rapid Streams*, dated 1863, although he does not say who their creator was.

The Maxwell's Red's body is hare's flax ribbed with fine gold wire, and the hackle and setae are red cock.

The Maxwell's Blue's body, on the other hand, is hare's flax ribbed with silver wire, and it has a medium to dark blue dun cock hackle and setae.

Cutliffe did not name the flies, but gave them in a long list of patterns which had been tried and proven by himself and other anglers. In his dressing for the red fly he recommended that the red be dark and rusty-looking, and that a dark 'rusty' blue be used for the blue fly. Both patterns are tied on size 14 or 15 hooks (old numbers).

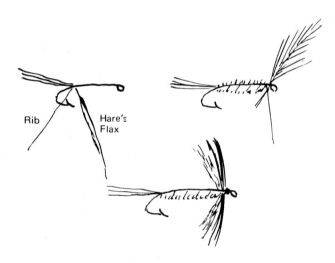

No. 25

Masson Grub

DURING a fishing visit to the River Deveron at Turriff in Aberdeenshire, I heard tell of a grub fly that was killing a lot of sea-trout and the occasional salmon.

I traced its origin to Ian Masson, an experienced angler and professional fly tyer, who has a tackle shop in that little town. He was kind enough to present me with a copy of the pattern and this is the one (dressed on a single hook) which I am using in the illustration.

Ian dressed this fly as an approximation of the docken grub, which is such a favourite bait for trout and sea-trout. But he has also tied the pattern in small sizes (as small as 12s) which have taken fish, so that the Masson Grub seems to have attractions beyond its similarity to the docken grub.

Right from the day it was introduced the Masson Grub has been taking sea-trout. Ian and other anglers have used it most successfully on the Deveron's pools and it has taken fish from the Spey as well.

Indeed, Ian told me that he has had orders from anglers in England who had heard of the fly's success.

It is not a difficult pattern to dress. The first step in tying it is to wind on three or four turns of fine oval or round gold tinsel. The tail, tied on next, consists of several fibres of light barred teal or mallard, and the body consists of white wool, ribbed with fine gold oval tinsel. The original pattern had a body made from dubbed sheep's wool of a fine white texture.

I submit, however, that a further improvement might be achieved by using Electron White Depth Ray fluorescent wool, ribbed with the oval gold tinsel.

355

The hackle, which should be sparingly put on, consists of a couple of turns of black hen or hennycock hackle, just long enough in the fibres to reach the end of the hook, but in no sense thick enough to hide the white body. Finally, the head is painted red.

Ian usually dresses the fly on a size 10 or 8 (old numbers) hook, single or double.

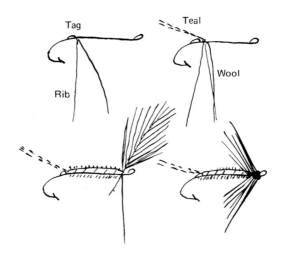

356

No. 26

Heather
Moth

OFTEN in July and August, when the heather moths come out and are blown on to the surfaces of the northern lochs of Scotland, the trout (and even sea trout) will readily take a fully-hackled pattern like the Heather Moth.

This pattern is also used with success by anglers who fish it dry on a greased line, when caddis flies are hatching in the lowland lochs of Scotland.

It can also be used successfully for sea trout in night fishing.

Normally, when fishing it in the lochs of the far north, it is dressed on a size 8 (old number) hook, but it can be usefully tied on a size 12 or a size 10, and it is likely to get its best results when fished as a bob fly or top dropper on the wet-fly cast.

There are one or two variations of the original pattern, but only in minor respects. At times, the tail consists of a snippet of dyed red feather or a small golden pheasant topping, but the most common appendage is a few fibres of barred teal plumage, tied in short.

The body is also subject to changes. In most cases, grey monkey fur, grey dun seal's fur, or blue cat's fur is used, but I have also seen Heather Moths dressed with an ordinary grey wool body. Whatever material is used for the body it is ribbed with oval or round silver tinsel.

The original dressing of the Heather Moth had a Scots Grey or dark grey and white grizzle cock hackle, dressed fully in palmer style down the body, but later versions have made use of an ordinary grey dun or a badger hackle. They all seem to serve an equal purpose.

Tie in the fibres of barred teal plumage for the tail. Then tie in

357

the ribbing tinsel and dub the wool (or fur) on to the tying thread, which should preferably be grey or white. Then wind on the wool or fur.

Tie in the grizzle hackle at the neck and wind it down the fly's body, fixing it in with the ribbing tinsel, which should then be wound up the body in evenly-spaced turns between the hackle fibres.

A further hackle may be tied in at the throat to give the fly a better-tapered appearance.

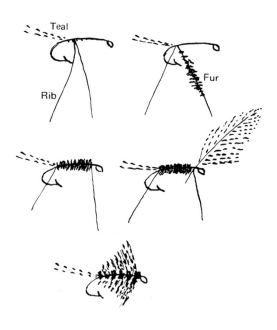

No. 27

Bourach

I BELIEVE this bright and attractive-looking fly had its origin on the River Spey. Indeed, I have been informed by a North of Scotland fly tyer and angler that it was used with marked success by Sandy Campbell, a former keeper on the Aberlour House waters of that famous river.

It is a colourful pattern which can be used for sea-trout as well as salmon and it is particularly good for grilse fishing in fairly fast water.

This pattern lends itself to a slim and slender dressing. Do not use too much hair for the wing, and put on the long-fibred blue hackle in beard fashion to accentuate this slimness.

The tail consists of a bright blue hackle point, and the body can be either embossed silver tinsel (without ribbing) or flat silver tinsel, ribbed with fine oval silver tinsel.

Make the wing with little more than a dozen fibres of bucktail dyed pale yellow or primrose and dress it on single and double hooks from size 8 (old number) upwards. An attractive sea-trout pattern can be dressed on a low-water 10.

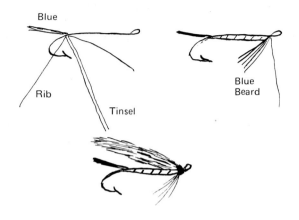

Blue

Rib

Tinsel

Blue
Beard

No. 28

Sharpe's
Favourite

ONE OF THE MOST successful anglers ever to fish the Aberdeenshire River Don was the late Mr. Alan Sharpe, the well-known tackle dealer and angling broadcaster

In Sharpe's Favourite he had a pattern on which he got a lot of trout and sea-trout from the Don and other rivers in the north of Scotland.

It is, in fact, a variation of the Greenwell Quill theme, with a body consisting of undyed peacock quill stripped of its flue, a furnace cock or hen hackle, and a waterhen wing. The tail consists of three fibres of the furnace hackle.

Tie in the tail and then put on a couple of turns of fine flat silver tinsel as a tag and wind on the stripped quill.

In using quill for a body, it makes a nicer looking fly if you employ a dark thread so that the windings of quill, put on slightly apart, give the fly a segmented look.

Now wind on several turns of the furnace cock or hen hackle—and add two corresponding pieces of waterhen wing feathers.

The fly is tied on hooks ranging from 14 to 12 (old numbers), and the pattern can be used on the tail or the bob position of the wet-fly cast. It can also be used as a dry or floating fly, in which case a cock hackle is used and the wings are given a slightly upward set.

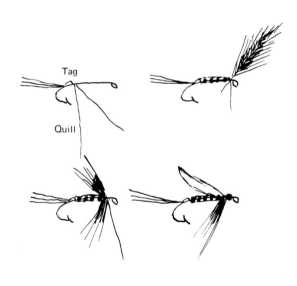

No. 29

Assassin

MY THANKS for particulars of this fly are due to Major Vivian Bailey, author of a most interesting book, *Come Fishing and Shooting*.

It was Miss Megan Boyd of Kintradwell, Brora, who first directed my attention to the pattern. She urged me to get in touch with Major Bailey, and, in the course of correspondence with him, I learned that reference to the Assassin was made in his book.

In his letter to me Major Bailey said he believed that Miss Boyd is the only professional fly tyer who knows the correct dressing. He added that when one asked for the fly of this name in tackle shops one got something quite different.

The Assassin has a short golden pheasant crest feather for a tail. Before this is put on, wind on a tag of fine oval or round silver tinsel. The body is flat silver tinsel, ribbed with oval silver tinsel.

The hackle consists of speckled grouse plumage and blue-barred jay, both tied in as beard hackles, the jay on the outside of the grouse.

There is a break half-way down the body where a yellow hackle is tied in and wound on. The wing of the fly, which extends only half the length of the body, is dark bronze speckled mallard.

In the case of larger dressings of the fly it is usual to add a golden pheasant topping or two over the back of the winging feather, but this is a refinement that can very well be done without.

Major Bailey informs me that he has killed salmon on the Helmsdale, the Brora, the Beauly, the Dee and the Spey with the Assassin, and that as a trout pattern it has taken fish from rivers and lochs all over England and Scotland.

In his book he mentions that he was given the fly originally by his friend Frank Howker while he was fishing the River Gwash in Rutland and that he immediately took trout with it.

This pattern can be dressed on salmon hooks from size 8 upwards and can also be used in smaller sizes for trout fishing.

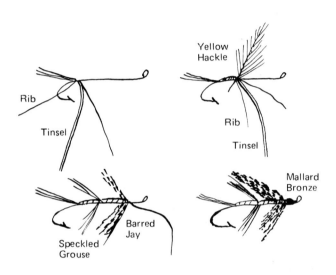

No. 30

Devonshire Doctor

ONE OF the most attractive-looking hackled patterns ever to emerge from the West Country, the Devonshire Doctor has a fine reputation as a trout killer.

Like so many of the West Country patterns which are dressed with a cock hackle, it can be fished either wet or dry, and seems to do particularly well when fished just below the surface in fast water.

In sharp contrast to the soft and sparsely-hackled North Country patterns, those of the West Country are usually quite heavily hackled with stiff-fibred feathers with a degree of sparkle about them.

The Devonshire Doctor is a case in point. The Coch-y-Bonddu or Dark Furnace cock hackle with fairly long fibres should be given at least four turns. The body, which should be tapered from head to tail, was originally made from black rabbit's flax, ribbed with fine, flat, gold tinsel. One should explain that the black flax was shaved from the black rabbit fur or hair. Nowadays almost any soft black fur or hair is used.

The flat gold tinsel—three or four turns round the body—should show quite prominently.

The whisks, which should be tied in before the body fur and tinsel are applied, consist of three or four fibres of Coch-y-Bonddu hackle.

This fly should be dressed on hooks ranging from 14 to 12 (old numbers) and every effort should be made to ensure that the hackle has a really dark centre and bright points.

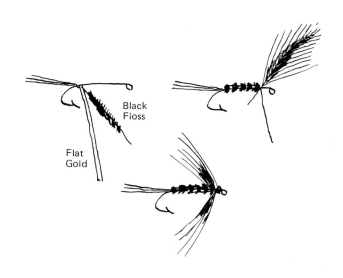

Black Fioss

Flat Gold

No. 31

Driffield Dun

NAMED AFTER the famous Driffield Beck, this is an extremely popular Yorkshire dry fly. And like most of the North Country flies it should be sparsely dressed to give its best results.

The tail of the fly consists of two or three pale ginger cock hackle whisks.

For the body use pale blue rabbit's or mole's fur, either lightly dubbed on to yellow silk so that the silk shows through the fur or with the fur put on first and ribbed afterwards with a piece of unwaxed yellow tying silk. If you use a minimum of fur to give the fly a very slender body you can then use the yellow thread to rib it carefully and neatly to produce an attractive-looking body for the fly.

The wings of the Driffield Dun are made from slender strips of pale starling, and these are tied forward (facing back towards the eye of the hook) and a pale ginger cock hackle is used for the legs of the fly.

There is a tendency among some fly-tyers to dress this fly with double wings—two on each side to give them 'body'—but, in my opinion, this should be avoided. The whole object of the exercise is to achieve a lightly-dressed fly, which will sit up daintily on the surface like a natural insect.

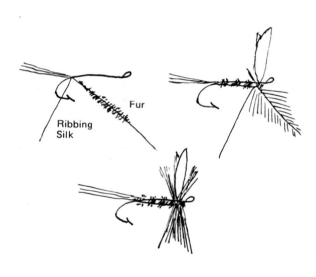

No. 32

Old
Charlie

REGARDED in some quarters as a tolerable hair-winged version of the Thunder and Lightning and in others as a variation of that great favourite, the Hairy Mary, Old Charlie can be used with good effect for salmon and grilse from midsummer until the end of the season. It is particularly good as an autumn pattern.

It was designed by Douglas Pilkington of Stow-on-the-Wold, and enjoys a splendid reputation on the River Spey, and other rivers, either as an orthodox pattern or as a low-water fly.

Start off the dressing by winding on a flat gold tinsel tag. Then add a tail of golden pheasant crest (or small topping). There is no necessity to add a butt. The body is composed of dark claret floss silk, ribbed with oval gold tinsel Do not make the ribbing too close, but in wide-spaced turns.

The hackle is hot orange cock and a suitable dye for this can be obtained from reputable suppliers of fly-dressing materials. The hackle can be wound on in the ordinary way or tied in as a beard.

Natural brown bucktail, preferably with black tips, is used for the wing, which should extend to the end of the hook in the normal pattern or to the end of the abbreviated body in the low-water fly.

Some anglers use black-barred red squirrel for the wing in the smaller patterns.

Tie in small jungle cock feathers for the cheeks, one on each side of the hair wing, and, if you wish, you can give the fly a head of red varnish, though this is not essential.

Dress the fly on hook sizes ranging from 8s to two-inch irons in both sinking and low-water patterns.

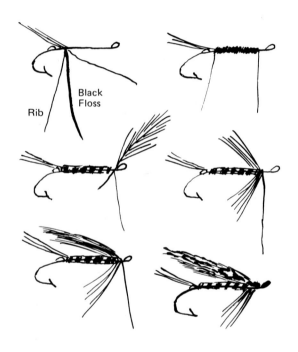

Black
Floss

Rib

No. 33

Half
Stone

ONCE, at Loch Awe, while fishing for trout with sunk flies, a friend of mine took a number of fish when other anglers were having a rather lean time. Yet the fly my friend was getting his trout on, the Half Stone, is, in fact, a West Country pattern, originally intended for river fishing. He put it on his cast in one of those moments of frustration when fish are looking at nothing!

The Half Stone, as I understand it, was first tied as a representation of a caddis or sedge fly, but, fished on the tail of my friend's wet-fly cast, it was probably taken by those Loch Awe trout because of its nymph-suggesting appearance.

Some old dressings of the Half Stone have a honey dun hackle and omit the mole's fur or water rat fur used as a thorax for the more orthodox pattern. The dressing details for the fly used by my friend were: Tie in at least three fibres of rusty, blue, dun cock hackle for the tail. Then wind on a piece of primrose or yellow floss silk round the tail half of the body. The other half of the body consists of mole's fur (slatey shade) or water rat's fur, dubbed on to yellow tying silk.

This is not a very difficult fly to dress and I have found that in the absence of a natural, rusty, blue cock hackle a white one, with shiny edges, dyes very well in a suitable blue dun shade.

Dress this pattern on size 14 to 12 old number hooks and keep it as sparsely dressed as possible if you are fishing it as a sunk fly.

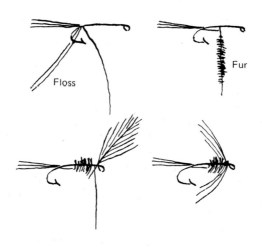

No. 34

Countess of Seafield

AMONG the many requests for salmon-fly dressings that Miss Megan Boyd of Kintradwell, by Brora in Sutherland, receives in her capacity as a professional fly tyer, that known as the Countess of Seafield is a great favourite. During a visit to her workshop she gave me the details of this attractive-looking pattern.

One surmises that this fly was tied in honour of the lady whose title it bears. It is certainly regarded as a good salmon pattern on the River Spey and on other northern rivers.

Miss Boyd dresses it mainly on size 1 light irons and the wing

370

is put on in Ackroyd fashion; that is, to lie low over the back of the body.

Tie in a tag of several turns of oval silver tinsel. You can also put in a black wool or ostrich herl butt after fixing in a golden pheasant crest feather (small topping) for the tail, but this is not strictly essential.

The rear two-thirds of the body is composed of embossed silver tinsel, ribbed or unribbed, and the remaining third is yellow seal's fur (or wool) ribbed with oval silver tinsel. Tease out the fur or wool with the point of a dubbing needle.

Now tie in a bright blue cock or hen hackle (as in the Teal and Silver), either by winding it round the throat of the hook in the orthodox way and snipping away the uppermost fibres, or by putting it on in beard fashion after reversing the hook in the vice.

The wing is made from corresponding narrow strips of cinnamon turkey, and, as already indicated, these should be tied in to lie low over the body.

Although Miss Boyd chiefly dresses this pattern on size 1 hooks, presumably it could be tied in smaller sizes for grilse and sea-trout.

You can make a hair-winged variation of the fly by using brown bucktail for the wing.

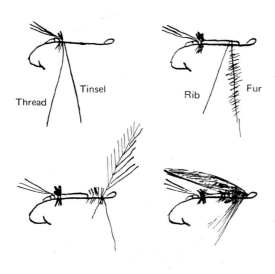

No. 35

Prince Charlie

PRESUMABLY NAMED after the original Bonnie Prince Charlie, this is one of the older patterns which has enjoyed a revival in recent years.

I can remember a time when it was regarded as one of the best flies that could be used on Loch Awe and Loch Ard in the spring months. Now, when so many anglers tie their own flies and are inclined to fall back on old dressings with a view to testing their worth, this pattern has been getting notice and justifying the new faith that is being placed in it.

It is one of the simplest flies to dress. Tie in a short red floss silk tail, and use the same red floss for the body, ribbing this with even and tight turns of flat gold tinsel. Strive to keep the body slim.

The hackle is black hen, which should be put on sparingly. For the wings use the grey mottled feather from a partridge's tail, taking a piece from each side and matching them into a slim wing.

This has proved a good tail fly and can be tied in hook sizes ranging from 15 to 12 (old numbers) singles. It seems to give best results when there is a good wave on the water.

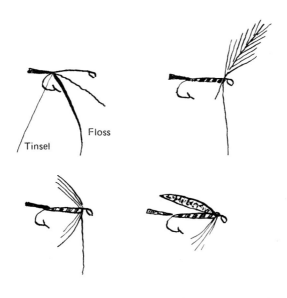

Tinsel

Floss

No. 36

Black Shrimp

VARIATIONS of the Shrimp Fly are legion, but the Black Shrimp is enjoying a considerable vogue among those who fish for salmon in north of Scotland rivers.

I was given to understand that its inventor was a retired Inverness sea captain, who was also reckoned to be responsible for other worthwhile salmon flies.

But I have since learned that it owes its origin to a Mr. John Cathcart, of Inverness, whose original dressing was a combination of the Sweep and the Shrimp.

Mr. Cathcart took 13 salmon on one day with his version of the Black Shrimp—from the River Ness.

The pattern given here is only slightly different from Mr. Cathcart's, and is also a good killer.

Instead of the brownish-red golden pheasant feather normally used for the ordinary shrimp flies, this one has a large black henny cock hackle which is tied in and wound-on as in the sketch. You could also use the golden pheasant feather dyed black if you were short of a black hackle with the necessary length of fibres.

Before you put on the tail hackle you tie-in several turns of flat silver or oval silver tinsel as a tag. Then, after the tail hackle has been applied, you tie in a piece of silver oval tinsel for ribbing the body.

The body is in two parts—bright orange floss nearest the tail and black floss silk nearest the head. A bright yellow hackle is then tied in, and this is followed by the insertion of the two jungle cock feather wings.

All that remains to be done now is to tie in another black henny cock hackle in front of the wings and finish off the fly's head with a whip knot. The head is varnished with black cellulose varnish.

This fly can be dressed on hooks up to $1\frac{1}{2}$ in. It does well on a size 6 low-water double or even on an 8 Limerick single.

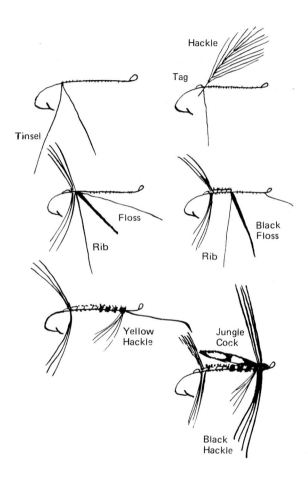

No. 37

July
Dun

THIS IS A SMALL dark olive dun which, as its name suggests, most often makes its appearance on the water in July, or possibly in August. Because of its smallness it is often mistaken for the iron blue dun. It is a very old pattern, and is most often used as a dry fly, to be floated over trout or grayling.

The tail of this fly consists of several fibres of medium olive cock, the same feather being used for the hackle. For the body use a piece of heron herl dyed yellow, and rib this evenly with the finest gold wire.

Try to give the fly a thinnish look and tie it on very small hooks—never larger, say, than size 16 (old number).

The wings, which should be short enough to correspond with the minuteness of the natural fly, are made from strips of very dark starling. Some fly-dressers use single wings while others prefer to have them doubled, but the latter, I think, make for a rather bulky fly, when the natural insect is comparatively small.

You can dress a hackle version of the July Dun by using the same body and setae but a darkish dun cock for the hackle.

For the spinner you can use gold-coloured floss, ribbed with fine gold wire, for the body. The hackle is ginger cock, as are the setae, and the wing is pale starling or bunched fibres of blue dun cock.

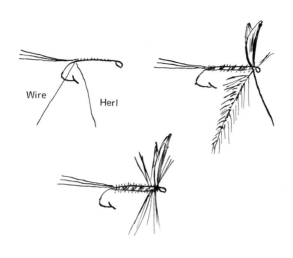

No. 38

Hunter

DURING correspondence with Miss Megan Boyd, the Brora salmon-fly dresser, she introduced me to this fly, which, at the time, she knew only as the Red and Black White Wing.

Miss Boyd was kind enough to suggest that I contact Captain Roddie Casement in Hampshire for further information about the pattern.

This I did and the good Captain went out of his way to obtain as much information as he could about the fly. He told me that it was first loaned to him by a gillie near Galashiels. This gillie reckoned it was a first-class fly to have on at the "grey dark"— that half-hour just before complete darkness.

In a subsequent letter, Captain Casement informed me that he had been in touch with the gillie in question and had ascertained that the fly's correct name was the Hunter and that it should be fished at dusk or in slightly-coloured water.

It was used mainly on Highland rivers with great success and had originally been tied by gillies to try on the River Tay. Incidentally, Miss Boyd later told me that it was also a favourite on the Tweed.

To dress the Hunter fly, tie in the ribbing tinsel. Then wind on red floss silk for the first (rear half) of the body and black floss for the remaining half.

The rear half is covered or veiled with a blood-red hackle, put on palmer style, and the other half of the body (the black one) with a black cock hackle, again put on in palmer style.

Both halves are then ribbed (through the hackles) with the ribbing tinsel, and a throat hackle of barred blue jay or spotted guinea fowl dyed blue is put on.

The winging feather can be from white swan, goose or turkey and the fly can be dressed in various sizes to suit conditions on the rivers where it is to be fished.

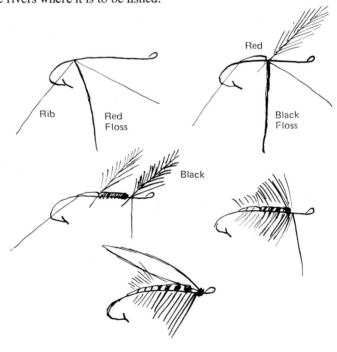

No. 39

Dark
Watchet

THE LATE T. K. Wilson never tired of singing the praises of this fly for trout fishing on his beloved Yorkshire rivers.

Regarded as an imitation of the diminutive Iron Blue Dun it fishes best in April and May when that insect is often seen about the water, even on the coldest and roughest of days.

It is dressed in the traditional North Country style with a soft hackle that works in agitated fashion in the water. Being an imitation of such a small natural fly it should be dressed on a tiny hook and for the same reason it should be rather sparsely dressed.

The materials for dressing the Dark Watchet, also known as the Little Dark Watchet, are not particularly difficult to come by. The hackle consists of a feather taken from the outside of a coot's wing. An alternative hackle, and one very often used, can be obtained from the neck of a jackdaw. Twisted strands of orange and purple silk, scantily dubbed with water rat's fur, are used for the body.

Although the original pattern had an orange head this is not regarded as strictly necessary in the modern fly, though, if you wish to be a perfectionist, you can use part of the orange silk for the head and coat this with clear varnish.

This fly can be dressed on size 16 to 14 short-shanked hooks. Stroke the hackle fibres back towards the tail of the fly so that they slope over the bend.

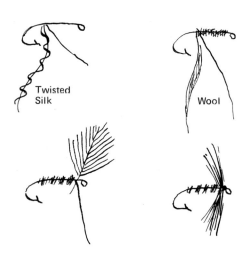

Twisted
Silk

Wool

No. 40

Hen
Blackie

ONE OF THE BEST-KNOWN of the whole array of Clyde patterns, the Hen Blackie (it gets its name from its blackbird wing), will take trout from the start to the end of the season.

Dressed in the sparse Clyde style in small sizes (never bigger than size 14, old number, hooks), it is a great favourite on that river and many a fine trout it has taken for me from that beloved stream.

I have also caught trout with it while loch fishing, and I can particularly remember a day on the Carron Reservoir when I got four brace of good fish with this fly on a dull and scoury day.

Dress this fly on size 16 hooks for preference, with some 14s for the rougher days, and use a minimum of materials.

First tie-in and wind on a piece of well-waxed yellow gossamer tying silk. If you are so inclined you can preface this operation by tying-in and winding-on one or two turns of oval or flat gold tinsel as a tag, but this is not strictly essential. The fly has no tail.

The winging feather is obtained from the secondary feather of a hen blackbird and should be tied-in with the shiny side outwards to lie flat, in sedge-like style, over the back of the fly's body, extending slightly beyond the end of the hook.

The narrower the wing and the closer it is to the back of the fly, the better the Hen Blackie appears to perform. For the legs use black hen hackle, put on very sparingly after the wing.

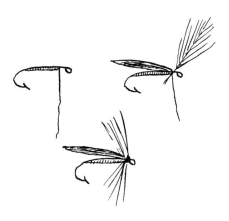

No. 41

Pot
Scrubber

WHILE on a fishing holiday in the Highlands I learned about this fly and was attracted to it by its comical name. Subsequent inquiries elicited the information from Alan Clavering of Lairg, in Sutherland, that to the best of his knowledge it was first tied by a gillie on the Lower Conon (Hydro-Board water).

Mr. Clavering unfortunately cannot recall the name of the man who invented the fly, but he assures me that it has often done the trick when other salmon flies have failed. He has used the fly with success on the Rivers Borgie, Shin, Cassley and Brora—and it has done well on the Oykel, too.

Mr. Clavering kindly sent me the pattern which is shown in the photograph.

The Pot Scrubber is not a particularly difficult fly to dress. It has a short, silver oval tinsel tag, a golden pheasant topping (small) for its tail, and the body consists of bronze or copper-coloured flat tinsel, ribbed with oval silver tinsel.

The original pattern, I understand, had its body made from a piece of a metal pot scrubber (which gave the fly its name).

The hackle, which may be cock or hen, is brown and it can be put on in the orthodox way or as a beard. The wing is grey squirrel tail, showing the brown, black and white parts of the hair.

Tie in the silver tag first, then the small topping (for the tail), and wind on the bronze flat tinsel. Rib the flat tinsel body with the oval tinsel in tight, evenly-spaced turns.

Tie in and wind on the hackle in the ordinary way or put it on as a beard (under the neck of the hook only). This latter method, I think, gives a neater head to the fly.

I have not yet tried this fly but I am told by anglers who have that it is a killer fished in various sizes for salmon.

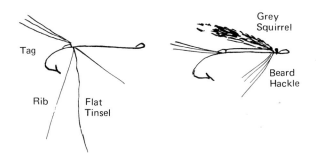

Tag

Rib

Flat
Tinsel

Grey
Squirrel

Beard
Hackle

No. 42

Green
Peter

THIS IS ONE of the most popular of the Irish flies for fishing
for trout in the big loughs. Every season it gets a lot of fish from
Loughs Conn, Mask, and Corrib, as well as other waters.

The dressing I am giving now was passed to me by Mr. Pat
Quinn, the well-known Castlebar tackle dealer, while I was on a
fishing holiday in Ireland last summer. Pat gets a great many fish
with the Green Peter, tied on a size 10 or 8 (old number) hook,
and in his shop are pictures of him with some of the big catches
he has made.

The fly used by Pat Quinn has a green seal's fur body, ribbed
with very fine oval gold tinsel, but there are some dressings of
the fly which have a slip of olive-green feather over the seal's fur
body.

The wing is speckled grey pheasant and this should be tied to lie down well over the back of the fly's body. The hackle, which is ginger hen, is tied in after the wing and is put on fairly thickly. In some cases mallard scapular feather is used instead.

This is all there is to the Green Peter, but there is a companion fly, known as the Dark Peter, which has a black seal's fur body with a little green seal's fur mixed in with the black. The only other difference is the use of a Coch-y-Bonddu hackle instead of the ginger one.

Then, of course, there is the Blue Peter. This one has the same wing, a ginger hackle and a silver-ribbed blue seal's fur body, with ginger hackle tied over it in palmer style.

All these flies will take trout from the waters I have mentioned, and are well worth a trial by every angler who visits the Irish loughs.

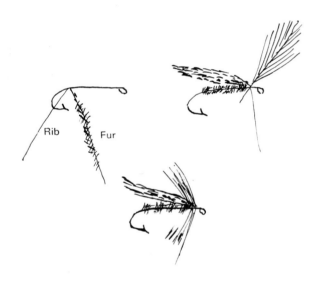

No. 43

Campbell's Fancy

ON BRIGHT days when there is a good wave on the surface of a lake or reservoir a gold-bodied fly will often take a trick. And this one, which originated in America, has proved to be successful not only in such conditions, but as an evening pattern in the summer months.

As flies go it is one of the most attractive-looking patterns that exists, a fancy fly rather than an imitation of any special insect, though, of course, it might be mistaken by the trout for some kind of fish fry.

Friends who have tried it for sea-trout say that it does well at dusk.

In some respects it is our old friend the Teal and Gold, which some anglers affirm can be as deadly as the possibly better-known Teal and Silver, but the hackle of the latter is blue or black, according to taste, while this one has a Coch-y-Bonddu hackle.

Tie in a short golden pheasant crest feather as a tail, then wind on the flat gold tinsel (it can be ribbed or unribbed).

Having formed the body, tie in and wind on the Coch-y-Bonddu hen hackle, which has a black centre with ginger tips.

Now take two corresponding strips from a piece of barred teal plumage to form the wing—and if you are tying large sizes of the pattern take wide-enough strips of the teal feather that you can fold (once) before tying them in against each other to make the wing.

All that remains now is to finish off with a whip knot and to varnish the head with shellac or cellire varnish.

This pattern can be dressed on hook sizes ranging from 14s to 6s (old numbers).

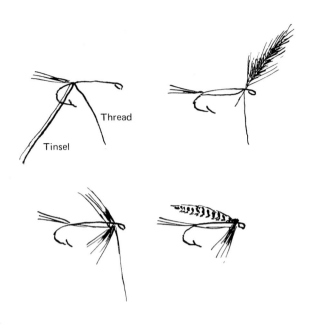

Thread

Tinsel

No. 44

Devil

LIKE MOST ANGLERS, I am a sucker for the fancily-named fly,
and I was amused, during a holiday in Donegal, to find one
with the rather descriptive name of Hidden Death!

I don't know whether any such claim can be made for the Devil,
but I was told by an angler who does much of his fishing on Lough
Conn that he gets a lot of his trout every season with this pattern.

Fundamentally, I suppose you could call it a Grouse and Black, except that it has a topping of dyed red feather along the upper edge of the wing.

The fly I saw was dressed on a size 8 hook. It had golden pheasant tippets for its tail, and the body was made of black floss silk, closely ribbed with fine flat gold tinsel.

The hackle was black henny cock—and I must admit that it looks a most attractive-looking pattern, which I intend to copy in smaller sizes for future use in my own part of the country.

Here is the method of dressing this fly: Tie in the tippets, then fix in a piece of the ribbing tinsel and wind on the black floss silk (or black tying silk at a pinch). Rib the body and tie a black henny cock hackle rather sparingly.

Now tie in the wings, consisting of two corresponding pieces of speckled grouse tail feather or brown speckled hen, and surmount these with a folded piece of swan or goose feather dyed blood red.

I am told that this fly will take anywhere on the cast, but is usually fished as a central fly on a three-fly cast.

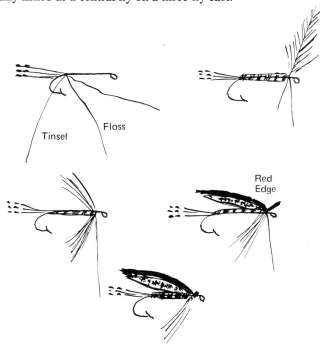

No. 45

Beacon Beige

ORIGINALLY, this fly was simply known as the Beige. It was given the title Beacon Beige by Peter Deane, who regards it as the best-ever imitation of the Olive Dun. Chalk-stream anglers (and the trout in these streams) hold it in very high esteem.

Those who use the Beacon Beige insist on it being very lightly dressed. Mr. Deane improved on the original pattern by using an Indian game-cock hackle of a dark shade through the Plymouth Rock (or grizzle) cock hackle and he recommends that the game-cock hackle should be fairly long in the fibres.

It is not a particularly difficult fly to dress, though good grizzle hackles are now in short supply or very expensive to obtain.

The tail of the fly consists of about four fibres of the Plymouth Rock hackle, which is grey-white with dark markings.

The body is made with the well-marked peacock quill from the eye feather of that bird, stripped beforehand of its flue, and tied and wound in to show the segmented body.

Put on the Plymouth Rock hackle first, then wind on the Indian game-cock hackle (or any really dark red-brown cock hackle with hard sharp fibres), mixing this among the fibres of the first hackle.

Do not put on too much hackle. The fly should be dressed as lightly as possible, with not too much of the Indian game hackle through the Plymouth Rock hackle, and it should be dressed on hook sizes up to 12s on light-wire hooks.

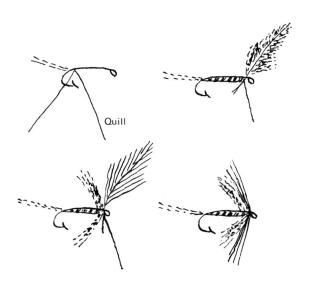

Quill

No. 46

Gold
Zulu

ALTHOUGH it has not quite achieved the popularity of the Black Zulu, that grand old favourite of the Scottish loch-fisher from which it was developed, or for that matter of the Blue Zulu, known by some as the Wee Blue Devil, the so-called Gold Zulu is regarded by some loch-fishers as a suitable companion for both on a wet-fly cast.

Regarded primarily like the other Zulus, as a bob-fly or top dropper, it also fishes well as an intermediate fly with the Black Zulu on the tail and the Blue Zulu on the bob, and a cast like this is especially worthwhile on those windy days of big waves when there is a dull scad on the water.

The Gold Zulu can also be fished on its own as a dry fly on hot, sultry days in summer and autumn.

It is easily dressed, with a red feather, silk (floss) or wool tail, a peacock herl body, ribbed with fine flat gold tinsel, and a Coch-y-Bonddu (red-black) hackle running the full length of the body.

Some fly-dressers tie in the hackle by the tip at the tail and wind it up the body, but I prefer to run the hackle down the body, from the throat, over the herl body, and to fix it in with the ribbing tinsel before winding this in evenly-spaced turns up to the neck.

Dress this fly for trout on size 16 to 14 (old number) singles and doubles. It does best for me on 16 doubles.

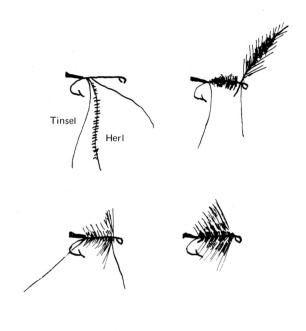

No. 47

Skunk Tail

HERE is a fly that enjoys a good reputation on the River Deveron, where it is known to account for some of the biggest salmon when dressed either as an ordinary hair-winged pattern or in tube style up to an inch in length.

It is not unlike the Thunder Stoat, a variation of the Stoat's Tail, which I have already referred to in this series, and I would like to think that it will get such a favourable reception from fly dressers as the Thunder Stoat was given when I made it the subject of one of these articles.

The principal difference between this fly and the Thunder Stoat is that the Skunk Tail incorporates the slight use of Depth Ray fluorescent floss. This is tied in and wound on as a tip for the body.

Use a dark, preferably black, tying thread when dressing the Skunk Tail. Tie in a tail consisting of a small golden pheasant crest feather, then add the tip or tag of neon magenta D.R.F. floss. Now tie in the oval silver ribbing tinsel and the black floss silk, which is to be used for the body.

Wind on the black floss and rib it with the oval tinsel. Fix in a black henny-cock hackle, either in the orthodox fashion or in beard style.

The wing consists of a slender bunch of any good black hair. Black squirrel is probably the best, but in a fast water I prefer black bucktail or even a coarser hair dyed black.

Some fly-dressers believe that they improve the pattern by adding some fibres of neon magenta fluorescent material as a sort of underwing for the squirrel, but this is a matter of taste. I have also seen dressings of the Skunk Tail which had a bright magenta cock hackle instead of the black one.

After the hair wing has been tied in, place a well-marked piece of jungle cock on each side, and, after finishing off the head of the fly, paint it with black cellulose.

This pattern can be successfully dressed on low-water singles of from three-quarters to one inch or on low-water doubles of equal size.

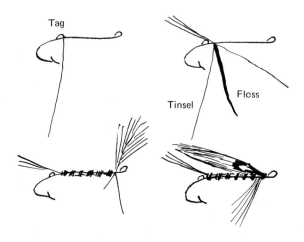

No. 48

Sooty Olive

HERE IS ONE of the better-known Irish patterns that kills a lot of trout in Lough Conn every season. It is particularly deadly in late spring and early summer, dressed on a size 8 or 10 old number hook, and fished as top dropper on a two- or three-fiy cast.

I was introduced to it during a fishing holiday in Ireland, when my boatman, Pat Rawlings, told me that, in his opinion, the Sooty Olive had few equals as a trout killer.

Sure enough, when I tried it I got several trout of 1 lb and upwards from Lough Conn, and even more trout when I fished it at Lough Mask later on.

Some fly-tyers dress this fly with a small golden pheasant topping for the tail, but I am assured that the barred tippet fibres from the same bird serve just as well. And the fish did not seem to cavil at the tippets on the fly I was using.

The body is made of rough, brownish-olive-green wool, mohair, or seal's fur, ribbed with evenly-spaced turns of fine oval gold tinsel. For the legs use a shiny black, henny-cock hackle, sparsely applied. In fact, the neatest dressings of the fly have the hackle put on in beard fashion (below the hook only).

The wing is made from greyish-rooted bronze-speckled mallard plumage. It is a good plan to double corresponding pieces of the mallard feather for the wing. The doubling gives strength to the fly's wings and, provided you take care to keep the fibres together, by tying them in soundly, makes a neat and durable fly.

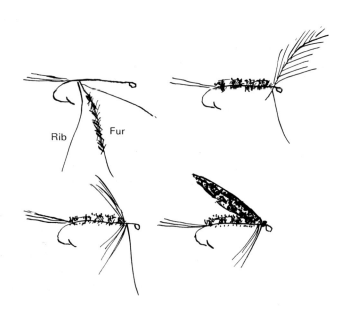

Rib

Fur

No. 49

Hawthorn

IT IS as a floating fly that this pattern does its best work. And when these flies come on the water they evoke considerable interest from the fish.

Their presence is particularly pronounced where rivers or lakes are bordered by trees or heather. They are big flies and should, therefore, be dressed on 12 (old number) light wire hooks, using cock hackles to give them the necessary buoyancy.

The late Courtney Williams put considerable stock on the Hawthorn fly as a trout killer. He gave the fly a body of black ostrich herl, a long-fibred cock hackle, and starling wings. This is the most popular dressing.

But Roger Wooley preferred the body to be made from two strands from a black turkey tail feather, showing the quill in the winding-on process so that the body had a shiny black appearance.

In addition, Wooley tied back the turkey tail fibres to represent the thick legs of the natural insect and added a black cock hackle to ensure proper buoyancy. He also made the wing from strips of jay primary wing feathers.

Both patterns have their adherents, but I think that the one given by Courtney Williams is the more popular and I shall settle for his dressing.

Tie in herl from the black ostrich feather, giving it a fairly thick appearance. Then tie in the two corresponding pieces of starling wing feather and add the long-fibred black cock hackle, as shown in the sketch.

This pattern can be used equally well for river and lake fishing, being at its deadliest when the natural insects are on the water.

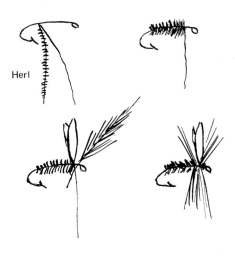

Herl

No. 50

Dark
Needle

INTENDED as a representation of a Stone Fly, the Dark Needle is a favourite North Country pattern. It was greatly esteemed by the late T. K. Wilson, one of the most knowledgeable anglers ever to cast a line on the rivers of Yorkshire.

Needle flies are so slender, with semi-transparent wings, that they are almost indiscernible on the water. Yet, when they are in flight, they look much larger than they actually are.

There are two dressings for the Dark Needle. One has a claret, waxed silk body; the other has an orange waxed silk body. Both have a small dark dun-coloured hackle, taken from the shoulder of a starling wing, and the fly has a head formed of a turn or two of magpie herl.

This fly and the Light Needle, which has an orange waxed tying silk body and is hackled with the flank feather of a young starling, are very popular for fishing in the rivers of Yorkshire, but while the natural insect is seen often enough on or near still water, I have never known the artificial to make any consistent kills of fish.

Tie in the claret or orange waxed tying silk very thinly, then add the small dark dun feather from the shoulder of the starling wing, making sure that the fly is sparsely dressed. Add the head of magpie herl (one strand) and fish the fly wet. Dress the fly on a size 15 (old number) hook.

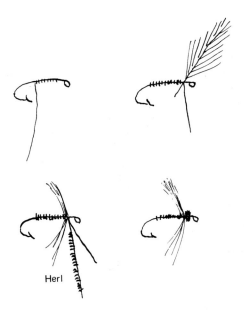

Herl

Index to Patterns

Printed and bound in Great Britain by
Fakenham Press Limited, Fakenham, Norfolk